VALUES-BASED

MULTINATIONAL

MANAGEMENT

LEE A. TAVIS AND TIMOTHY M. TAVIS

VALUES-BASED MULTINATIONAL MANAGEMENT

*Achieving Enterprise Sustainability through
a Human Rights Strategy*

University of Notre Dame Press
Notre Dame, Indiana

To Sparky and Jane

CONTENTS

FOREWORD

Since its first meeting in October 1978, I have followed with care the efforts of the Program on Multinational Managers and Developing Country Concerns through its conferences and the multi-volume series with the University of Notre Dame Press. Over the years, the core issue remains the same—the persistent desperate circumstances for so many people in our world. In terms of dealing with the situation, however, much has changed.

Information technology has made the world a global village, with all of the positives and negatives a village entails. In our current universe, we all know how one another lives. With enhanced information and communications comes a new political risk within countries, between countries, and through international terrorist networks; the balance of power is subtly shifting from governments to civil society; while some groups and poor countries have broken through the barriers to advancement, many remain mired in poverty; the HIV/AIDS pandemic is brutalizing the already poor.

Building on ideas of development, this book looks at the evolving global structures and interprets their meaning for multinational managers. When the village becomes global, the entrepreneurs in that village need to be attentive to what is expected of them and assume those responsibilities.

The growing emphasis on technology reminds me of my work with the United Nations Conference on Science and Technology for Development in the early 1980s. Our focus at that point was to advance science and the grassroots use of that technology. Although the early signs of the computer and communications explosion were in evidence, I did not anticipate the rate of technical advancement or its massive impact on our lives. With improving access to this technology, the power of the individual poor can increase, while, ironically, the strength of legitimate institutions to represent them (governments, labor unions, etc.) is decreasing.

The emphasis on human rights in this volume remains a constant. As I have reminded the diverse interactive conference participants (managers, missionaries, activists, academicians, policy advisors) in each of the fourteen Program workshops, save two, "If you want peace, work for justice." In our country we have made huge strides but understand how far we still have to go. All institutions in our society have a moral responsibility to promote human rights. This volume shows why a human rights policy also makes financial sense for business. Its focus on the multinational manager is right on target, given the growing power and opportunity of multinational companies.

Reverend Theodore M. Hesburgh, C.S.C.
University of Notre Dame

This volume addresses the values concern of multinational managers. Always a difficult balance, the values dimension of multinational decisions is becoming more complex with the worldwide integration of economies and peoples. The digital revolution that drives the integration process known as globalization shows no sign of abating. In this broader environment, a more informed society is changing its mind as to what it expects of the business enterprise. At the same time, with globalization, the business enterprise with its remarkable adaptability is gaining power relative to the nation state. As the state slowly loses its policy freedom and thus its regulatory power, its ability to represent the values of its citizens erodes. With this increasing power for the multinational enterprise comes increasing responsibility.

In meeting its responsibility, management must first reassess the appropriate role for its firm in the rapidly changing global environment. As with all major business decisions, values are an essential component, although difficult both to discern and to articulate.

The agenda for action is to strategically position the firm in the new setting. This consists of anticipating the trends of technical and social change in order to advantageously meet the macro demands not only of the present but also those of the next decade. Carrying out this agenda is a true managerial challenge, particularly as we work our way through the effects of macroeconomic trauma. Strategies that fit the firm to its future, and specific uniform corporate standards that become the global rules of the organization, must be established today. Resources need to be committed; managers must be chosen, developed, and integrated; flexible organizations must be created now in order to implement strategies.

The argument unfolds in the following steps.

Part I presents the problem of evaluating the corporate environment. Chapters 1 and 2 assess the digital revolution as the driving force of change in the multinational corporate environment and its integrating impact on global economies and political regimes, as well as cultural values and social structures. As the digital revolution continues, so will its economic, political, cultural, and social effects. These changes lead to a long-term transition in corporate governance—a regulatory void—and the need for principles based on social values as distinct from a reliance on compulsory external regulation. The multinational enterprise, as the institution most adaptable to global change, must assume the responsibility associated with this enhanced power.

Part II shifts to the problem of strategically positioning the firm in this new dynamic environment. Changes in cultural values and social expectations as a function of the digitally enhanced information revolution, joined with economic integration and the demand for political participation, call for a fundamental reassessment of corporate strategies, as outlined in chapter 3. In this process, the basic market model must be extended to incorporate a strategy of long-term enterprise sustainability, and beyond that to consider normative departures from the market model. Given the diversity of the societies operationally integrated within the multinational enterprise network—consisting of multiple business units around the world—the strategic extension of the basic market model as well as its implementation calls for an in-depth understanding and sensitivity to local operating settings. This understanding is best accomplished through partnering with NGOs—the topic of chapter 4.

Part III addresses establishing a strategy of human rights. A human rights standard, we argue, is the most universal, enduring, appropriate, and workable social standard for the enterprise. The concept of human rights has deep global roots in both religious and secular traditions. A moral statement of human rights as it has evolved in Catholic social thought, among other traditions, is presented in chapter 5. This body of teachings on social morality in a human rights context represents a dramatic reversal in the history of the Catholic tradition. The secular tradition of human rights has roots in the liberal rights theories of the seventeenth century, also discussed in chapter 5. A modern, detailed statement of social values in a human rights framework, hammered out at a critical moment in world history, is the Universal Declaration of Human Rights, outlined in chapter 6.

Part IV discusses implementing a human rights standard. The United Nations Global Compact is a code based on the Universal Declaration of Human Rights and the ensuing activities triggered by the Declaration, which is specifically formulated for the business enterprise. The content of the Compact, its universality, and its applicability to business decision making are critiqued in chapter 7. A study of the United Nations Global Compact as it is being implemented in a large Swiss pharmaceutical enterprise, Novartis, is the topic of chapter 8. The Novartis study exemplifies a corporate adoption of human rights as the social standard for a multinational enterprise. Chapter 8 analyzes the application of general principles of human rights to the specific business enterprise, the determination of implementing guidelines for the firm, and the tensions created at local operating locations.

Part V addresses the challenge of managing the firm as a community. Coping with a human rights strategy and, for that matter, any social standard can be a major managerial challenge, as reflected in the Novartis study. Arguably, this best takes place in an organization managed as a community. Two dimensions of this broad topic are covered. Chapter 9 considers the transition from the idea of an individual (understood in terms of the secular view of human rights) to that of a person (understood on a religious view). Drawing on the psychological distinction between the individual "drive for more" and social embeddedness, and the importance of the person as distinct from the individual in religious traditions, it underscores the need for emphasis on the person. The tension between obeying organizational rules, such as rules implementing specific human rights standards, and personal flourishing in a multinational environment is the topic of chapter 10. This tension remains at the heart of much intrainstitutional conflict. The notion of the enterprise as a community of persons is useful in bridging these tensions. The ethics of each involved person are central to this community.

In this sequence of steps in the book, the breadth of the global change in the environment of the business enterprise leads to a focus on human rights as the most appropriate strategy for the long-term sustainability of the business enterprise. The analysis continues to the issues of implementing that strategy within the firm.

Managers will want to proceed sequentially through the volume—beginning with the reality of the new business environment as outlined in Part I, following the argument through the return/risk tradeoffs of positioning the firm in that environment in Parts II through IV, and ending with the more conceptual treatment of managing the firm as a community in Part V. Academics who use the book as a second course in business ethics may want to begin with Part V. Here, the psychological and religious dimension is added to the moral philosophical basis of the traditional first course in business ethics. The sequence of Parts I through IV will then build on this foundation.

ACKNOWLEDGMENTS

Many colleagues have provided counsel and comments on parts of this manuscript: Matt Bloom (organizational behavior), John Uhran (computer engineering), LeRoy Krajewski (management information systems), George Howard (psychology), Edward Trubac (economics), Kevin Misiewicz (accountancy), Jeff Bergstrand (international economics), Hal Culbertson (peace studies), Klaus Leisinger (executive), Yuliya Shcherbinina (ethics), James O'Rourke (communications), Rev. Oliver Williams, C.S.C. (ethics), Thomas Bausch (management), Timothy Fort (theology and law), Ted Romaine (engineering), and Georges Enderle (ethics).

Three people deserve special appreciation: John Caron for his commitment to the activities of the Program on Multinational Managers and Developing Country Concerns since its inception in 1978; Thomas Tavis for his careful analysis of the argument from the perspective of a research librarian; Jule Poirier for her patience in drafting and redrafting the manuscript, editing all of it, and keeping track of notes and their correct bibliographical references. We also thank Rebecca DeBoer for her patient and exacting editorial work and Marge Gloster for her inspired work on the cover.

For any errors making it through this filtering process, the authors cheerfully blame each other.

PART I

THE NEW MULTINATIONAL ENVIRONMENT

The interrelationships of our world are changing in fundamental ways. Global integration has become a reality, with sweeping economic, political, social, and cultural effects. Much of this change is caused by the digital revolution—computer technology and its impact on information systems. Power balances are shifting as multinational managers adopt technological and information advances and adapt to the sweeping changes in the global system. For their part, national governments are losing the freedom to determine policy as they increasingly become part of the integrating global system.

Chapter 1 analyzes the unrelenting changes. The digital revolution is defined as the driving force. The nature of systemic changes and the relationship to the revolution modify the environment of the business enterprise.

Chapter 2 assesses the future of the digital revolution and its continuing influence. It considers strategies of adapting, protecting, or rejecting, along with their potential for success, and details the adaptability of the multinational enterprise.

Part I concludes with the need for adjustments in institutional responsibility to match the changing global system, particularly for the multinational enterprise. The world finds itself in a regulatory void as national governments lose their policy freedom and global governance networks are slow to develop. In this environment we must think in terms of principles-based responsibility as distinct from rules-based, externally imposed requirements.

CHAPTER ONE

Global Integration

Its Driving Force and Pervasive Impact

The process of open interaction among individuals and institutions across the world that has come to be known as globalization has changed the lives of these individuals and their institutions. The driving force of global integration is the digital revolution. With the implementation of integrated circuits, computational memory and speeds have doubled every two years. Among the multiple effects of this technology is its influence on the availability of information. The reach and pervasive influence of this information technology over the last quarter century is molding our institutional interactions and changing their balances of power. With the continued advance of computer technology and its influence on the availability of information, this rate of change will continue, even as the effects of the global recession work their way out of the system.

I. THE DIGITAL REVOLUTION

The development of the integrated circuit in 1968 initiated the "digital revolution" in its current phase. The remarkable pace of advancement has penetrated every facet of our lives and interactions within our various communities.

Computation Technology

The introduction of integrated circuits began the era of increasing calculation speeds and ever-smaller circuits that continues today. The pace with which computation technology has progressed since that time is startling.[1] In 1965, Gordon Moore, one of the inventors of integrated circuits (and then chairman of INTEL), predicted an exponential growth in computing power, known as Moore's "Law of Integrated Computers." He predicted that transistor-die sizes would be cut in half every twenty-four months, meaning that both computing capacity (i.e., the number of transistors on a chip) and the speed of each transistor would double every two years. As it turns out, Moore's predictions have held.[2] Indicators of this progress include the following:

- As of the end of the last century (2000), "Computers are about *a hundred million times* more powerful for the same unit cost as they were at the half-century mark.[3]
- Measured as the calculations per second that can be purchased for $1,000, the calculations were ten per second in 1950 and 10^8 in 1999.[4]
- The cost of a megabyte of storage fell from $10,000 in 1958 to less than $0.001 in 2005.[5]

This exponential rate of change is difficult for us to grasp. It begins slowly but becomes very large very quickly. Taking 1968 as a base rate, computing speed would increase every two years, first by a factor of 2 in 1970, then 4 in 1972, then 8, 16, 32, . . . and would be up to 512 times faster in 1986 and 1,024 times faster in 1988. In 2006 the multiplier would be in the neighborhood of 500,000.[6] Compare this rate of change to the industrial revolution, which took generations to take hold.[7]

moves it beyond the control of all but the most powerful and determined governments and governance networks.

Social fractures have been associated with major technological break-throughs throughout history—the invention of gunpowder and the industrial revolution are examples—but the interconnectedness and rate of change brought about by current technology is unprecedented. Globalization has led to a crisis mentality. The integrated information of financial markets has allowed the financial crises to move quickly from one country to another; organized crime and terrorism thrive on communications technology; economic cycles are closely connected among countries; the economic rate of change makes people more vulnerable. The resulting tensions have erupted in meetings of multilateral institutions and economic summits and were abundantly evident in the recent economic malaise. The potential for peace in today's world depends on our ability to introduce social, economic, and environmental concerns into the marketplace.

There are two ways of looking at the distributional results of technologically enhanced economic change: (1) the overall distribution of benefits, and (2) the incidence of poverty. The absolute gaps in income among countries and peoples have increased with economic integration. In 1970 the ratio of income per capita for the world's richest 10 percent compared to the poorest 10 percent based on country averages was 19.4 to 1.[27] By 1997 this ratio had increased to 26.9 to 1.[28] As measured by the Gini coefficient, a standard measure of inequality, household surveys indicate that between 1988 and 1993 dispersion increased dramatically.[29]

The economic dislocation associated with economic globalization and reflected in the dispersion of income is tied to the rate of change of the process. The rapidity with which markets have been opening and the intensity of the competition for a place in the market, all driven and supported by technological development, create enormous opportunities for those who have access to and can cope with the globalizing institutions, but lead to exploitation and marginalization for those who do not and cannot. Raimo Väyrynen states, "As a rule, actors controlling specific, mobile and tradeable resources benefit from globalization, while those stuck to fixed assets that are not competitive in the international market see their incomes decrease."[30]

The incidence of income poverty in our world and its impact on human development are unnerving. Human development is broader than income and wealth. It involves health, education, food and nutrition, the inclusion of women and children, the environment, and security. Klaus Leisinger in a recent essay points out that

> more than a billion people do not have access to safe water and even more lack access to sanitation, and communicable diseases (tuberculosis, HIV/AIDS, diarrhea, measles, malaria, schistosomiasis, and infections of the lower respiratory tract) create a health burden of more than 57 million deaths and 610 million death and disability adjusted life years (DALYs). Poverty is not only a cause, an associated factor, and a catalyst of ill health, it is also its result. Poverty keeps the poor in ill health and ill health keeps the poor in poverty—a vicious circle. And there are challenging times ahead. The world population will grow from today's more than 6.5 billion to more than 9.2 billion by the year 2050. More than 98 percent of this population growth will occur in the less-developed countries.[31]

With respect to infant and maternal mortality, Leisinger observes,

> The *WHO World Health Report 2005* reports that "each year 3.3 million babies—or maybe even more—are stillborn; more than 4 million die within 28 days of coming into the world; and a further 6.6 million young children die before their fifth birthday. Maternal deaths also continue unabated. The annual total now stands at 529,000—often sudden, unpredicted deaths which occur during pregnancy itself (an estimated 68,000 as a consequence of unsafe abortion), during childbirth, or after the baby has been born—leaving behind devastated families, often pushed into poverty because of the cost of health care that came too late or was ineffective." While a baby girl born in Japan today can expect to live for about 85 years, a girl born at the same moment in Sierra Leone has a life expectancy of only 36 years. In some countries the situation actually worsened in the 1990s, and worrying reversals in newborn, child, and maternal mortality have taken place. Overall, 35 percent of Africa's children are at higher risk of death today than they were ten years ago. Every hour, more than 500 African mothers lose a small child—in 2002

alone, more than four million African children died. Those who do make it past childhood are confronted with adult death rates that exceed those of 30 years ago. Life expectancy, always shorter in sub-Saharan Africa than elsewhere around the globe, is shrinking. In some African countries, it has been cut by 20 years and life expectancy for men is less than 46 years.[32]

The World Bank describes these conditions in terms of "inequality traps." It notes the persistence with which "economic, political, and social inequalities tend to reproduce themselves over time and across generations."[33]

At the turn of the century, the countries of the United Nations captured the broad human rights dimension in a series of specific "Millennium Goals." Eight goals set in 2000 were to be achieved by the year 2015 in terms of eradicating extreme poverty and hunger; achieving universal primary education; promoting gender equality and empowering women; reducing child mortality; improving maternal health; combating HIV/ AIDS, malaria, and other diseases; ensuring environmental sustainability; and developing global partnerships. In 2007, midway through this period, the United Nations reported on progress based on data available during the first third of the fifteen-year period.

The good news is that "the proportion of people living in extreme poverty fell from nearly a third to less than a fifth between 1990 and 2004."[34] If this trend continues, the goal of halving the proportion of people whose income is less than $1 a day will be achieved by 2015.[35] The picture for the other goals is mixed. For example, child mortality is declining while the number of people dying from AIDS is growing. Leisinger points to the huge remaining gaps. He cautions, "Even under the best case scenario of achieving the Millennium Development Goals, hundreds of millions of people in future generations will continue to live in misery."[36]

How can an increase in the dispersion of income and a modest decrease in poverty both hold at the same time? The answer is the increase in overall productivity. In statistical terms, the expected value of the distribution of income and consumption has increased as well as its standard deviation. The productivity-driven distribution moved to the right at the same time that it broadened. Income poverty can be represented as a threshold at the lower tail of this distribution. With globalization, the improvement in the mean has been great enough to offset most of the increase in dispersion, thus modifying the effect of this dispersion on the poor. The World Bank notes: "As countries become richer, on average the incidence of income poverty falls."[37]

The moral issues of poverty are different from those associated with the dispersion of income. Clearly, poverty and the oppression of human development is unjust, particularly in the presence of such great global affluence. It is a violation of human rights. Only the most ardent supporters of unfettered markets would disagree, although others might want to allow the growth benefits of globalization to "trickle down." While there is reported progress in human development, the sad reality is the loss in opportunity. With the dramatic increase in productivity, we should have been able to do better.

The morality of the increasing global dispersion of income and wealth (as distinct from poverty) is more controversial, involving the standard deviation of the distribution as distinct from the area below a threshold. The observed dispersion is not itself immoral. Much of it is a function of effort and skills. The moral consideration enters in terms of a second-generation right of usable access to the resources necessary to enhance one's economic position. This includes access to the economic system and to the education necessary to take advantage of that access. It is the discrimination, exploitation, marginalization, and denial of opportunity contributing to the dispersion that is immoral. From our privileged perch, it is easy to miss the reality of what it means to be shut out, caught in persistent, hopeless poverty.

Two decades ago, for those of us working in development economics, this inequality, especially the numbers and circumstances of the desperately poor, was a moral issue. Our frustration was over how little of the global increase in productivity was reaching these people, who were exploited in the process or, with greater damage, marginalized from global integration. Today it is still that, but with an added dimension—the political risk. With enhanced information reaching most people, the poor now understand fully their comparative living standards, the lack of access to opportunity for themselves and for their children, the institutions and political apparatus that stand in their way, and the alternative ways of achieving opportunity. This defines political risk. This threat of political unrest challenges autocracy and foments terrorism.

Spread of Liberal Democracy

"In a very real sense, the 20th Century was the 'Democratic Century.'"[38] In 1950 only twenty-two countries—14 percent—representing less than a third of the world's population were classified as democratic. By 2000, 120 countries—nearly two-thirds of the population—were classified as electoral democracies.[39] How is this democratization associated with globalization, and is it sustainable?

Democratization Waves

Democracy is currently in what Samuel Huntington identified as its third wave.[40] The first wave commenced with the American Revolution and lasted until after World War I, when much of Europe slipped into fascism and military dictatorship.[41] The second was triggered by the decolonization, primarily in Africa, that followed World War II. This second wave receded as many of these newly democratic regions were replaced by dictatorships in the 1960s.[42]

This third impetus for democracy coincided with global market integration, although the cause-and-effect relationships are murky.[43] The initiating factor was the economic success of European unification. As Jan Black puts it, "This new wave of democratization might be traced to Western Europe in the mid-1970s. Having developed strong domestic economies and a strongly democratic vocation, having discarded the costly last throes of straightforward colonialism as opposed to neo-colonialism, and having found economic strength and unity, the European Community exerted a strong pull on the continent's unconverted fringes."[44] Democracy in Latin America can be attributed to the post-Vietnam-conflict United States, and in central and eastern Europe to the implosion of the former Soviet Union.[45]

Information technology has made national borders more porous to ideas and preferences as well as to trade and investment. Citizens worldwide are demanding greater participation in their governments. There has also been substantial pressure from developed-country democracies, the United Nations, and its intergovernmental (multilateral) institutions for greater democracy in national governance.[46]

Islamic Countries as an Exception

The Islamic countries of the Middle East are examples, among many others, of exceptions to the trend toward democratization. In 2005 there was not a single democracy among the sixteen states of the Arab Middle East.[47]

One limitation is the stage of development of these countries.[48] They are poor and have a legacy of extreme differences in income and wealth. Their recent quarter century of growth, which ended in 1985, was based on extensive governmental controls—protected markets, large governmental bureaucracies, and a bias against agriculture.[49] Globalization forced Middle Eastern countries out of this model in much the same manner as globalization ended Latin American state capitalism.[50] In the Middle East, unlike other countries, there has been no productive upside to globalization. Islamic countries have stagnated economically. As of the mid-1990s, average earnings had not increased in real terms from those in 1970.[51] These countries have been marginalized by the economic integration of the globalization process.

A country's stage of development is clearly a factor in democratization. In assessing the potential for democracy in Islamic countries, Abdolkarim Soroush identifies economic development as a necessary condition: "The primary condition for the realization of democracy is the liberation of human beings from the elementary needs and necessities of life. It is true that human beings have always opposed inequity and demanded justice (democracy being a modern manifestation of this perennial human quest), but justice can prevail only where its seekers are not weighted down by poverty and insecurity."[52]

The presence of oil is another "inhibiting factor." In 2008, of the twenty-three oil-dominated economies, not a single country was a democracy. Seven of these nondemocracies are in the Persian Gulf.[53] The large, concentrated cash flows associated with oil allow autocratic regimes to gain and maintain power, particularly in developing countries.

A factor that sets the Islamic countries apart from other poor, marginalized, postcolonial, and, in some cases, oil-rich areas in Africa and Asia is the influence of Islam on the politics of these societies. Is there a unique feature of Islam as a religion or as a historic civilization that dampens or blocks democratization? The core question is whether a reli-

gious democracy is possible. Are rules governing personal and social behavior based on divine revelation and interpreted by the state compatible
with the grassroots participatory ideal of a Western democratic state? The
idea of rights and their correlative responsibility is fundamentally different in Islam. Responsibility, not rights, denotes the relationship between
the ruler and the ruled. In Bernard Lewis's view, "The exercise of political
power is conceived and presented as a contract, creating bonds of mutual
obligation between the ruler and the ruled."[54] In these bonds, the focus in
Islam is on justice as distinct from the Western emphasis on freedom.[55]
And, as Lewis notes, "Democracy usually evolves out of a movement toward freedom."[56] Moreover, in spite of the strong caveats against arbitrary
rule in the Islamic tradition, Islamic political regimes throughout history
have been autocratic.[57] "The dominant political tradition," Lewis observes,
"has long been that of command and obedience and far from weakening,
modern times have witnessed its intensification."[58]

Notwithstanding the historical precedent and continuing tension between the Western ideas of religion and democracy and the teachings of
Islam, however, the teachings on the relationship between the ruler and the
ruled in fact support the grassroots participation so important in democracy. The tradition of mutual consent—*shura*—is central to the governing
process. As one Islamic scholar observes, "The meaning of *shura* is the solidarity in society based on the principle of free consultation and genuine dialogue, reflecting equality in thinking and expression of opinion. Through
public and private consultation, the governor (the leader) should seek active
advice and input from his followers prior to making a decision."[59]

Soroush argues that religion and democracy in Islamic countries are
mutually reinforcing. He concludes one of his essays with the words, "This
essay originated in the question of the possibility of combining democracy and religion; but it went on to articulate their affinity and need for
each other. Notions of liberty, faith, dynamism of religious understanding,
and rationality of worldly affairs were evoked to attest to the possibility,
even the necessity, of such an auspicious reconciliation. . . . A religious
reign over hearts was distinguished from a legal rule over bodies."[60]

We conclude that it is the lack of economic development, the presence
of oil, and external political involvement, more than Islam, that accounts
for the lack of democracy in the Middle East. Larry Diamond agrees:
"The obstacles to democracy in the Middle East are not the culture, or the

religion of Islam, or the society, but rather the regimes themselves and the regions' distinctive geopolitics."[61] Survey evidence in Muslim countries supports the notion that Islam is not incompatible with democracy.[62]

Democracy's Depth and Fragility

Elections are the core of democracy. It is necessary that they take place in a free environment with open, unfettered, informed interaction among the candidates and the populace. The conditions of an ideal election are not unlike those of an efficient financial market.[63]

Still, the idea of democracy goes well beyond the mechanics of an election. Liberal democracy also includes the opportunity for participation of the electors in the decisions of the elected government officials. It implies access to policy discussion and review through the media and other channels. Extending the notion of democracy beyond election procedures embraces conceptually different, less measurable components and engenders substantial disagreement.

A working democracy assures civil as well as political rights. Amartya Sen notes:

> *Political freedoms*, broadly conceived (including what are called civil rights), refer to the opportunities that people have to determine who should govern and on what principles, and also include the possibility to scrutinize and criticize authorities, to have freedom of political expression and an uncensored press, to enjoy the freedom to choose between different political parties, and so on. They include the political entitlements associated with democracies in the broadest sense (encompassing opportunities of political dialogue, dissent, and critique, as well as voting rights and participatory selection of legislators and executives).[64]

Those who equate democracy with freedom would include Sen's full set of instrumental freedoms. In addition to political freedoms, these include economic facilities, social opportunities, transparency guarantees, and protective security.

Democratization often becomes entangled in uneven social change and political agendas (external as well as internal), making its path difficult to discern. In considering the sustainability of democracy, Huntington's use of the term "waves" indicates his cyclical view of the phenomenon. Both of the first two waves did recede, with the first lasting 150 years and the second only twenty years.[65]

Currently there appears to be a pause or even an ebb tide in democratization. Freedom House classifies countries according to their performance on political rights and civil liberties. In addition to free and fair elections, its categories of political rights includes governmental accountability and a government free from pervasive corruption. Civil liberties include several categories of freedoms (freedom of expression, of religion, intellectual freedom, freedom of assembly, freedom to form organizations); the right to own property; and equality (of opportunity, of gender, and in the treatment of minorities). Based on a country's rankings against these criteria, they are classified as free, partly free, or not free.[66] Based on its classifications, in 2006 Freedom House reported a "profoundly disturbing deterioration in democracy."[67] Between 2006 and 2007, according to another measurement poll, thirty-eight countries experienced reversals in their ratings, almost four times the number that showed improvement.[68] Diamond uses the term "global democratic recession" to refer to this phenomenon: "That half of the most important states outside the securely democratic West are authoritarian regimes or slipping away from democracy, testifies to a worrisome turn in the global democratic trend. So does the growing backlash against international efforts to promote democracy."[69]

Still, the drive for participation and empowerment fueled by the availability of information and the structural stimulus from economic integration will continue. The factors that triggered the "third wave" remain. The equivocal nature of the democratization process, combined with the relentless drive for economic integration (which generally supports democratization, but may sometimes undercut it), ensures that the long-term trend will be toward democracy, even though short-term patterns will continue to exhibit ebbs and flows.

The Social Effect

The technological factors that so effectively drive the positive results of globalization also create social fractures. To date, the spread of technology has been uneven, contributing to the aforementioned maldistribution of income associated with economic productivity. In addition to the old distinctions between developed and developing countries, there are now new winners and losers in this digital revolution since access to information is uneven—a phenomenon known as "the digital divide." In addition to this divide, the influence of the Internet on personal relationships and community involvement is a source of concern to many. This section addresses questions of access to the Internet and its influence on personal relationships and civil involvement.

The Digital Divide

The maldistribution of access to the Internet, while a function of many economic variables, is a direct result of uneven access to information as a component of structural access to opportunity. This digital divide embodies direct geographic, gender, and class distinctions as well as those of income.

As noted, the number of Internet users has exploded to over a billion globally. However, use is highly concentrated. The 238 million users in North America in 2007 represented 70 percent of the population—an amazing penetration. In the Middle East the figure was just 17.4 percent and in Africa only 4.7 percent; globally, the average was 20 percent.[70]

Historically, there have been differences in population segments as well. Computer use is dominated by the United States, thus making English the Internet language.[71] For most countries, Internet users are located in specific urban areas and are richer, better educated, and younger than non-users, and tend to be male.[72] With the development of multifunctional handheld devices, however, these statistics are changing.

Personal Relationships and Community

Are the isolated hours interacting with a machine changing the nature of our personal relationships? Has this isolation dampened our commitment to local communities? We may be at a turning point in the answers to these concerns, given the rapid growth of virtual communities.

Isolation
A person's interaction with his or her computer is quite intimate. Long hours are spent, day and night, interacting with machines. This inter-

action is a source both of great satisfaction and of frustration. How many of us have e-mailed a colleague two or three offices down the hall rather than walk the corridor to speak personally with her? With this behavior comes a broad concern that the decline of person-to-person interaction associated with Internet use will diminish our social skills. As of 2001, the preponderance of evidence from sociological studies allayed this concern. The evidence suggested that even though Internet involvement could shift the user from a group-based to a network-based society, it often reinforced existing patterns of behavior and enhanced social ties.[73]

Participation

The Internet melds online communities of shared interests with our traditional geographic communities. Kjell Nordstrom and Jonas Ridderstrale have described online communities in terms of new tribes. "Our old society was geographically structured and so were the tribes. . . . The new tribes are global. They develop with people who are relevant to you, no matter where they are. Now, we also see *attitude-based* and *competency-based* tribes." They also argue that "the tribal pioneers are often found in groups considered outcasts and marginal in the geographically structured world." To them, this leads to individualism and social fragmentation.[74]

Again, as of 2001, the evidence did not support a movement away from geographic communities associated with Internet use. Summarizing available sociological studies, Paul DiMaggio and his co-authors conclude, "The Internet has no intrinsic effect on social interaction and civil participation." They go on to note that the "Internet tends to intensify already existing inclinations toward sociability or community involvement, rather than creating them *ab initio*."[75]

Virtual Communities and Individual Expression

Observations based on evidence through 2001 were made before the development of virtual communities. With the so-called Web 2.0, users moved beyond their own PCs and e-mail to interacting with the Web in search not only of new information but also of extensive new personal contacts. In 2006 Andreas Kluth referred to the frenetic picture: "As we head into 2007, there are by some counts more than 400 social-networking sites, all trying to become the next MySpace; more than 200 web-video sites, all trying to become another YouTube."[76]

In its "Person of the Year" issue for 2006, entitled "YOU," *Time* magazine captured the nature of three virtual websites:

- YouTube has become video blogging. While it was not designed for this purpose, it has become "the public video diary of a generation of teens and twenty-somethings."[77] "It's the combination of two simple things— easy, cheap recording and easy, free distribution that makes YouTube so potent and its impact so complex. . . . It's a surveillance system. . . . It's a spotlight. . . . It's a microscope. . . . It's a soapbox."[78]
- "FaceBook is a social networking website that has become—for many people—a way of doing what people used to do by gossiping and talking on the phone, but a lot more efficiently and publicly."[79]
- Second Life is a virtual site where individuals can build their own personas called avatars. *Time* calls it a "cartoon location built by enterprising users" that has "created the perfect capitalistic system in which you pay for fake stuff (clothing, housing, hookers) with real money . . . but Second Life is different enough (flying! teleporting! cloning!) that it functions as a therapist's couch on which you learn about yourself by safely exploring your darkest desires."[80] In fact, an island named Brigadoon in Second Life is home to a large community of people with autistic spectrum disorders (ASD).[81]

Virtual reality is crossing the boundaries between real and imaginary. Corporations are creating three-dimensional online personas or avatars.[82] Litigation has been brought in U.S. courts over a real-estate investment in Second Life.[83] The software taps and makes public a remarkable image of individual creativity. At the same time, it tests the limits that society will allow in individual expression. When we empirically analyze the sociological effects of these phenomena in 2015, the personal and communal impact will undoubtedly be different from that of 2001, summarized above.

Cultural Erosion

Information technology appears to be contributing to a global cultural commonality. With the increasing accessibility of information about the lives of other people across the world, unique traditional cultural characteristics and practices as well as value systems are bound to be modified.

Our interest here is the ways in which culture affects society. William Glade sees "culture" as "referring to the complex of such things as attitudes, values and preferences, beliefs, systems of cognition, model personality orientations, prevailing behavioral expectations, and expressive traits."[84]

Unique traditional cultural practices have been disappearing for some time, as the tentacles of modernization reach further into remote areas.[85] Much of this traditional cultural leveling is due to the spread of American lifestyles and attitudes. As noted, the Internet is predominantly in English. Music, movies, Internet videos, and products are largely from the United States. The extent of U.S. cultural penetration is extensive and resented by many. For example, the French Minister of Culture remarked in 2005 that "Hollywood movies account for 85 percent of movie tickets sold around the world. . . . In the United States, only 1 percent of shown movies come from outside the United States," a situation regarded as an "asymmetry of cultural power."[86]

The Regulatory Void

The regulatory void begins with the loss of policy freedom on the part of the nation state. Porous borders lead to a decrease in a country's ability to regulate and control the activities of the multinational firm. Set against this observed trend is the slow development of international law and of global organizations able to take over the regulatory function. The loss of policy freedom has been dramatically demonstrated with the implosion of the former Soviet Union and, more subtly, with the demise of Latin American state capitalism. Beyond these examples, there is a gradual loss of policy freedom in developed as well as developing countries. There is also a nascent movement to fill this regulatory void on a global scale through global governance networks. These networks take a good deal of time to evolve, however. The net result is a period of regulatory transition—a regulatory void.

Loss of National Policy Freedom

The key factor in economic integration has been the deregulation of national product and financial markets. The opening of product markets, so important to international trade, has been matched by deregulation and laws creating more favorable climates for foreign direct investment, particularly in the 1990s. From 1991 through 1999, 94 percent of the 1,035 changes in national laws across all countries were directed toward creating these more favorable global investment climates.[87] Around the world, bilateral investment treaties increased from 181 in 1980 to 1,856 by the end of 1999.[88] In the process of stimulating economic globalization, national governments passed much of the control over the allocation of resources in their countries from regulators to the marketplace—from government-led to market-led development. The result was that with economic globalization, the policy freedom of the nation state declined.

Often referred to as a "loss of sovereignty," this shift in power has been the subject of extensive debate. Kenichi Ohmae and Jean-Marie Guéhenno, for example, both declare the "end of the nation state."[89] Others claim that globalization has actually led to enhanced activities on the part of national governments, at least among the developed countries.[90] Ann-Marie Slaughter views this process as the state disaggregating:

> From this perspective, the State is not disappearing; it is disaggregating. Government officials and institutions participating in transnational government networks represent the interests of their respective nations, but as distinct judicial, regulatory, executive, and legislative interests. They respond to and interact with the growing host of non-State actors; they can link up with their sub-State and supranational counterparts. This disaggregation provides flexibility and networking capacity, while preserving the fundamental attributes of Statehood— links to a defined territory and population and a monopoly on the legitimate use of force. That is the core of State power, power that remains indispensable for effective government at any level.[91]

For Väyrynen, too, the relationship between globalization and sovereignty in the international structure is complex but not exclusive:

> Globalization is not an alternative to sovereignty, but it rather provides a new context in which it is embedded. . . . In the future, a state will be less of a corporate actor and more of a decisional arena in which various forces meet to resolve national and transnational problems. Sovereignty remains the dominant organizing principle

of international relations, but politics and decision making become more diverse and complex. Networks, coalitions, and transactions between states become new units of analysis.[92]

He addresses the loss of policy freedoms in terms of agenda-setting power: "Sovereignty is not disappearing, but its nature is changing. The globalization process has lowered national barriers and transaction costs, leading to a closer integration of national and international societies. As a result of this development, the agentive power of the State has declined, or has become more strongly conditioned by the State's relationship with domestic and transnational social and economic forces."[93]

This loss of agenda-setting power applies to developed as well as developing countries, although developing country governments have long been accustomed to being in a less powerful position in this and other areas.[94] Global economic integration, as institutionalized in the World Trade Organization (WTO), can severely limit the economic policy freedom of these countries.

If economic growth is to be stimulated, market deregulation must be accompanied by policies that work toward domestic market efficiency through competitive structures and information flowing to all market participants. An effective banking system, private property rights, the enforcement of contracts, and anticorruption policies, all based on an efficient judiciary, are critical if openness is to contribute to economic development. In this sense, countries with institutions that have not historically relied on open market policies—countries of the former Soviet Union or those characterized by Latin American state capitalism or Asian government-led development—or that were never particularly effective (a definition of underdevelopment) experienced the greatest constraints on development policies. The conditions set by the World Bank and the International Monetary Fund limit funds for social investment. The cost of meeting WTO requirements can be large.[95] In these respects, global economic integration limits national economic freedom for the developing world and, through resource limitations, social policy freedom.[96]

This loss in the power to regulate the multinational firm leads to a regulatory void, which international bodies or networks are attempting to fill. While there has been substantial activity at the international level, the question remains as to the extent to which global governance can assume the regulatory function in response to the declining policy freedom of national governments.

Global Governance

Global governance begins with international law.[97] Beyond intergovernmental agreements involving treaties and governmental agencies, institutions of civil society are increasingly involved in global networks.

International Governmental Relationships

"Domestic law and international law are both law, but they are very different forms of law."[98] International regulation is not a replacement for the nation state. In the international arena, there is no political institution equivalent to a sovereign national government that can legally constrain the activities of the business enterprise, other than the case of the European Union.[99] International affairs are guided by a plethora of bilateral and multilateral agreements among nation states. Between 1946 and 1975 the number of these agreements more than doubled, from 6,351 to 14,061.[100] These agreements, extensive as they are, still do not have the characteristics of national government.

The United Nations and its sixteen specialized agencies have many of the attributes of government. They were created by agreement among most national governments at that time, and they have decision-making power. Their continuance, however, in contrast to the nation state, is conditioned on the acceptance of the membership.

The numbers and density of international relationships among domestic governmental institutions have increased in recent years. These forms of governmental collaboration are tied to democracy, in that governmental institutional collaboration across borders is most common among liberal democratic economies. Judicially, there is cross-fertilization of decisions and cooperation in dispute resolution among judicial organizations.[101] Governmental agencies increasingly collaborate in the areas of security regulation, banking and insurance supervision, criminal law enforcement, environmental policy, and antitrust policy.[102]

In addition to international law and intergovernmental collaboration, civil society is increasingly involved in global initiatives, often through private institutions and networks.

Involvement of Civil Society

With globalization, private institutions have become a significant factor in global governance. There are two broad institutional components in this civil society—the business enterprise and the nongovernmental organization (NGO). Both groups are becoming far more active than in the past, often in collaboration or confrontation with one another.

Many of these networks focus on social and environmental responsibilities and standards. From the business perspective, they can be motivated by a sense of social responsibility; the protection or enhancement of the industry's reputation; an attempt to forestall external regulation; or a desire to promote a particiular brand image. The commitment begins with the individual enterprise expressing its objectives in the form of corporate credos, statements of values, or specific guidelines in detailed codes of ethics or conduct.[103] A 1995 study of U.S. firms indicated that 34 percent of those surveyed had a formal written credo, 53 percent a statement of values, and 91 percent a code of ethics or conduct.[104] Among non-U.S.-based multinationals, however, less than 50 percent had a formal written ethics statement.[105]

International private networks are a logical extension of these individual corporate efforts.[106] An example of an international statement of aspirations is the Caux Round Table (CRT). The CRT was founded in 1986 by a group of senior executives from Europe, Japan, and North America.[107] The Caux Principles for Business were published in 1994 and have been implemented in dozens of firms. The principles are a living document, in that the CRT continues to meet on a regular basis and is finding increasing acceptance by non-CRT members, who recognize its basis in corporate leadership. There are two problems, however, with the Caux Principles: they are too general, and there is no enforcement provision.[108] Specific codes of conduct address both of these concerns.

An example of a code-based monitoring-enforced network consisting of multinationals, universities, and advocacy groups is the Fair Labor Association (FLA). The FLA developed from the White House Apparel Industry Partnership (AIP), a unique combination of government, business, labor, and other NGOs convened by former president Bill Clinton and charged to end the sweatshop conditions in the apparel industry.[109] The AIP issued a Workplace Code of Conduct and Principles of Monitoring.

It also designed the Fair Labor Association as the mechanism for certifying and supervising independent monitors. Regarding the monitoring process, David Schilling states: "The AIP had serious, often heated, discussions about independent monitoring: Who will do it and how will it be administered?"[110] As the network structure moved from the AIP to the FLA, disagreements over monitoring and the payment of a sustainable living wage led the labor representatives and some of the human rights groups to drop out.[111] The FLA is currently the most active group monitoring conditions in apparel manufacturing plants across the world.[112] Membership consists of 23 major-brand participating companies and suppliers, 5 founding NGOs, 33 affiliates of the NGO Advisory Council, and over 194 colleges and universities.[113]

As private networks move to become governance networks, governmental agencies are involved. An example of a broader international membership network is drawn from the chemical industry. The "Responsible Care" program developed by the Canadian Chemical Manufacturers Association sets standards for the handling of chemicals.[114] These standards are being broadly implemented, with much encouragement from developing country governments. The International Counsel of Chemical Associations (ICCA), consisting of national chemical associations, has been instrumental in formulating its own standards beyond those set by the International Organization for Standardization (ISO). Many of these restrictions were set in conjunction with Greenpeace and are reflected in the Intergovernmental Forum on Chemical Safety (IFCS), which developed from the United Nations Conference on Environment and Development. As Virginia Haufler notes, "This reflects a complicated interrelationship among the members of a private sector regime (ICCA), and other nongovernmental organisations (Greenpeace), and governmental institutions (IFCS and individual governments)."[115] Through these kinds of networks, business has a voice in the rules and guidelines of the global economy.

Substantial network efforts have been devoted to international standards. A powerful network is the International Organization for Standardization.[116] Members of the ISO come from national standards bodies,[117] some governmental and others private.[118] For example, the U.S representative, The American National Standards Institute, is a federation of businesses, governmental agencies, other standards groups, labor, consumers unions, and academics.[119] The ISO 9000 quality management system standards and the ISO 14000 for environmental management systems reflect major industrial input.[120] This is an important example of intense business involvement with civil society and governmental groups.

Achieving Legitimacy and Authority

The maturation of a global governance network implies legitimacy and authority. Legitimate authority can be based on an effective democratic form of government, in which the governed accept the authority of the elected officials. It can be assigned to international networks by these governments. The European Union and the United Nations come the closest to meeting the requirement of assigned authority. Governmental cross-border networks are attempts to gain input into international regulation that will affect the country. These are logical extensions of national policies to international levels. Through involvement in mixed government/private networks, national governments attempt to influence the network and to gain access to information and technology that is more available in the private sector. Multinational firms and NGOs seek governmental involvement for legitimacy and authority. Beyond the legitimacy anchored by national governments, global governance networks must earn legitimacy and authority based on transparency, accountability, and performance. In a governing sense, legitimacy can exist without the procedural basis of democracy. As with democracy, however, non-elected networks are judged on their "effectiveness in producing valued outputs."[121]

The reality is that global governance networks are slow to develop, as we have pointed out. They are particularly slow to achieve full legitimacy and authority, and they are specialized. Although improving in organization and power, these networks cannot be expected to provide the coherent regulation offered in the past by the nation state or the enforcement of such regulation. Väyrynen describes the rules of global governance in terms of "soft law":

> In general, one can predict an increase in flexible and diverse, but less binding international rules (as manifested by the growing role of "soft law"). Actors often resort to soft law in the absence of well-defined institutions and precedents, or because of the sheer complexity of the issues. . . . Compliance with transnational norms is achieved more by

monitoring, persuasion, and capacity-building than by formal enforcement mechanisms.[122]

The Future

The economic collapse triggered in 2008 has drawn intense scrutiny to regulatory efforts. In the financial sector, regulation failed to keep up with the evolution of financial institutions and instruments in the "shadow banking system." As markets became global, regulation remained local. In the United States and Britain, these factors were exacerbated by libertarian views of the markets' self-regulating capabilities. As the financial market collapse spread to the product markets, the competitive weakness of individual enterprises became apparent. In some cases, such as automobile emissions, this weakness was a function of regulatory shortcomings as well as lack of management foresight.

As officials attempt to find new national regulatory architectures combined with international collaboration, regulation will change. Maturing regulation will draw on enhanced information, will tend to assure more transparency, and will be more articulate in its requirements. The most extensive and clearest change will be in the financial sector, where various mechanisms of governmental involvement attempt to find a balance between controlled stability and market innovation. For the product markets, added reporting demands and controls will be required of firms involved with government stimulus programs. Beyond that, for most countries and companies, changes will consist more in the articulation of existing rules than in the imposition of new ones.

In summary, the global system, driven by technology, will return to its integrated growth patterns. Government involvement in the financial sector will persist. Alternatively, in product markets, the regulatory void will continue for most multinational enterprises, as nation states continue to lose policy freedom, awaiting the authority of global governance networks.

This lack of uniformly applied authoritative social guidance places the multinational manager in a difficult position. Multinational managers confront both the absence of uniformity and the absence of a level playing field in competition with other firms, yet must also strategically position their firms today for a world as it will be in five to ten years and beyond.

CHAPTER TWO

Responding to the Future

Continued exponential growth in computational technology is assured, thus driving advancements in information and the ways we visualize the world around us. This chapter anticipates the future of computational technology and its information dimension, along with its globalizing effects. It assesses alternative reactions to this future in terms of adaptation, protection, or rejection. Faced with such great technologically driven opportunities and risks, combined with the unsettling nature of the macroeconomic crisis rippling through the system, one is reminded of William Butler Yeats's verses: "Things fall apart; the centre cannot hold; / Mere anarchy is loosed upon the world."[1]

I. TECHNOLOGY

Computation Technology

A useful way of anticipating the future of computational technology is through the concept of a "natural life cycle of technologies."[2] The history or life cycle of a technology can be plotted on an S-curve, from early modest performance and slow progress to exponential improvement and then to maturity. As a specific technology approaches maturity, investment turns to the development of new technologies; the market will jump from a maturing to a developing S-curve. One can discern three nested S-curves in current computation technologies: the development of layered chips, as the single chip reaches maturity; nanotechnology moving toward exponential growth; and quantum computing in its very early stages of development.

The increase in speed and the decrease in size of integrated circuits, based on the increasingly higher resolution of optical lithography, has been dramatic, to the extent that electron tunneling (the leaking of electrons through insulating barriers that have become too thin, causing micro-shorts within a highly miniaturized computer circuit) is becoming a problem.[3] Current extensions are expandable silicon-based chips and multiple layers of chips. Memory chips are now being stacked to six tall in order to reduce the density of storage.[4] It is anticipated that cubical chips will approach hundreds or even thousands of layers.[5] At the present rate of advancement, even cubical silicone chips will soon reach their material limits and the peak of their technological S-curve.

We are already seeing the beginnings of an investment jump to nanotechnology. Nanotechnology should assure the continuation or even acceleration of Moore's Law. In nanotechnology, individual atoms and molecules replace lithographically drawn transistors.[6] Most current efforts focus on ordered molecular structures.[7] These nanoparticles are measured in terms of nanometers, billionths of a meter—about the length of ten hydrogen atoms. A massive amount of research in nanotechnology is underway. In the United States, for example, governmental research on nanotechnology is the largest federally funded science project since sending a man to the moon. The governments of Japan, Western Europe, and developing countries such as India, China, South Africa, and Brazil are also contenders. It is estimated that over half of such activities are governmentally funded, although corporate expenditures are gaining rapidly. In the United States, for example, about 90,000 nanotechnology patents were registered by 2003.

By 2004, nanotechnology was already being used in over two hundred consumer products. This technology can enter the production process at any of three levels: first, nanomaterials, which are the basic raw materials for the next two levels. An example would be the clay nanoparticles produced by Southern Clay Products. Second, nano-intermediates, products that incorporate nanomaterials or nano-sized features. Examples include stain- and odor-resistant fabrics, memory chips, or composite materials that include nanomaterials in their makeup. And third, nano-enabled end products made with nano-intermediates. Examples include clothes made from stain- and odor-resistant fabrics, computers made with nano-intermediate chips, or the 2004 Chevrolet Impala, which used nano-intermediates in its side moldings.[8]

Nanotechnology is close to becoming the computational base for information technology. With companies such as Hewlett-Packard studying the use of individual molecules as components in switches and transistors in order to create a new type of memory, new memory chips could be produced in the near future, followed by major changes in computer logic chips. Computer chips would be in the class of nano-intermediates, as would fuel cells and solar cells. Such breakthroughs could cut the cost of electricity by 50 percent, increase fuel economy, and produce better catalysts.

Revolutionary quantum computing is based on the laws of quantum physics. It has been the topic of increasing research since the 1970s and appears to be approaching a reality much sooner than experts believed was possible. In quantum computing, four possible values "unique to the ambiguous world of quantum mechanics," known as "qubits," replace the 0 and 1 of digital computing; the result is that "huge calculations can be done using a manageable number of qubits."[9] A number of research groups are working on quantum computing, each with its own approach. In 2007, for instance, a Canadian company, D-Wave Systems, introduced its version of a small quantum computer, the "Orion"[10] (some remain skeptical of the Orion computational approach and usefulness).[11]

It is anticipated that such developments will enable a continuation of exponential growth in computer technology through this century. Kurzweil forecasts that "a $1,000 personal computer will match the computing speed and capacity of the human brain by around the year 2020."[12] And as we learn more about the functions of our brains, it is logical to assume that there will be more interconnections between computers and our bodies. Computers have already been attached to a person's brain, using the brain as a controller.[13] Broader computer links to the brain are under development.[14]

Information Technology

The continuing growth of computation technology will, of course, have its effect on information. The rate of change in information technology will be less rapid, however, since there is more social interaction involved. In the near-term, remarkable advances are being made in telecommunications and virtual reality. Programming approaches are being modified to take advantage of new hardware capabilities. Core changes in the Internet itself are longer-term and less assured. Finally, management information systems and their effect on organizational structure will draw on these developments.

Technical advances in communications are well underway in terms of mobile, multifunctional input/output, voice input/output, and visualization. A relatively new communication device, for instance, is the multifunctional cell phone such as the Apple iPhone or the Palm Pre. These kinds of devices are replacing the personal computer as the primary form of access to the Internet. They are approaching the full integration of the Internet with a person's PC, including language translation capabilities.[15]

The trend toward immersive experience of information continues. As illustrated in developments in computer games and computerized video games, "we are moving from visual to virtual—visual, auditory, even to haptic interfaces and virtual tactile environments."[16]

The efficiency of software programming is also being challenged. One response is to improve the design of individual software projects and automate much of that development.[17] In a study undertaken in 2002, the National Institute of Standards and Technology concluded that software failures cost $59.5 billion a year and that 25 percent of commercial software projects are abandoned before completion. The Software Engineering Institute at Carnegie Mellon concluded in a 1994 study that, on average, there are 100 to 150 bugs per 1,000 lines of code.[18] In addition to these technical concerns, a frequent complaint is that software designers have no understanding of real people and create software that does not fit user needs or is incomprehensible to most users.[19]

Anticipating how the Internet itself will evolve is more speculative. Internet development is a marvel of collaboration among many users. A major part of this information explosion was the "end-to-end principle" followed by the early designers in the 1970s, who structured the Internet to be as open and simple as possible, minimizing the software inherent in the Internet iself and relegating applications to the users at the "ends" of the communications.[20] This structure enabled numerous innovations, such as "the Web, peer-to-peer file sharing, and Internet telefony" that were unanticipated in the 1970s.[21] These innovations, however, have been made at the edge of the network, so to speak. The desired simplicity of the Internet has prevented innovation at its core. While innovation at the edge will continue, innovation at the core of the Internet will be forced upon us by the massive increases in the sheer volume of data that are expected over the next few years:

> That the system has scaled up well enough to handle almost 1 billion users and blazingly fast fibre-optic links is nothing short of amazing. But as the Internet has grown, so too have problems such as spam, viruses, and "denial of service" attacks that can cripple large websites—not to mention the challenge of accommodating all kinds of new devices, from cars to mobile phones to wireless sensors. "We've pretty much exhausted the tweaks we can do," says Tom Anderson of the University of Washington.[22]

Present core innovations in their early stages include flexible routers that can "learn" new protocols and multiple Internets running in parallel. Core modifications will undoubtedly challenge the simplicity of the end-to-end principle. Moreover, insofar as the modifications reduce the openness of the Internet or increase the control of information, there are important implications for the exercise of free speech.

Paralleling fundamental changes in the Internet, management information systems will be upgraded. This will have a continuing influence on organizational structures. For example, IBM is working on self-adjusting systems, described as "computer systems that regulate themselves in much the same way our autonomic nervous system regulates and protects our bodies."[23] Computers will take care of themselves by automatically adjusting to changes in their environment. Defining characteristics include the following: "An autonomic system must configure and reconfigure itself under varying (and in the future, even unpredictable) conditions"; it must "perform something akin to healing"; it must "know its environment and the context surrounding its activity, and act accordingly." In the more distant future, increased information capabilities will match some of the remark-able dimensions of exponentially growing computation technology.[24]

Technical Assessment

One of the strongest confirmations of technological projections can be found in the views of people directly involved, such as Bill Joy, a cofounder of Sun Microsystems. Rather than question the predictions of a techno-logical future, he expresses alarm over its implications.[25] Many share a sense that technology may be advancing more rapidly than our ability to understand and to cope with it.

We simply do not know where this technology will ultimately take us. The self-replications of genetically modified organisms, nanoorgan-isms, and intelligent nanorobots have led to doomsday predictions. Joy endorses John Leslie's pessimistic anticipation in his book *The End of the World* and Ray Kurzweil's more sardonic assessment. As Joy remarks, "The philosopher John Leslie has studied this question and concluded that the risk of human extinction is as least 30 percent while Ray Kurzweil believes we have 'a better than even chance of making it through' with a caveat that he has 'always been accused of being an optimist.'"[26] The possibility of the intentional creation of harmful self-replicating organisms or devices by terrorists or military groups, as well as the unintentional creation by benign groups, is ever present.

II. THE IMPACT OF GLOBALIZATION

As computation technology continues its exponential growth and is re-flected in the changes in information technology, the integrating effects—economic. political, social, and cultural—will also continue. Some of these responses to technology will move forward like a steamroller; some will be fragile; others will experience starts and stops.

Economic Integration

Economic integration will continue under the pressure from information technology. While there will be efforts toward national isolation associated with the collapse in the international financial system and its spread through global product markets, efforts that will cause temporary slow-downs or even setbacks, the incessant underlying force for globalization will ultimately prove unstoppable.

Uneven Distribution

Some of the news with respect to the uneven distribution of the fruits of global productivity associated with economic integration is finally good. This unevenness will be modified through market mechanisms as the digital divide is gradually overcome. Many who have been marginalized by their lack of access to information are gaining access to e-mail and the Internet.

Attempts to make personal computers more available in developing countries, for example, have been spearheaded by the MIT Program "One Laptop Per Child."[27] A simple, rugged computer has been developed that can be powered with a hand generator, and the program is striving for its goal of distribution in developing countries at a cost of $100 per computer, with an emphasis on children learning by doing. These laptops use an interactive technology known as "mesh networking," whereby each laptop can interface with others in the network without utilizing the Internet. The whole network then gains access to the Internet when a single node is connected.[28] An inexpensive computer is also being pursued on a commercial basis by Intel,[29] originally in collaboration with the MIT group but now independently. Another effort involves placing multiple, simultaneous users on a single computer.[30] In terms of software, Microsoft has developed a scaled-down, less expensive version for Windows for use in developing countries. For isolated communities, experiments are underway to assess the feasibility of reaching the Internet through satellite connections powered by solar panels.[31]

The major impact on the digital divide, however, will be through advancements in the technology and use of cell phones and evolving mobile multifunctional devices. Cell phones are probably the best example to date of developing-country technological leapfrogging, eliminating the high cost of landlines. In addition, reasonably priced access to the Internet is beginning to be available. As of the end of 2006, "emerging markets today account for more than half of the world's total telecom connections."[32] As reported in 2005, for example, there were an estimated eight mobile phones for every hundred people in Africa, and twenty-seven mobile phones per every hundred people in the Philippines.[33] Gartner Research predicted in late 2006 that mobile connections would increase by 1.5 billion in the next five years, with 87 percent of the increase coming in emerging markets.[34]

The rural poor of the developing world have proven ingenious in adapting what was once the urbanite's high-tech accessory to their circumstances and needs. Women with phones in Bangladesh villages rent time on their phones to other villagers.[35] With access to cell phones, farmers and fishermen are able to check local and regional market prices and work to reduce the exorbitant fees of the middleman. These phones broaden trade networks, reduce transactions costs, and eliminate the need to travel. Concern over the availability of networks to service these mobile phones is allayed by the fact, as estimated in 2008, that a whopping 77 percent of the world's population live within the range of a mobile phone network.[36]

The use of cell phones evolving to smartphones, then, completes the technological leapfrog by making web-based technology available to the technologically less-sophisticated person. Still, technical penetration into remote areas and the full use of that technology by isolated people remains a challenge.[37] As mobile devices provide greater access to the Web and access becomes more straightforward, both elements of the digital divide—access and capability to use that access—will be overcome.

Lifting the poor from their poverty trap is the good news. The challenging news is the demand for associated resources and the associated degradation of our environment. Thomas Friedman notes that as hundreds of millions move out of abject poverty and others move into the middle class, this creates a huge new demand for "'things', all of which demand lots of energy, material resources, land, and water and emit lots of climate changing greenhouse gasses from the time they are produced to when they are discarded."[38]

Democratization

The long-term prognosis for democracy is still positive, in spite of the many setbacks. People want democracy, an idea fueled by its possibilities and performance. Global democratization will continue, although slowly and with many starts and stops.

Information technology continues to be a driving force for democracy. As Edward Lucas notes, "The Internet has provided citizens with vastly more information about their elected representatives: their voting behavior, their source of finance, their outside interests, the content of every public speech they ever made."[39] Local information increases with Web 2.0. Blogs have become a major source of information that would not appear in the more formal media. According to an early 2008 estimate, there were over nine million active blogs, with forty thousand added each day.[40] Blogs and cell phone text messaging are playing a significant role in elections.[41] As governments become more efficient in using the Internet interactively to provide public services, moreover, the necessary standardization and availability of information to Internet viewers become major impediments to corruption.

Larry Diamond proposes three factors that will determine whether the "third wave" of democratization continues. He stresses that democracy begins with individual determination: "for democracy to endure, . . . leaders and citizens must internalize the spirit of democracy." The other two factors are socioeconomic rather than individual. "One will be gradual economic development that lifts levels of education, formation, and autonomous citizen power and organization. The second will be the gradual integration of countries into a global economy, society, and political order in which democracy remains the dominant value and the most attractive type of political system."[42] As we have argued above, economic integration and development are both driven by the continuing pace of the digital revolution. In the long run, if economic integration and information availability, supported by personal idealism and determination, continue, the trend toward democratization should also continue.

Cultural Erosion

Cultural erosion can be analyzed in terms of cultural layers: tastes, traditions, language, and values. Tastes are easy to observe in terms of dress, entertainment, food, and so on. In the traditional town of Bangdong in the Indonesia highlands, for example, it is stunning to see the main street dominated by U.S. brand labels—larger than life, three-dimensional signs advertising Levis and other products. Traditions reach deeper than tastes, and their loss can be painful. One is reminded of the musical *Fiddler on the Roof.* Language is often more resistant to change than either taste or traditions. Nevertheless, as the French have discovered, it is surely not immune to erosion.

Values can be the most persistent of these cultural layers. There is a psychological reason for this. The idea of narrative consciousness suggests that our early cultural learning is through stories, which then become a filter for our acceptance of counterviews later in life. (The concept of narrative consciousness and its resistance to different values are topics of chapter 10).

To the extent that cultural distinctions are based on religious beliefs, these will be most likely to endure. Differences between certain values of the Islamic world and of the West, for example, will endure as they have for centuries. These distinctions spill over into the political and economic realms.

Added Regulatory Complexities

Advances in technology raise almost unimaginable challenges for current regulatory structures. They will change the nature of control for existing regulatory agencies. They cut across present regulatory fields, such as pharmaceuticals, the environment, chemicals, health and safety in the workplace, and the right to privacy. Nanotechnology and genetic patenting provide two examples.

The strong emphasis on nanotechnology, combined with its risks for health, safety, and the environment, intensifies the debate over the need for tight regulation to protect against risk versus the potential for regulatory interference in the development of that technology. A related dimension is the ongoing debate over a strong patent system that supports small innovators; it may also lead to multiple small patent holders, which could have an inhibiting effect on the technical efforts of large companies.[43] Some regard nanotechnology as an opportunity to form a new creative regulatory approach, along with the emergence of a new technology.[44]

An interesting pioneering attempt to regulate nanotechnology was underway in Berkeley, California, as of 2007.[45] The issue of regulation arose when a federal research lab affiliated with the University of California filed an environmental impact statement for its planned molecular foundry. After years of discussion, the new city council regulation focused on size and transparency. Businesses (excluding Lawrence Berkeley National Laboratories and the University of California) are required to report annually any products they use that are composed of materials with at least one dimension of 100 nanometers or less. Given the competition within the private sector to bring nanoproducts to the market, this blanket requirement for transparency could be problematic.

Another regulatory issue as a result of current technological advances is the potential protection of life forms. Our current patent system privatizes the "genes of plants, animals, and microbes as well as entire organisms. For example [as reported in 2007], more than 20 percent of human genes have already been patented and most of these patents are held by corporations."[46] Continuing new discoveries in biology greatly complicate the process.[47] Here, the perennial patent problem of finding a balance between incentives to promote creativity and research and the social need for access to the results is taking on a new meaning.

For the corporate world, the massive problem of regulating technology underscores the importance of analysis and responsibility on the part of the enterprise. Technological responsibility is captured in the "precautionary principle." This principle states that the developer or implementor of a technology must anticipate and hedge against future damage from that technology even if there is no present scientific certainty that such damage will occur. Applying this principle to the environment, the United Nations Rio Declaration states: "Where there are threats of serious or irreversible damage, lack of full scientific certainty shall not be used as a reason for postponing cost-effective measures to prevent environment degradation."[48] The precautionary approach is applied directly to corporations through the United Nations Global Compact, a voluntary social and environmental code (the topic of later chapters).[49]

III. RESPONSES TO GLOBALIZATION

Individuals and institutions have responded in different ways to globalization: some adapt, others protect, while a third group rejects the process of globabilization. These strategies hold different promises for the institutional or individual future. In assessing these responses, brief examples will be given.

Adaptation

Adaptation can be a challenging but promising strategy. It begins with a realistic assessment of the shifting technical, political, and cultural, as well as economic, environment. Adaptation is not acquiescence, nor is it an attempt at raw dominance. It is the art of pursuing self-interest with a focus on the long term, while acknowledging the interests and relative power of others. The effective adapter takes time to understand the background and context within which counterarguments are made and power is positioned. Understanding positions that are in disagreement represents a moral as well as an opportunistic approach.

Few institutions fully meet this ideal, as is so apparent throughout history and in today's daily news. Still, many of the firms simultaneously operating across national boundaries and in multiple countries and cultures have demonstrated a remarkable ability to adapt: an ability fully challenged for banks and business enterprises on the shifting ground of financial and product markets as well as the uncertainty of governmental reaction.

Multinational firms have globalized their production and service structures, modified their managerial structures, and adjusted well to new informationally driven social demands. The management of these banks and enterprises have adopted technology and adapted to its integrating force: services are outsourced and offshored; production structures are globalized in search of efficiency and cost advantages; research and development now take place in numerous locations across the world; management structures are information-rich, interactive, decentralized networks; interinstitutional collaboration is extensive in terms of strategic business structures; collaboration with nongovernmental organizations and full global governance networks are growing. Indeed, multinationals have been the instruments for the dramatic increase in productivity and integration.

Foreign direct investment is the mainstay of global productivity and integration. As a percentage of gross domestic product (GDP), foreign direct investment (FDI) inflows have grown substantially in recent decades (see Table 2.1). The pattern of direct investments is similar to that observed with per capita GDP. Growth in developing and least developed countries is surpassing that of the developed countries, albeit from smaller bases.[50]

Table 2.1   Foreign Direct Investment Inflows as a Percentage of Gross
Domestic Product

	1990 (%)	2005 (%)
World	1.0	1.9
OECD	1.0	1.6
Developing Countries	0.9	2.7
Least Developed Countries	0.3	2.6

Source: Human Development Report 2007/2008, p. 293.

A second dimension of FDI flows is their relationship to official development assistance (ODA). In all cases tabled above, the increase in FDI is
matched by a decrease in ODA.[51]

Cross-border mergers and acquisitions, including the acquisition
of privatized government enterprises, provided the basis for these FDI
patterns—a more than seven-fold increase in the thirteen years from
1987 through 1999. About half the number of cross-border mergers and
acquisitions—70 percent of the value—were horizontal. The vast majority
of this activity involved acquisitions—97 percent.[52] Mergers and acquisitions (M&As) continue to focus on cross-border deals. In 2007 cross-
border M&As represented 40 percent of all M&As. This is an increase
from 20 percent in 2000 and 30 percent in 2005. While private equity
M&As slowed at the end of 2007, corporate M&As maintained vigor.[53]

A recent trend is the increase in multinational direct investment from
emerging economies. These accounted for 14 percent of FDI outflows in
2006, even though FDI emerging economy inflows substantially exceeded
the outflows. Most of these flows were in the form of takeovers. Much
of this activity was an attempt to acquire technology. These emerging
country multinationals are bringing their own, in some cases unique, approaches to managerial adaptation.[54]

As with global trade, these patterns have been distorted by macroeconomic turbulence. Private capital flows in 2009 are expected to be less
than half of their record 2007 levels, along with trade. However, continuation
of the underlying technological drivers ensures that long-term patterns will

be a reflection of those reported above, as the global economy regains its balance.

Managers have adapted their organizational structures. While firms continue to emphasize the commonality of goals, policies, and procedures across their networks, the idea of control from a central core has changed. Managerial philosophies have shifted from hierarchical structures to heterarchical ones. The command and control systems typical of the post–World War II internationalization of mass production have given way to decentralized networks. Today's multinational organization consists of multiple business units—subsidiaries and affiliates—with greater authority and responsibility.

In response to the dramatic growth in developing country economies and their direct investment inflows, recent organizational thinking focuses on the need to respond to local uniqueness but in a way that is not overwhelmed by complexity. McKinsey & Company describes the challenge as follows:

> Striking an appropriate balance between the protection of local value and the integration of selected cross-country processes and functions is challenging; the organizational response to create the right linkages must be subtle and avoid blunt centralization. Companies should also consider geographic clustering, ensure clear accountability where it really matters—in linchpin roles—and build common ways of working in critical cross-border processes while allowing the local units to maintain their own cultures.[55]

The potential for new organizational structures is supported by enhanced information networks. Extension and refinement of these networks continues. As another recent McKinsey article states, "Given the vast resources going into storing and processing information today, it's hard to believe that we are only at an early stage in this trend. Yet we are. The quality and quantity of information available to any business will continue to grow explosively as the costs of monitoring and managing processes fall."[56] These internal information networks themselves lead to a flattening of the organizational structure, since they delimit the information-gathering and coordinating role of middle managers.

Multinationals are also involved in ongoing coordination with other enterprises in the form of global supplier contractual networks, joint ventures, or strategic alliances, thus extending the reach of the individual multinational network. Supplier relationships have become more permanent for many multinationals. In production, quality control is so highly coordinated that the final quality assessment of a component is actually conducted in the contracting assembler's plant.[57] Component production scheduling is also undertaken by the contracting firm in many cases.[58]

Joint ventures are shared undertakings between two firms or between a firm and the state. Joint ownership provides a sense of permanence, although the joint venture partners remain with the venture only so long as it continues to fill their needs. Joint ventures between multinationals and indigenous enterprises are prone to conflicting purposes and management control issues.[59]

Strategic alliances are targeted to specific purposes, generally for technologized development or market penetration. Given the cost and complexity of technology and the rapidity with which it becomes outmoded, even the large multinationals find it difficult to commit human and material resources to risky ventures. In marketing, product life cycles are so short that products need to be simultaneously introduced in many national markets.[60]

With technologically enhanced interactive relationships, these kinds of intercompany formal relationships are giving way to less formal innovative networks that are particularly effective in capturing innovation within the firm, horizontally across corporate boundaries, throughout the supply chain, and with customers. McKinsey predicts:

> Technology tools that promote tacit interaction ["work that involves negotiations and conversations, knowledge, judgment, and ad hoc collaboration"], such as wikis, virtual team environments, and videoconferencing, may become no less ubiquitous than computers are now. As companies learn to use these tools, they will develop managerial innovations—smarter and faster ways for individuals and teams to create value through interactions—that will be difficult for their rivals to replicate. Companies in sectors such as healthcare and banking are already moving down this road.[61]

The effectiveness of adaptation has led to an increase in the power of multinational enterprises, balanced against the regulatory void and the loss of labor power. This shift in power places an added responsibility on multinational management. As we will stress throughout, adaptation calls for cross-cultural understanding, the willingness to engage in dialogue, and the search for universal principles.

Protection

A policy of protection, or protectionism, is an alternative strategy. It can begin with the same environmental assessment as adaptation. Governments, institutions of civil society, and individuals all want to make their own decisions and have long attempted to protect their interests from global pressures, although with mixed success. Protectionism tends to be a characteristic of the nation state as it attempts to represent the perceived interests of its citizens or its leaders.

Economic Protection

As the successor body to the General Agreement on Tariffs and Trade, the World Trade Organization, created in 1995, is the key body promoting marketization on a global scale. The Doha Round of negotiations, launched in 2001, was intended as an ambitious effort to make global markets more inclusive and to help the poor by boosting growth in developing countries, who now comprise two-thirds of WTO membership.[62] Given the fragility of the WTO, however, these negotiations were suspended in July 2006 and collapsed in July 2008.[63]

The reasons for the collapse appear to be clear. Although the United States had made a bold proposal to reduce farm subsidies and agricultural tariffs, the EU did not match the U.S. proposal, and neither met the demands of the developing countries.[64] For their part, the large emerging economies were unwilling to reduce their tariffs sufficiently, particularly on industrial products and on farm goods.[65]

Following the suspension and collapse of Doha, analysts have argued that trade liberalization will be assumed by regional agreements rather than the global approach of the WTO. At this point, most members of the WTO are also members of at least one regional agreement, with nearly two hundred such agreements in force at the end of 2006. The ten ASEAN countries, for example, have bilateral agreements with one another, and all, in effect, have bilateral agreements with China. Other agreements exist with India, South Korea, and Japan. At the time of the Doha collapse it was estimated that East Asia would have seventy of these free trade agreements.[66] While bilateral agreements are easier to negotiate than multinational ones, they can be damaging to developing countries since the more powerful country in the agreement dominates the other. Also, bilateral agreements can distort trade rather than create it. Beyond its consequences for trade, the collapse of the Doha Round also portends greater problems with future environmental treaties.

A more recent phenomenon is the intense pressure for economic nationalism resulting from the 2008 global economic collapse. It can take many forms: bank lending restricted to national clients, subsidization of local industries, national supplier requirements as part of stimulus packages, competitive devaluation, health and safety standards imposed for imports, and antidumping fees, as well as tariffs. Hopefully, the lessons of history will give pause to the political protectionists. Protectionist trade barriers fueled the Great Depression, which was one of the factors leading to World War II. In the global economic environment, open economies have been more productive than closed ones.

In the long run, economic protectionism cannot withstand the technologically driven pressures for economic integration. Developed countries cannot afford to isolate themselves from the dynamism of the developing world. Emerging countries are growing fast economically, as reflected in Table 1.1. Protectionism is exactly the wrong economic policy for the United States. Parag Khanna correctly argues that the United States is no longer the world's single economic power but is competing with the EU and China in a new "geopolitical marketplace." In this competition, the forty or so "second world" countries become the swing states that are critical to the success of the three central powers. This is not a world for isolation or protection.[67]

Political Protection

Two very different examples demonstrate the broad range of attempts to protect local societies against political influence. The first, the rejection by

French voters of the European Union constitution in 2005, was an attempt to protect themselves from the sweeping political unification of Europe. The second, China's control of the Internet, is an attempt on the part of the central government to thwart the internal political discussion that is sweeping the Chinese Internet.

Countering governmental policy, French voters rejected the European constitution in May 2005. This rejection was based on fear—"fear of globalization, fear of trade opening, fear of a new world, fear of the movement of people from Central Eastern Europe and further afield into Europe."[68] While France may well change her position as discussions of the constitution continue, with this rejection she relinquished much of her leading role in the development of the European Union.

The Chinese example is one of dichotomous policies. On the one hand, the Internet has flourished in China with the support of the central government. On the other, the Chinese government is attempting to control discussion on the Internet that it considers politically dangerous. Internet use in China is widespread: there are more Internet users in China than in the United States. Cell phones are used extensively, primarily to interact with the Internet. With this rush of Internet activity, politically oriented online communities have developed, thus posing a threat to the central government and triggering attempts to control them. Over a thousand words are banned from use on the Internet in China. There are police Internet departments in numerous cities and provinces, with 38,000 Internet police as of 2005. The role of these police is to find "heretical teachings, futile superstitions, and information harmful to the dignity and interests of the state."[69] Censorship has been erratic in practice, with costs and logistics problems, allowing people to slip through the system during periods of intense activity. Bill Gates, among others, argues that economic forces work against such censorship: "If your country wants to have a developed economy . . . you basically have to open up the Internet."[70]

Cultural Protection

As we have argued, the Internet is accelerating the cultural erosion that has been underway for a long time. Many resist it. Few people have been as determined to protect their way of life, for example, as the French.

Much of their effort is focused on protecting the French language. There are rules on how much advertising content must be in the French language. On French radio and televison, 40 percent of all songs must be sung in French. A government committee has been established to identify French equivalents for English expressions.[71]

France also shares in the global concern over the spread of "American" (i.e., the United States) culture through the export of music and movies. Entertainment is the second largest export of the United States.[72] In 2005, France, joined by Canada, spearheaded a resolution in the United Nations Educational, Scientific, and Cultural Organization designed to protect cultures, particularly those in developing countries that are threatened. This resolution was a thinly disguised effort to give countries the option to limit the spread of U.S. cultural influence. The resolution has "given voice to widespread concern about the perils of excessive domination by American popular culture."[73]

Will these efforts stop cultural erosion in France? Surely not, although they may slow the process. On a personal note, the authors were living in France in 1973, when the French government published a list of three hundred English words that were in common usage and announced that if any one of these words was used in communication with a governmental agency, the agency would not respond. The authors were convinced that their French vocabulary increased by three hundred words that day.

Rejection

Protection phases into rejection. This is in evidence among certain Islamist groups in the Middle East. The same combination of economic, political, and religious factors that impede democracy in some Islamic countries underlies a rejection of globalization, framed under the rubric of "the West." The intensity of this rejection is demonstrated daily not only in these countries but across Europe, continuously simmering with periodic outbreaks.

Much of this is due to religious fundamentalism. The separation of church and state that has evolved in the West, and its causal factors of technologically supported modernity and secularization, pose a challenge to Islam. The Islamic tradition does not accept this separation nor its underlying factors. This is the core of the rejection by idealistic Islamist radicals.[74] One scholar argues that "no Islamic state can be legitimate in the eyes of its subjects without obeying the teachings of the *sharia*. A secular government might coerce obedience, but Muslims will not abandon their belief that state affairs should be supervised by the just teaching of the holy law."[75] The spread of information about the West, including the "decadence" of Western society as depicted in films and music, fans the intensity of this rejection. Another scholar observes, "Most Islamic fundamentalists believe that Western culture encourages individuals to abandon what they regard as traditional values, such as the primary importance of the family; the authority of the father; and the sanctity of religion. The fundamentalists resent the influence of Western businesses, consumer goods, missionaries, and such cultural ideas as individualism and *secular* (nonreligious) government."[76]

Economic conditions in the Middle East and for Muslim minorities in other countries exacerbate their cultural rejection. Economic stagnation in the Middle East since the mid-1980s, combined with a young population facing high rates of unemployment, with little or no financially viable future, fuels their frustration. With domestic political voices thwarted, anti-Western behavior becomes an outlet for this rage. Across Europe, young Muslims find themselves in these same circumstances.

Against these understandable religious, economic, and political reasons for frustration with the West among the world's Muslims, the radical fringe passionately (and opportunistically) feeds on this discontent. An articulate Sunni activist provided the manifesto for radical fundamentalism in the mid-1960s. In his book *Signposts Along the Road*, Sayyid Qutb redefined the Islamic notion of *jihad*. *Jihad* traditionally meant the Muslim's internal struggle against tendencies to disobey the will of Allah.[77] Qutb promoted a militant interpretation of *jihad* as Islamic holy war against nonbelievers.

James Johnson has provided a useful assessment of the radical view of *jihad*:

As originally conceived, the emergency *jihad* of individual duty is comparable to the western idea of the *levée en masse*. Contemporary radical Islamists, however, have turned it into something quite different: a justification for perpetual unrestricted war against America in particular and the West as a whole. . . . On the radicals' interpretation, the world of Islam is currently experiencing invasion from the West by a variety of means: military, economic, political, and cultural. There is no caliph to take action against this, and existing Muslim rulers are too corrupt, too weak, or too much the tools of the West to take defensive action; so the duty to defend Islam becomes that of every Muslim as an individual. All citizens of the United States or of other Western countries, and all who support the alleged aggression against Islam are equally enemies: in short, there are no noncombatants among them, and the rules of restraint operative in the *jihad* of collective duty do not apply here.[78]

Johnson points to the persistence of this idea:

> Now, this conception makes the juristic *jihad* of individual duty into something it was not intended to be. The state of emergency is not temporary but enduring; the "invasion" is not that of a military force crossing the border of the territory of Islam with evil intent but a complex of different types of western influence and presence in traditionally Muslim lands, which the radicals regard as inherently evil whatever their character or purpose. And the distinction is erased between those two, in Western societies, who actively and directly take part in the activities characterized as "invasion" and those who do not. The radicals' reinterpretation of the emergency *jihad* of collective duty to make it a justification for terrorism hijacks it for their own ends. There is no common ground here, and so long as this conception of *jihad* persists, none is possible.[79]

Sayyid Qutb also argued strongly against compromise with outsiders[80]— an important point for the discussion of universality in chapters 5 and 6. Still, even if we set aside the radicals, the intensity of the general Muslim reaction and the growing distrust of European and American majority cultures make dialogue difficult and even dangerous. More than in any other clash of fundamental beliefs, the Islamic and Judeo-Christian traditions exemplify two groups that reject their members who are willing to conduct a dialogue with those of the other tradition.[81] This view is massively amplified by the political situation in the Middle East, and sadly ironic given the two traditions' common Abrahamic roots.

An example of a contemporary Muslim thinker who has been rejected by Muslim colleagues as well as by many in the West is Tariq Ramadan. He argues for participation in Western society but for protection of Muslim identity. He regards the two cultures as having much in common. In a 2007 interview he stated, "We have this construction today that the West and Islam are entirely separate worlds. This is wrong. Everything I am doing now, speaking of connections, intersections, universal values we have in common, this was already there in history." Extending his position, he asserted, "Whatever your faith . . . you are dealing with your fundamental principles. The message of Islam is justice. The neo-liberal order leads to injustice. The point is to extract universal principles from one's faith, but in politics it has to be a personal decision. The danger of my discourse in France is that I am telling people to be citizens. Muslims are still treated as aliens. I'm telling them to vote." In spite of this position, he said, "My fiercest critics come from majority Muslim countries. Traditional Salafists condemn me for being against Islam."[82] Ramadan has also encountered rejection from one of the leading governments of the West, the United States. In 2004 the University of Notre Dame appointed Ramadan to a faculty chair in Religion, Conflict, and Peace Building, but in July, after Ramadan had sent all of his family possessions and enrolled his children in local schools, the Department of Homeland Security denied him entry.

A second example demonstrates how small groups can reject technological advancement yet survive. The Amish in the United States have a long-standing opposition to technology. They refuse to use powered agricultural machines, autos, and electricity. This ban now extends to computers in most communities. One would expect the young Amish to be searching for global information and be drawn away from their lives of simplicity, community, and faithfulness, particularly after their traditional venture into the outside world (the rumspringa period) at the age of sixteen. This is not the case for the majority. More than 80 percent of these youth return to be baptized into the church as adult members of the community.[83]

The message is that rejection can lead to isolation and isolation pushes toward conflict. The Amish have handled their religious and cultural uniqueness by maintaining a close dialogue with their surrounding environment, thus achieving their own rules in terms of social security, education, and child labor.

In summary, the rapid pace of computational innovation will clearly continue and will be reflected in changes in information technology, although the latter will be modified by social interaction, and will likely proceed in a stepwise manner rather than smoothly. Globalizing effects will persist, too, albeit at different levels of scale and pace. Economic integration will regain its pace, and its unequal impact will be mitigated as the digital divide is technologically reduced or overcome. For the same reasons, cultural erosion and democratization will proceed. A troubling, anarchistic tendency is that individuals will become more isolated from their geographic communities and more narcissistic, which poses a major challenge to organizational management. Protection and rejection may work in specific situations, but not as a broad-based strategy. In this environment, only small fundamentalist groups may succeed with a strategy of isolation. As a religion, Islam, of course, will succeed as it has for centuries. In competing with the United States, the EU, Latin America, some of southern Africa, and much of Asia, the political and economic structures of the Middle East will be forced to change.

Returning to the issues of multinational management, there is no evidence that effective regulation will be in place in a reasonable strategic timeframe. Given all of the globalization pressures, national governments in the long run will continue to lose policy freedom and the capacity of regulatory control, complicated by intermediate attempts at economic protectionism. International law will grow, but only slowly, as global governance networks gradually increase their authority and remain focused on specific issues. This is unfortunate, since corporations need guidance in their social policies and a level competitive playing field, particularly in relation to environmental efforts.

The reality of the regulatory confusion necessitates the move from a system of imposed rules to one of principles-based responsibility. Management still needs guidance from society as to what is expected of their firms. In the past, this guidance has been in the form of enforced regulation from domestic governmental agencies. With enforcement blunted, this guidance now needs to be in the form of general principles.

PART II

REDEFINING THE ROLE OF
THE MULTINATIONAL ENTERPRISE

The digital revolution creates a challenging environment for multinational management. To date, multinational enterprises have, as a group, proven to be the most adaptable institutions of our global society. The role of business in this new, information-rich, economically integrating world is critical. There are clear signals that global society is asking more from the business enterprise than merely economic productivity. It is asking for a greater social role. With legal regulation in a period of transition between less powerful national regulation and evolving global governance networks, management is also searching for new sources of social guidance.

A first step for management is to assess the appropriate role of the enterprise and to strategically position the firm to serve that role—the topic of chapter 3. Interacting with nongovernmental organizations can be a critical element of this process. NGO agendas reflect changing social preferences. In many ways, they are the formal voices of the social preferences in civil society, bearing widely diverse messages reflecting the diversity of civil society. Partnering with NGOs can provide two benefits for the multinational enterprise. Internationally, such partnerships can help lay the foundation for transparency and broad legitimacy for the enterprise. On the local level, indigenous NGOs may have deep roots in the community and thus may act as guides for the management of the local business unit in understanding the community. The potential for business/NGO partnerships is analyzed in chapter 4.

The evidence presented in Part II underscores the need for a social standard that is universal, enduring, and considered legitimate across broad ranges of global society. A human rights standard, we argue, has the greatest potential for success.

CHAPTER THREE

Assessing the Appropriate Role
of the Enterprise

The appropriate role of the business enterprise is framed within its economic, political, social, and cultural environment. This environment simultaneously provides economic opportunities for the firm and constrains its activities. Driven by dramatic changes associated with the digital revolution, the transformation of the business environment signals a subtle shift in the role of the enterprise as prescribed by society and as viewed by management.[1]

This chapter analyzes the appropriate role of business in its environment and assesses the resulting responsibility of the enterprise as defined by management. The spectrum of reaction, ranging from a market-driven response to one based on moral judgments, is arbitrarily divided into three kinds of corporate responsibility: (1) pursuing the traditional market model of the firm; (2) extending that model to recognize the shift in social expectations for the business sector; and (3) conceptualizing the role of the firm as arising from a managerial sense of moral responsibility.

Fundamental changes are taking place in the ways that both society and management view these three kinds of corporate responsibility and the preferred balance among them. Each management team must assess its environment, define an appropriate strategy, and implement this environmentally sensitive strategy, if the team's enterprise is to flourish.

The three appropriate roles and the managerial implications are outlined in Table 3.1. It should be noted that the analytic distinction of the three kinds of roles and responsibilities does not necessarily capture a policy or decision within a single category. Many policies and decisions will include dimensions of each.

The argument will unfold in four ways:

- Analysis of three appropriate roles within the changing parameters of the global economic, political, social, and cultural system;
- Assessment of managerial responses to those shifting parameters in specific business cases;
- Brief comparison of this three-part structure to the current literature on business ethics, economics, and corporate social responsibility;
- Considerations in selecting an appropriate role.

I. ALTERNATIVE CORPORATE ROLES

The consistent and clear objective of the basic market model to "optimize productivity," as developed in economic theory and finance, provides a concise basis of comparison. In this role, management reacts to the drive of external market pressures within the constraints of governmental regulation. Some firms in commodity markets, unable to differentiate their products, find themselves forced into this model through the product and financial markets. Other management teams (a term including boards of directors), influenced by theorists such as Ronald Coase, M. C. Jensen, W. H. Meckling, and Milton Friedman, set their policies and make their decisions in these terms.[2]

The second category, "ensuring long-term enterprise sustainability," is guided by an assessment of long-term social preferences. Its intent is to capture what are perceived as the fundamental shifts in the expectations

Table 3.1 Appropriate Corporate Roles

	Optimize Productivity #1	Ensure Long-Term Enterprise Sustainability #2	Pursue Moral Enterprise Behavior #3
Appropriate Roles:			
* Relation to Market Model	Basic Market Model	Extension of Market Model	Normative Dominance over Market Model
* Social Basis	Governmental Regulation	Legitimacy through Universal Societal Principles	Unique Stakeholder Needs
* Corporate Governance	Financial Market Dominance	Board and Top Management Dominance	Enterprise Community
Managerial Implications:			
* Reflected Values	Efficiency	Enterprise Legitimacy	Moral Judgment
* Strategic Positioning	Product Differentiation	Set of Universal Values	Collaborative Efforts
* Performance Metric	Wealth	Reputational Capital Less Costs	Imputed Cost

of society for the fictitious corporate citizen. A correct, actionable assessment of social trends positions the firm for market success in the long term, which is then reflected in the productivity of internal stakeholders and their pride in their firms.

The third category, "pursuing moral enterprise behavior," is a managerial departure from the market model. It is guided by the moral judgment of enterprise personnel in those cases where they identify a need that can be uniquely served by their firm, beyond the demands of the market or society.

The selection of the most appropriate corporate response, or the balance among these responses, is sometimes controlled by the governance structure of the market, as noted in the case of commodities. In most situations, however, there is some freedom within the constraints of the market, in that management teams can opt for extensions of the market model or departures from the model. This conceptual and real space for freedom of decision is designated as "the managerial area of discretion."[3]

Optimizing Productivity

In the perfect model of economics and finance, product markets force managers to maximize their productivity as a competitive necessity for the survival of the enterprise. Financial markets then allocate resources to those firms they expect to survive and flourish.

Governmental laws and regulations provide four necessary functions in this model. One set of such laws focuses on contractual transactions among market participants. Another is directed to ensuring that markets are efficient. A third legislates fiduciary responsibilities. In the fourth set, governmental regulators impose constraints on the behavior of market participants, reflecting the governmental responsibility to represent the needs and preferences of society. In this theoretical model, managers are analysts, not decision makers. Their actions are dictated by the markets that drive them against the constraints imposed by governmental regulation.

Some industries, such as agricultural commodities or bulk chemicals, are driven by relatively efficient product markets. For most industries, however, product market imperfections allow some managerial freedom to differentiate a product or service. In addition, few enterprises face clear and effective regulatory constraints. Social regulation is a very difficult process; regulators attempt to interpret social preferences and translate them into uniformly applied rules enforced by law. Market imperfections and regulatory ineffectiveness move some decision-making authority from regulatory bodies in the idealized perfect market system to managers in the basic market model, as discussed in the following two sections.

A Perfect Market System

Briefly put, a perfect market system would be one where markets are efficient and the regulation of market participants is effective. To be efficient, a market must be competitive in a structure where full information flows to all market participants. In this way, all market participants are free to make informed choices among a variety of real or potential alternatives. The conditions for effective regulation are that the regulations must reflect the consensus of society as resolved through the various interest groups, including business; they must be uniformly applied and enforced, and clearly signaled to the entrepreneur; and they must have the intended consequences.

In this ideal system, the efficiency of the markets would drive the allocation of resources to their most productive use, while the constraints on market participants would ensure that the other noneconomic, social goals of the society are met. Management is assigned the task of optimizing economic productivity, while the government and other social representatives are assigned the task of constraining corporate activities in order to protect society from the damage of unfettered markets. The driving mechanism in this perfect system is the market. When buyers have many alternative sources of existing or potential supply and full information about each source, the less efficient producers, who must shave quality or increase price, are quickly driven from the market. As management scrambles for whatever advantage it can gain, its activities must be bounded by effective regulation if the less powerfully represented interests in the society are to be protected. Thus, in this system all managers are pushed by the informed competition in the marketplace to continually butt against the effective constraints imposed by regulation. Optimal productivity is assured by the demands of the efficient marketplace, while the broader interests of society are protected by effective regulation.

There is a clear separation of roles here—productivity for the firm and social objectives for the regulators. There is no freedom of action on the part of the manager; he or she must select technology and allocate financial, material, and human resources in a way that optimizes productivity within the imposed constraints.[4]

This is a power outcome. Managers and their firms are subject to the absolute power of the efficient marketplace, as constrained by the absolute power of the regulators. Managers serve the task of optimizing productivity, but, since this is a forced outcome, they have no productivity responsibility. Neither are they responsible for the broader, social objectives, since they are pushed against the regulated constraints. This is why the manager is an analyst, not a decisionmaker in this ideal system. In this perfect market system, values would have to come from either the market or the government rather than from the manager. But since the market itself is amoral, social values that constrain the market must be expressed through governmental regulation.

Basic Market Model

Of course, no system works this way. Some markets are efficient, but most are not. Even under conditions of relatively competitive structures and efficient information, most markets, particularly product, service, and labor markets, are in a constant process of adjustment and permanent disequilibrium. In this sense, we observe widespread market failure.[5]

With the economic meltdown triggered in 2008, many firms found themselves struggling to survive in this basic market model. Facing a liquidity crisis, financial institutions focused on short-term survival at the expense of productivity in their risk/return trade-off. Their move back to productivity is occurring within a new set of regulations covering a broader set of institutions and instruments, and enforced by a more determined set of regulators.

In product markets, the auto industry is an example of survival. In the United States, industry productivity slipped over a period of time in terms of cost control and failure to anticipate and act upon underlying global market trends. As demonstrated in this case, the demands of the basic market model are unrelenting. The crisis management of governments has drawn those governments into market stimulus that is reminiscent of the Keynesian model of the 1930s. As the effects of the crisis and stimulus work through the system, governmental regulation is still central to the workings of the basic market model.

Creative destruction: capitulistic economic development arises out of é destruction of some prior order

Regulatory Structures

The corporation is an artificial person created by the state, with rights and duties defined by law. In order to enhance economic productivity, the corporation is given rights such as unlimited life and limited liability. Its duties are to stay within the constraints established by business law and regulation. Two dimensions are central to the basic market model: (1) social regulation and (2) the fiduciary responsibility of those representing the firm. These constraints on market participants begin with the domestic regulatory regimes, and extend to international law.

Social Regulation

In the United States, social behavior is regulated by a range of federal and state legislation and codes: consumer safety through the Federal Trade Commission, workplace safety through Occupational Safety and Health Administration, environmental protection through the Environmental Protection Agency, and so on.[6] The aim of these requirements is external accountability. They set minimum behavioral standards and punitive measures for noncompliance. The critical internal organizational mechanisms of accountability are not included. The recent development of "reflexive law" is an attempt to bridge this gap. "The reflexive legal models ask corporations to be more attentive to legal and ethical norms by making them into self-regulating institutions with legal oversight examining the sufficiency of their moral maturity."[7]

Reflexive legislation includes the Federal Sentencing Guidelines and the Sarbanes-Oxley Act. The Federal Sentencing Guidelines, particularly in the 2004 amendments, move beyond the requirement of compliance programs to "mandate that companies develop legal and ethical corporate cultures."[8] Similarly, Sarbanes-Oxley holds senior executives responsible not only for the veracity of financial reporting but also for establishing procedures to assure the effectiveness of ethics programs.

Responsibility to Owners

The United States is undoubtedly the most shareholder-focused country in the world. Managers and directors have a fiduciary duty, a primary obligation, to the owners of a company's shares. These duties are based on the *[handwritten annotations in margins: "property ⇒ life, liberty estate" (top right); "Wealth of Nations ⇒ John Locke assumes existence back to 2nd treatise on civil government } social contract"]*

notion of <u>private property</u> as it has evolved in philosophy and common law. In 1932, A. A. Berle and Gardiner Means described this responsibility as follows: "Taking this doctrine back into the womb of equity, whence it sprang, the foundation becomes plain. Wherever one man or a group of men entrusted another man or group with the management of property, the second group became fiduciaries. As such they were obligated to act conscionably, which meant in fidelity to the interests of the persons whose wealth they had undertaken to handle."[9] Members of the board and managers, as officers of the corporation, thus become agents of the owners as principals. As agents, they are directed to execute the lawful duties of their principals—the owners. Given the number of shareholders in large corporations, their combined objective function would, indeed, be complex. The only common denominator may well be the value of the shares—the metric so emphasized in finance.

Still, as Timothy Fort notes, "The Business Judgment Rule allows for managers to utilize discretion of what might be in the long-term interest of shareholders," and "Courts acknowledge that managers have significant leeway in determining how shareholders are best benefitted."[10] Ryan York argues that the business judgment rule substantially reduces the requirements of the fiduciary duty to shareholders: "In fact, according to the Delaware Supreme Court, 'under the business judgment rule director liability is predicated upon concepts of gross negligence.' . . . In itself, the business judgment rule provides a nearly insurmountable ban for shareholders seeking recovery from directors for their breach of fiduciary duty."[11]

Explicit legal departures from the primary obligation to shareholders are the "other constituency statutes" passed by individual states. These statutes, which originated in the 1980s as anti-takeover laws, were strongly endorsed by the management of takeover targets at that time. The statutes allow directors to consider nonmonetary factors when judging tender offers. "Nonmonetary factors which boards of directors may consider include the interests of the company, its subsidiaries and shareholders; the interests of employees, creditors, customers, and suppliers; and the interests of the local state and national communities."[12] Pennsylvania was the first state to enact such a statute in 1983. By 1999, forty-one states had enacted some form of other constituency statute. These statutes vary substantially state by state. They can be categorized as "(1) permissive,

(2) mandatory, (3) those involving a conclusive presumption of validity of directors' determination, and (4) bondholder protection."[13]

Other Nations

The aggressive competition in the marketplace and the nature of social regulation as described above have become known as Anglo-American capitalism. In other countries, domestic competition is often muted by market structures, and social regulation can be far more inclusive. Germany is the model of continental Europe's social market economies. Under the German regulatory framework, termed *Ordnungspolitik*, regulation is very specific. It evolves from the corporatist form of German government, whereby the "social partners" (government, employer, and employee associations) form a social contract and embody it in the legal structure of institutional interactions. The duties of government agencies are carefully specified in the law, as well as the requirements for the firms subject to their regulation. Once the regulation is in place, governmental intervention that does not fit clearly within the guidelines is not allowed. Compared to the Anglo-American model of regulation, German regulators are viewed primarily as auditors, whose purpose is to ensure conformance to a set of clearly stated legislated requirements.[14]

In the growth years leading up to 2008, the competitiveness of Anglo-American capitalism was impinging on social market economies. Ironically, the global economic crisis is drawing Anglo-American governments into the marketplace with an enduring presence more characteristic of that in social market economies.

Corporate Governance

The advantage of the market model is its single purpose—that of optimizing productivity within the regulatory constraints as a means of enhancing shareholder wealth. Optimizing productivity is clearly a necessary condition for all enterprises. Firms must survive in the short run if they are to achieve long-term sustainability. There is a sense of urgency in meeting these market requirements, an urgency arising from the product markets as reinforced by the financial markets. In their relentless pursuit of small relative financial gains, financial analysts continually assess the future direction and risks for each enterprise. Once they perceive a management team as losing its competitive edge, their assessment will be reflected in the share price, thus forcing a change in policy or in management itself. Thus, the financial markets provide a key governance structure in the market model, where governance is implemented by the group that directs the activities of the enterprise toward its defined purpose.

Only when the enterprise meets the challenges of productivity does long-term sustainability become an option. At that point, astute management looks beyond the short-term pressures to achieve long-term growth and sustainability for its enterprise.

In the basic market model, the values pursued are those reflected in laws and regulation. First, society wants the productivity for which it created the corporation—an instrumental value ensured by regulation directed toward efficient markets. At the same time, social regulation seeks to represent intrinsic social values by constraining the activities of the firm. Rigid adherence to shareholder goals adds a distributive requirement.

These requirements can become complex. Fort, commenting on business law in the United States, observes that it "entails a bewildering number of ways that the legal system holds business accountable for its actions. This includes, for instance, basic rules of contract, property, and tort law."[15] In addition, "Regulation from environmental to consumer protection to minimum wage laws, to name just a few, also provides minimum floors for public trust in business."[16] He argues that "it is highly doubtful that any managers could possibly know of all the applicable regulations relevant for their work."[17] Courts nevertheless will hold them liable.

Ensuring Long-term Enterprise Sustainability

This second corporate role is an extension of the basic market model. It builds on the social contract for the business enterprise given that expectations change over time. Sustainability means achieving and preserving the legitimacy of the firm, as judged by local communities and the broader society.

There are two dimensions to this legitimacy. As noted above, society formally grants the rights and constrains the activities of the corporations through the corporate charter and legal regulations. Beyond these rights and duties embedded in the law, other groups in civil society and, indeed, those working at the firm are constantly judging the activities of the organization. While the corporation must fulfill the minimal legal requirements if it is to keep the license to operate, it must also maintain the broad social and local community judgment of legitimacy in order to ensure long-term sustainability.[18] Social judgment and local acceptance contribute to internal worker pride in the company and worker motivation, since the enterprise personnel are part of these external communities. Legitimacy then leads to an enhanced reputation and reputational capital.

A Social Contract

Long-term enterprise sustainability is based on the idea of a contract between society and the artificial person—the corporation—that it has created. Social contract theory can be described or critiqued in numerous ways. John Hasnas describes it as "an implicit agreement between society and an artificial entity in which society recognizes the existence of the entity on the condition that it serves the interests of society in certain specified ways."[19] In Helen Alford's terms, "Society provides legal and social space in the form of a license to operate."[20]

The early notion of a social contract was that of an agreement between individuals that gave rise to the state, as formulated in liberal rights theory. The seventeenth-century philosopher John Locke concluded that based on this contract, a sovereign authority could be created to protect the rights of the individual, and governments retained legitimacy only by protecting the rights they were established to protect.[21]

An extension of political and social contract theories is the idea that a social contract can exist within civil society, as well as between the individual and the government. As used here, this contract extends beyond corporate rights and responsibilities as defined by law to include "social expectations and critical attitudes prevalent in a social group, rather than in law."[22]

Meeting the social contract in this sense is an integral part of corporate management. The values underlying management decisions in terms of this contract are those of society, not those of the manager or the management team. Social values are the revealed preferences of society. In current usage, the term "values" is most commonly used in this descriptive sense, for instance, when researchers study the "value-attitudes of the group under study, as an effort to map its behavior more systematically."[23] Thus, we are concerned with empirically describable values of society as they affect the environment of the firm. The important question is how to measure these social values, not whether they are right or wrong. Even if one accepts the rights of society to direct the activities of the firm, the problem of identifying the tenets of this social contract, both those captured in the law and those extending beyond the law, and then translating those social values into action, may be the most challenging of all managerial tasks.

Reputational Capital

Reputational capital is the sum of the financial gain accruing to the enterprise over the long term as a result of its perceived legitimacy. It is a function of an organization's identity and image.[24] Two views of identity can be distinguished. Corporate identity reflects the perspective of top management and is directed to external stakeholders. Organizational identity, on the other hand, reflects the perspective of all members of the organization and is directed to internal stakeholders. The corporate and organizational views of identity are clearly related, since organizational members are "likely to carry their impressions of corporate identity into their organizational lives and compare them to their understanding of organizational identity as it derives from their direct experience."[25]

"Image" is generally described in terms of a company's product brands, since image refers to the way the company is perceived from the outside, including by consumers.[26] A measure of image value is brand equity. Brand equity can refer to the price of a branded good compared to a generic equivalent, or to royalty payments or licensing agreements. The most highly recognized brand valuation firm is Interbrand, which evaluates as many as twenty factors contributing to brand equity.[27]

Reputational capital is broader than brand equity. It involves shaping a unique identity for the firm and captures the internal as well as the external dimension of a firm's identity.[28] The *Fortune* list of the most admired companies in the United States addresses this broader concept.[29]

Reputational capital tends to be reflected in financial capital. Following a careful analysis of 127 studies of the relationship between corporate social performance and corporate financial performance, Joshua Margolis and James Walsh concluded that "a clear signal emerges from these 127 studies. A simple compilation of the findings suggest that there is a positive association and certainly very little evidence of a negative association, between the company's social performance and its financial performance."[30]

Market analysis of executive surveys supports the claim that there is a positive relationship between social attentiveness and financial performance. In a 2008 survey of 1,254 international executives undertaken by the Economist Intelligence Unit, companies that pursued a long-term sustainability strategy (based on social, environmental, and ethical principles) substantially outperformed those that did not—their stock prices experienced a growth of 45 percent over the previous three years. This compares to a three-year growth of just 12 percent for those firms that did not pursue such a strategy.[31]

From the viewpoint of enterprise management, the need is to select a set of social preferences that leads to increased reputational capital for their firms. A plethora of organizations provide standards and ratings targeted to consumers, employees, and investors. Each reflects its own specific interests and subjective measurements—product or workplace, principles or certification, environmental or exclusively social. The result is a diverse set of standards.[32]

The value of reputational capital is supported by the growth of social investment funds. Socially responsible investments are experiencing strong growth worldwide in both absolute and relative terms. Socially responsible investment (SRI) is defined as "an investment process that considers the social and environmental consequences of investments, both positive and negative, within the context of rigorous financial analysis."[33]

Socially responsible investing means different things to different people. Generally, in the United States, it includes positive or negative screening of potential investments; investing in overlooked areas in communities, such as small business, affordable housing, or microentrepreneurs; and shareholder advocacy. Among these three types of activities, screening of investments dominates the other two in terms of the value of assets involved.[34] In the United States, professionally managed SRI represented about 11 percent of assets (over $2.7 trillion) as of 2007 and continues to grow.

In addition to SRI investments in the United States, some general pension and mutual funds consider social performance in their investment decisions. The United Nations Global Compact has issued a Principles of Responsible Investment whose signatories commit to incorporating environmental, social, and governance issues in their investment analysis. In addition to these professionally managed funds, 50 percent of individual U.S. investors report that they consider social criteria in their investments.[35] The underlying lesson here is that the academic and professional investments communities are watching social performance and claims.

SRI in Europe has grown as well. In its 2008 report, the European Social Investment Forum concluded that, broadly measured, SRI assets under management across Europe had a value of $3.7 trillion (2.67 trillion euros). This represents a substantial growth in SRI of more than 102 percent over 2006 and 2007.[36]

In summary, the evidence indicates a positive relationship between reputational capital and a firm's product and financial market performance. Empirical confirmation of that relationship is muddied, however, by the many definitions of social performance, along with measurement difficulties. The challenge of management is to identify the most legitimate and enduring set of social preferences.

Stakeholder Relationships

The external and internal components of long-term sustainability are tied to the stakeholder power relationships of the firm. Stakeholders are defined as "those who can influence or are influenced by the activities of the firm." Stakeholders and their representing institutions that provide the base of their power are represented in Figure 3.1.[37] There is generally a difference in the power balance between the enterprise and its external, as distinct from internal, stakeholders.

External stakeholders are those in a position to influence the activities of the firm. In civil society, customers and the financial markets (owners and creditors) are the primary external stakeholders. Also included are the media, NGOs, trade associations, local communities, and subcontractors. In most situations, the government is the most powerful external stakeholder, although it is seldom identified as such. External stakeholders often hold the balance of power relative to the firm since they have other alternatives they can pursue—consumers can purchase other products, subcontractors have other potential contractors, trade associations reflect the views of other companies in the industry.

Figure 3.1   Enterprise Network Stakeholders

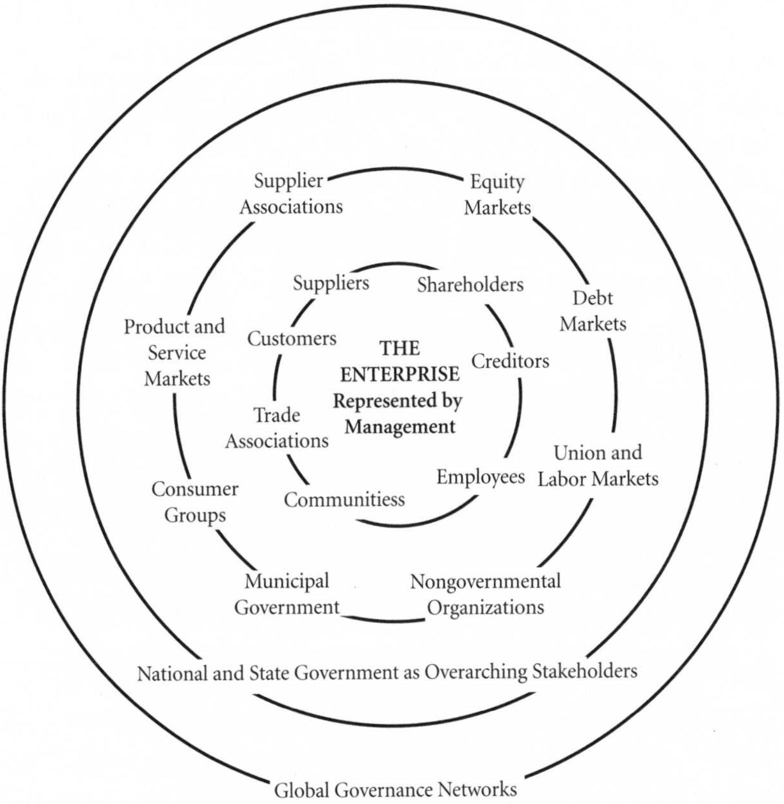

Source: Based on Tavis 2002a, p. 546.

Internal stakeholders (those directly influenced by the activities of the firm) include management and employees along with specialized subcontractors. Internal stakeholders are locked into the firm, compared to the external stakeholders. They hold firm-specific assets (i.e., valuable experience and skills related to the specific firm), assets that lose value if separated from the enterprise. Thus, internal stakeholders generally have less power relative to the firm. For management, this means that attention to the demands of external stakeholders must always be combined with sensitivity to the needs and motivations of, as well as the firm's responsibility for, the internal stakeholders.

Changing Social Judgments

As a result of the digital revolution and its broad ramifications, society is now much better informed about the activities of the business firm than it tended to be in the past, and it is extending its requirements for legitimacy. Concerned groups coalesce around this information. Many form nongovernmental organizations, whose programs are designed to bring pressure on firms for specific corporate action.

Two examples make this point. The first is the responsibility of apparel manufacturers for the working conditions in developing-country subcontracted plants. In the 1980s, working conditions in a subcontracted plant not owned by the contractor were seldom part of an apparel contract. Any conditions written into the contract created a legal liability for the contractor, since the contractor could become responsible for losses associated with those provisions. Society has now determined that working conditions in subcontracting plants are a responsibility of the contractor. Firms such as Nike were slow to recognize this trend and, as a result, suffered severe damage to their brand image. While Nike is today a leader in subcontractor workers rights and is extending that responsibility to environmental practices in its supply chain, the past damage to brand image endures.

A number of associations have evolved to ensure that apparel manufacturers meet this responsibility. Two have become the most influential—the Workers Rights Consortium and the Fair Labor Association. The Fair Labor Association (FLA, introduced in chapter 1) has been remarkably effective in improving the working conditions of developing-country apparel workers who produce for U.S. brand manufacturers. At its founding the organization, consisting of a few apparel manufacturers with a representation of universities, was boycotted by all but two NGOs. The FLA was strongly criticized by the student-based Worker's Rights Consortium (WRC) as being an industrial public relations gambit. Over time, however, collaboration among the manufacturers, a stronger university voice, and the inclusion of more NGO affiliates have led to effective action, legitimacy, and reputational capital for its members. Beginning with a list of companies who refused to reveal the location of their subcontractors, the FLA now not only lists the subcontractors but also publishes inspection summaries of the plant audits. The FLA and WRC now work together on local WRC plant remediation projects, and the FLA is accepted and recognized as an effective global monitoring and remediation group.[38]

As groups such as the FLA, the WRC, and the Ethical Trading Initiative[39] advance their own agendas, and as membership in such groups increasingly overlap, formal relationships among them will develop.[40] In that process, they could approach the authority of a global governance network.

A second example is drawn from the pharmaceutical industry. In the 1980s and into the 1990s, the purpose of pharmaceutical firms was broadly recognized as that of finding new drugs to prevent disease and enhance all our lives. Increasingly, across the world, society is coming to the conclusion that access to medical care is a human right and that pharmaceutical companies have the correlative duty to support that right. Pharmaceuticals are expected to reduce drug prices and, at the same time, develop drugs to treat diseases even if the firm's economic opportunities from a particular drug are limited. In short, society is changing its social contract with the pharmaceutical industry.

The social problem facing the pharmaceutical industry, it must be acknowledged, is far more complex than that facing the manufacturers of apparel. In pharmaceuticals, the buying motives are fundamentally different. In the case of many drugs, the disease, not the consumer, chooses the product, and its availability or affordability may be a matter of life or death. For other drugs, the consumer has only a narrow set of alternatives from which to choose. The necessity of a physician's prescription is also relevant to product choice. These factors lead to a different kind of purchasing decision from that existing with apparel buyers.

Pharmaceutical firms are responding in a manner that Thomas Costa describes as a paradigm shift for the industry. One multinational, Merck & Co., Inc., initiated the process with the production of a drug for a disease in the tropics. In 1987, Merck developed the antiparasitic drug MECTIZAN to treat onchocerciasis ("river blindness"), a devastating tropical disease. In spite of the fact that there was no possibility of commercial success for MECTIZAN, Merck management decided to pursue its development and clinical trials, overruling the objection of some members of the Merck management team and industrial association representatives who argued that developing a nonprofitable drug was not an appropriate role for a pharmaceutical enterprise. The drug has been remarkably effective with virtually no negative side effects. Merck has committed to offering

MECTIZAN free for all who need it for as long as they need it. Indeed, MECTIZAN is also proving effective in treating other tropical diseases.[41] This action on the part of Merck drew other voices to the issue and has led to so-called orphan drug legislation in the United States.

These kinds of corporate efforts are expanding dramatically. A major focus is the control of HIV/AIDS.[42] The producers of drugs for HIV/AIDS testing and treatment are involved in outreach programs to assist in the attempts to deliver effective therapies. Two examples, among many, are Bristol-Myers Squibb and Abbott.

The Bristol-Myers Squibb foundation is involved in the largest dona-tion program to date directed toward prevention and treatment of HIV/ AIDS in Africa. Since 1999 the "Secure the Future: Care and Support for Women and Children with HIV/AIDS" (STF) program has committed $150 million to over two hundred grantees as diverse as traveling theatri-cal groups, training programs for grandmothers who are caregivers, pro-grams to help orphans deal with the loss of their parents, and home-based care solutions across ten countries. Research advances include lower-cost tests to monitor HIV blood levels, new approaches to preventing mother-to-child transmission, and an extension to tuberculosis prevention. The emphasis is on replicable projects. STF monitors each of the grantees care-fully, as the STF overall strategy evolves.[43]

Abbott and the Abbott Fund have committed $100 million to the strug-gle against HIV/AIDS in developing countries. The Access to HIV Care program provides the firm's two protease inhibitors at a loss[44] and donates its Determine HIV rapid test to aid in the prevention of mother-to-child transmission.[45]

Other efforts of pharmaceutical firms address the issue of drug prices, through patient assistance programs,[46] drug donations in developing countries,[47] and leaves for executives to work in healthcare delivery.[48] However, although pharmaceutical firms are working individually with numerous NGOs and governmental agencies, interfirm collaboration has not reached the extent of the Fair Labor Association.

An example of a university-based collaborative effort is a series of work-shops and field activities that has been underway at the University of Notre Dame since 1987, including pharmaceutical companies, faith-based groups and other NGOs, multilateral institutions, and representatives from less-developed countries. The workshops and field research since 1987 have contributed to the growth of mutual trust as well as the determination to act. The most recent workshop, held in April 2005 and supported by Abbott, Bristol-Myers Squibb, Lilly, Merck, and Pfizer, focused on HIV/AIDS in the context of quality health care in developing countries.

These examples demonstrate the importance of sensitivity to changing social preferences concerning the appropriate role of the enterprise, long before these views are reflected in governmental regulation. As the forces associated with such reevaluation take hold, the social voice becomes louder, posing a correspondingly greater external and internal danger to a firm's reputational capital. Accurately recognizing these social trends early in their development is critical to the firm. Interaction with NGOs can prove to be a major asset in this process, as will be discussed in chapters 4 and 8. A firm has a window of opportunity before such issues become politicized, at which point meaningful progress becomes far more difficult.[49] In a very practical way, misjudgments in anticipating social preferences can result in serious damage to the perceived legitimacy of the enterprise, particularly since the expression of social beliefs involves fads and shifting ground, as well as activists' determination to challenge corporate responses. Some of the external social pressures for change originate from narrow self-interest or from unique features of a specific culture, while others have a more universal basis and are communicated broadly.[50] The challenge for management is to correctly identify those social trends that reflect universal principles, as distinct from temporary fads or local cultural phenomena.

Responding to social activism, of course, goes well beyond the apparel and pharmaceutical industries. An example of a firm that met the necessary efficiency requirements of the basic market model and looked toward sustainability through an increase in reputational capital is Wal-Mart. Setting the standard for efficiency in the domestic retail industry, even to the point of scheduling production in supplier plants, Wal-Mart has been able to meet its slogan "always low prices, always" and achieve the largest sales of any company in the world.[51] In the process, however, it has come into conflict with local communities over traffic congestion and over competition with local merchants and has been criticized for its employment practices.[52]

Wal-Mart is now demonstrating a concern for its social reputation through community activities and extensive public relations. The firm's performance in the aftermath of Hurricane Katrina drew praise from a wide range of groups, including many of its critics, as it contributed $20 million in cash, 1,500 truckloads of free merchandise, and food for 100,000 free meals.[53] The company is taking a leadership role in environmental responsibility and is using its demonstrated efficiency to identify new and often cost-saving environmental projects. It is driving environmental concerns down its supply chain in order to "create a more socially and environmentally conscious network of suppliers around the world." The goal as of 2008 was to make products 25 percent more energy efficient within three years.[54] In short, Wal-Mart is pursuing reputational capital for sustainability along with efficiency.

A uniquely successful example of interpreting social pressures for legitimacy and thus gaining reputational capital is The Body Shop. In 1976, Anita Roddick tapped into the growing expression of social concern about the environment. She created a cosmetics and toiletries retail operation of over two thousand stores with products and operations focused on environmental sustainability. Consumer packaging is minimal and recyclable; products are made from natural ingredients where possible, void of any animal testing, and with minimum use of synthetic chemicals; greenhouse emissions are minimized, even to the point of limiting the use of air freight and executive travel. These requirements extend throughout the supply chain, for example, to the promotion of sustainable palm oil production. The firm also participates in environmental advocacy programs.[55] Roddick was insightful in her early interpretation of social preferences. The reputational capital of The Body Shop grew with her commitment.

A test of sustainability is the long-term, dogged environmental approach of Stan Ovshinsky, the founder of Energy Conversion Devices. In 1957, Ovshinsky became convinced that society would turn to hydrogen as a source of energy and set out to "usher humanity into the hydrogen economy of the twenty-first century." ECD has operated in the black only once in its first fifty years of existence. Society now seems to be awakening to the need for alternative energy sources and the possibility of hydrogen as an energy source.[56] After years of struggle against larger companies with interests deeply invested in fossil fuels, ECD is now in a position to gain from its technical leadership.

Other companies focus on specific programs, often in conjunction with prominent NGOs to enhance their long-term reputational capital. An example is the relationship between Whirlpool and Habitat for Humanity: Whirlpool donates a refrigerator and stove for each Habitat for Humanity home built in the United States and Canada and for many abroad. Since its founding in 1976, Habitat has built approximately 165,000 homes, providing housing for 800,000 people in over three thousand communities. In 1999, under the leadership of its CEO, Whirlpool committed $25 million to this project in order to build reputational capital by donating products and inspiring employees.[57] Each year Whirlpool employees apply for the opportunity to spend a week working on Habitat homes. In 2005, 120 workers were selected from 450 applicants. The employee results are clear. "We've all grown from this. We're going to take a lot more away than we contributed."[58]

Corporate Governance

In this sustainability role, the corporate governance concepts of the market model still hold. Perceived legitimacy becomes reputational capital. The financial markets are sensitive to social judgments. A firm's social performance in its external environment also positively affects the internal stakeholders. Managers and workers are members of multiple communities, the business enterprise being only one of these, and they bring their judgments and beliefs to work.

Management's role is to discern subtle shifts in social expectations and strategically position the enterprise to ensure long-term corporate sustainability. In this, ensuring long-term sustainability through legitimacy and the achievement of reputational capital is a *sufficient condition* compared to the *necessary condition* of optimizing productivity.

Pursuing Moral Enterprise Behavior

This third notion of corporate responsibility departs from the basic market model and its extension in four respects. First, the pursuit of moral corporate behavior tends to have an internal basis, compared to the external pressures to optimize productivity or achieve social legitimacy. Pursuing moral enterprise behavior is strongly dependent on the individuals in the firm. Second, the objective of this responsibility is not to enhance the wealth of the firm through productivity, reputational capital, or motivation of personnel. This responsibility is based on a normative set of values directed to meeting unique stakeholder needs, particularly those of the internal stakeholders, over whom the enterprise tends to be dominant. The normative concern for unique stakeholder needs goes beyond the objective of enhancing their productivity to genuinely ensuring their personal fulfillment.

A third characteristic of this category is its departure from the contractual nature of both the stakeholder and shareholder theories. Stakeholder theory is based on the idea of a contractual relationship between each stakeholder and the enterprise. Contracts can be either explicit or implicit in nature.[59] Financial theory takes this contractual relationship a step further. Jensen and Meckling extend the pioneering work of Coase to define the business enterprise as a nexus of contracts. Indeed, in financial theory, the reason for maximizing shareholder wealth is the shareholder's distinction as the only stakeholder without a contract. When all other stakeholders have a contract with the firm, the shareholders bear the residual risk, and thus should receive the residual return.[60] In contrast, the moral enterprise model conceives of the enterprise as a community.

Fourth, moral behavior requires management to be proactive, as distinct from the reactive nature of other corporate responses. Within the social preferences that become the standards of the enterprise, there are unique local stakeholder needs that may call for a departure from uniform standards. Local exceptions are particularly important for multinational corporations, whose operations span and affect diverse cultures.

A normative departure from the market model depends on some freedom of action in spite of product pressures and regulatory constraints— some "managerial area of discretion." As noted earlier, there is a certain level of productivity that a firm must achieve, if it is to survive in our current global competitive environment. It is also essential for a firm to be attentive to evolving social judgments, as a means of maintaining its market position. Its success in doing so influences internal stakeholders through motivating productivity. Once a firm is positioned for productivity and long-term sustainability, it may have the additional freedom (the managerial area of discretion) to proactively pursue morally based activities that management judges to be the firm's responsibility, and to divert resources from enhancing shareholder wealth and long-term enterprise sustainability to these normative departures from the market model.

In this third category of corporate roles, management relies on its collective and individual moral judgment. A well-known case of pursuing moral corporate behavior under difficult circumstances involves Malden Mills and the determination of CEO Aaron Feuerstein. In 1995, Aaron Feuerstein's family-owned factory in Lawrence, Massachusetts, burned to the ground. Malden Mills was one of the four remaining textile mills still producing in New England. Following a brush with bankruptcy in 1982, the company had developed a technology for producing a fleecy, lightweight material used in outdoor clothing. Its product, Polartec, moved Malden Mills to the high end of the textile market and preserved the company from the severe competition that had forced most of the industry to the southern United States and to developing countries. The morning after the fire, Feuerstein announced that he would not only rebuild the factory in Lawrence but also continue to pay full wage and medical benefits during the estimated three-month reconstruction period. Feuerstein's actions were based on a sense of responsibility to the workers, both blue and white collar, and to the surrounding communities of Lawrence and Methuen, which would have lost fourteen hundred jobs.[61]

In this particular case, Malden Mills held a unique niche in the apparel market, a product differentiation that allowed it to compete on a noncommodity basis. Second, the mills were privately owned, thus providing a shield from equity market pressures.

A second example of CEO commitment is that of Ray Anderson of Interface, Inc., a publicly traded firm in an intensely competitive industry. Anderson founded the firm in 1973 to provide modular, self-adhesive carpeting for the commercial market. In the ensuing thirty years the company became the world's largest producer of commercial floor coverings and related interior products, with a workforce of 5,200, manufacturing facilities on four continents, and sales in 110 countries.[62]

In 1994 a book by Paul Hawken, *The Ecology of Commerce*, fundamentally changed Anderson's view of his company. His goal was ultimately to have no negative effect on the environment—a "zero environmental footprint"—in this intensely competitive industry and, further, to help restore the environment by influencing other companies. As of 2004, Interface management believed that the company was about a third of the way toward that goal: its carbon intensity (a measure of "clean" energy use) was down one-third, emission of greenhouse gases down 46 percent, the number of its smokestacks reduced by a third, effluent pipes reduced by 47 percent, and water usage down 78 percent per yard of carpet tile and 40 percent per yard of broadloom produced. Interface now leases carpets on a plan whereby the company recycles the used carpet when it is replaced.[63] With environmental savings estimated at over $200 million, Anderson sees this environmental approach as "not only the right thing to do, but the smart thing to do."[64]

Implementing this third category of responsibilities is more difficult than implementing the other two categories. The pursuit of moral corporate behavior is a substantial departure from the market model, and standards for action are difficult to discern. Given that a management team has the necessary freedom of action, or managerial discretion, within the market constraints, it falls on the team members to exercise their own moral judgments as to the direction of the firm over and above the activities that are rewarded by reputational capital, and to fundamentally reassess the relationship between the firm and those who comprise the organization. As noted earlier, normative departures call upon the distinction between values and morality. "Values" are measured by social preferences, which can be determined empirically, while "morality" refers to the rightness or wrongness of thinking or action. Julia Annas notes that it is "notoriously difficult to define morality. . . . It is possible, however, to identify characteristics of morality. . . . Such characteristics are (a) a distinction of kind between moral and nonmoral reasons, (b) a strict demand of responsibility ('ought' implies 'can'), (c) the prominence of *duty* or *obligation* as the basic moral notion, and (d) an essential concern for the noninstrumental good of others."[65]

The key factor in pursuing moral enterprise behavior is the interaction among those within the organization, considered as a community. Viewing the enterprise as a community departs from the contractual notion of both the stakeholder and the shareholder model, and is a different approach from our traditional organizational guidelines. Community involves the management of relationships rather than contracts—attention to the good of each person and his or her personal flourishing. Individual rights are defined and assured by the enterprise community, while individual responsibilities are determined with respect to communal goals. The enabling structures within which these personal relationships are nurtured must benefit the enterprise community as well as the individual (see chapter 10).

Individuals associated with each business unit are members of multiple communities—family, voluntary organizations, religious institutions—each with its own, perhaps subtle, differences in core values. Societies consist of overlapping and nesting communities, whose values are reflected in the institutions of that society.[66]

Corporate Governance

Governance for this enterprise role is based on a freedom of action within the confines of the market model. The underlying values are not those of governmental laws and regulation as in the basic model, or on broader social values observed for the enterprise sustainability extension of that model. The values in this normative enterprise role are founded upon the moral judgments of those within the enterprise.

II. COMPARATIVE APPROACHES

Many views of corporate responsibility are consistent with one or more of the appropriate roles described in this chapter. Three approaches that involve more than one role are those of business ethics, economics, and the movement of corporate social responsibility (with environmental protection as a distinct topic within social responsibility).

Business Ethics: Recognition of Market Opportunities

Business ethicists argue that managerial decisions must be based on moral principles. To them, motivation is central. Such deontological approaches (focusing on the rightness of intentions or motives as opposed to rightness of consequences), whether founded on reason or theology, are the starting point for all ethical decision making. Since the emphasis is on doing the right thing, this places most of the business ethics literature in the category of pursuing moral enterprise behavior. A major part of this literature, however, also recognizes the wealth-enhancing potential of normatively based actions. Lynn Paine, for example, presents a nuanced version of the view that "ethics pays."[67] Preferring the term "ethics counts,"[68] Paine focuses on the morality of the managerial decision but recognizes that it may well have a wealth-enhancing effect. While the motivation and determination of the manager are central, enhancing wealth is a possibility if not a probability. Thus, the managerial response begins on the right-most column of Table 3.1 (Pursue Moral Enterprise Behavior) and moves to the left (Ensure Long-Term Enterprise Sustainability). Ethics also has a great deal to say about the person and the organization—the topic of Part V in this volume.

Economics: Acknowledging a Social Fit

Ethics-oriented models entail a different direction of decision making than that typically observed in economic analysis. When economists consider ethics, their reasoning generally moves from left to right in Table 3.1—from achieving wealth through optimizing productivity to achieving wealth through ensuring sustainability, with little or no acceptance of normative departures from the market model. Their analysis remains firmly grounded in the utilitarian support of the market. Other ethical principles, such as trustworthiness, are supported insofar as they are necessary for efficient transactions. In analyzing a series of papers by economists and ethicists at a conference aptly named "Managing Ethical Risk: How Investing in Ethics Adds Value," Ralph Chami, Thomas Cosimano, and Connel Fullenkamp drew two conclusions. "First, ethical considerations are vitally important to the efficient functioning of individual businesses and entire economies. . . . Second, economic ideas and methodologies are essential to any discussion of business ethics."[69]

Corporate Social Responsibility: A Need for Focus

The literature and corporate reports on corporate social responsibility (CSR) are remarkably extensive and diverse. A 2007 Google search on "corporate social responsibility" found 34.4 million hits, and a search on "conferences on corporate responsibility" yielded nine million.[70] The CSR literature spans all three of the concentric circles proposed by the Committee for Economic Development as a model for CSR:

The *inner circle* includes the clear-cut basic responsibilities for the efficient execution of the economic function—products, jobs, and economic growth. The *intermediate circle* encompasses responsibility to exercise this economic function with a sensitive awareness of changing social values and priorities: for example, with respect to environmental conservation; hiring and relations with employees; and more rigorous expectations of customers for information, fair treatment, and protection from injury. The *outer circle* outlines newly emerging and still amorphous responsibilities that business should assume to become more broadly involved in actively improving the social environment (for example, poverty and urban blight).[71]

These concentric circles, outlined in 1971, trace productivity and sustainability roles with an emphasis on sensitivity to changing social preferences.

If we trace the development of the definition of corporate social responsibility over time, we find an increasing emphasis on its normative thrust as distinct from what is essentially a sustainability focus. The earliest definition in 1953, by Howard Bowen, supported the sustainability strategy: "It refers to the obligations of businessmen to pursue those policies, to make those decisions, or to follow those lines of action which are desirable in terms of the objectives and values of our society."[72] Over time, the moral requirements have become more prominent. In 1987, Edward Epstein defined CSR as "relating primarily to achieving outcomes from organizational decisions concerning specific issues or problems which (by some normative standard) have beneficial rather than adverse effects on pertinent corporate stakeholders. The normative correctness of the products of corporate action have been the main focus of corporate social responsibility."[73] In the current literature, although the concept of CSR may be informed by normative determination, it is primarily opportunistic in the sense of ensuring long-term sustainability for the enterprise.

Recently, Helen Alford, Barbara Sena, and Yuliya Shcherbinina have related CSR to the explicit moral base of Catholic social thought. In their analysis, however, they find it necessary to refine the notion of CSR in order to fit the normative dimension of Catholic social thought—passing from CSR through a concept of corporate citizenship to their definition of "sustainability." Drawing for support on the environmental origins of sustainable development, they note that "it [sustainability] also implies a unity between the ecological, social, and economic systems, and between the members of the human community, both those living today and those yet to be born. In this sense, the underlying ethical component in this term is closer to that of the Aristotelian-Thomistic tradition than it is perhaps in the other terms we have discussed. . . . The idea of sustainability, defined as it is with a focus on the human community, is perhaps the term that comes closest to that of the common good within [the Catholic social traditon]."[74]

Alongside the move toward normative managerial decision making, a backlash against corporate social responsibility is also evident. For example, speaking from a market-based perspective in a 2005 *Economist* survey, Clive Crook assaulted the movement from its basic idea to its practice.[75] While Crook, a strong market advocate and critic of CSR, reinforces our three-way classification of roles and responsibility, his conclusions illustrate the difficulty for many in moving beyond the basic market model to embracing the idea of sustainability and, even more so, a normative departure from the market model.[76]

In 2008 Daniel Franklin commented: "Three years ago, a special report in *The Economist* acknowledged, with regret, that the CSR movement had won the battle of ideas. In the survey by the Economist Intelligent Unit for this report, only 4 percent of respondents thought that CSR was a 'waste of time and money.' Clearly, CSR has arrived."[77] Part of the growth in emphasis on CSR can be attributed to the intensity of the discussion over climate change.

Environmental Responsibility

The wonder of nature surrounds us. So does pollution. The issue today is one of short-term versus long-term values—short-term consumption versus long-term effects such as growing shortages of fresh water and continuing contamination; ocean acidification; land and forest degradation; the extinction of species; and air pollution. Moreover, the poor are disproportionately hurt by degraded environments.[78]

Most firms are involved in some facet of environmental protection. Initially, their measures are an acknowledgment of the associated cost reduction, for example, in reducing energy use. Many creative cost-savings conservation practices and technologies are available.[79] At some point, however, these cost-savings programs turn into major outlays of resources and give rise to the need for reputational benefits, as in the case of Wal-Mart outlined above, following the sequence already described from the basic market efficiency model to long-term social sustainability strategies. For many forms of pollution, however, the necessary efforts cost more than the firm on its own can afford, either as a part of improving its efficiency or enhancing its long-term sustainability.[80] There are short-term and long-term market limits on what the firm can accomplish by itself. For an economy as a whole, the resources committed to substantive ecological efforts can involve a large cost and become a limit to economic development. Environmental protection is an area where effective regulation is absolutely essential.

Most of the current environmental concern is focused on greenhouse gas emissions and their connection to global warming—a topic of great concern and intense debate. The evidence of increasing amounts, particularly of CO_2, in the earth's atmosphere is clear. There has been an increase of approximately 18 percent between 1970 and 2008.[81] This presence will increase as the demand for energy continues to grow more rapidly (growing at 1.7 percent per year since 1985 and projected at 2.2 percent per year over the next ten years).[82] The connection between greenhouse gases and global warming is still debated in some quarters.[83] Nevertheless, as more people become concerned over the issue, it behooves multinational management to pay attention.

In a recent (2007) annual survey, McKinsey found that 55 percent of consumer respondents chose environmental issues, including climate change, as one of the three sociopolitical issues (from a list of fifteen) expected to attract the most attention over the next five years. This was an increase of five percentage points above the 2006 survey. Surveyed business executives are becoming increasingly aware of this consumer concern. Fifty-one percent of them classified it as one of their three most important sociopolitical issues—up a whopping twenty percentage points from the 2006 survey.[84]

Unlike corporate social responsibility, which can be narrowly focused in terms of its specific activities and location, efforts to control greenhouse gas emissions encounter the problem of the "global commons." The polluters seldom bear the negative consequences of their actions. Those bearing the negative effects can be very distant from the causes. In stakeholder terminology, those affected by corporate environmental degradation or enhancement are often only remotely connected to the firm and may even be members of future generations. Climate change is a collective problem that must be addressed collectively. The question is, Who will take care of this commons? In short, managing a firm's strategy regarding environmental efforts is unlike other dimensions of its social response. In the case of environmental protection, corporate responsibility requires an effective regulatory structure, with local requirements nested within a regional, national, and ultimately a global regulatory system. An advantage for regulatory efforts is that environmental impact measures are more precise than those for other social impacts.

Attempts to address the global commons through regulation have lagged far behind attempts to address the national commons in many countries. The Kyoto Protocol of 1997 was a landmark agreement, requiring 36 industrial countries to make what are relatively modest reductions in CO_2 emissions. While Europe has made substantial progress under the treaty, which was ratified by 156 countries, the United States refused to ratify the agreement.

With the Kyoto Protocol scheduled to expire in 2012,[85] international conferences are attempting to seek a broader and more effective agreement. Following the United Nations December 2007 conference in Bali, *The Economist* described the outcome as "a vapid statement of good intentions."[86] As of early 2009, the U.N. Copenhagen meeting scheduled for December 2009 was seen as perhaps the last opportunity to reach a workable agreement through the efforts of the United Nations.

The future of such treaties is uncertain. Developing countries are hesitant to set environmental standards because the cost will slow their economic development. Their attitude is that the developed world polluted the environment in its drive for economic growth and now unfairly wants to restrict this same drive in the developing countries. They point to the United States, with one-fifth of global carbon emissions, as the largest polluter, with only 5 percent of the global population and no uniform program for abatement. As developing countries experience the effects of global warming, however, their attitude is softening. Drought in the Amazon rain forest, for example, may force a reassessment of the historical Brazilian position that the Amazon is exclusively its concern.[87] The water sources for India and China, the Himalayan glaciers, are melting at an alarming rate. China, the world's largest carbon emitter, suffers from serious domestic pollution. Its 2006–2010 five year plan addresses pollution abatement with determination on a coordinated national basis (as with all Chinese policies).[88]

Within the United States as of 2008, leadership has fallen to the states and to fragmented voluntary efforts. California took the leadership with its far-reaching statewide greenhouse gas regulatory programs. Florida and others are following. In these cases, the regulatory state enjoys little of the environmental benefits from its own effort. In addition, the "leakage" potential, in the sense that polluters may move out of states with stricter regulations or import energy from states with less strict regulations, is significant.

Utility companies are forming their own interstate groupings. The Regional Greenhouse Gas Initiative is a program of ten Northeast and Middle Atlantic states to develop a mandatory market-based cap and trade program.[89] Led by the progress in the Northeast, similar interstate carbon-reduction energy savings accords are evolving in the Midwest (extending to Manitoba), Southwestern, and West Coast states.[90]

At the national level, environmental regulation has been surprisingly slow to develop. Congress did not act on early, repeated efforts to deal with carbon emissions. The Environmental Protection Agency up to and including 2008 did little to support regional, state, and local efforts or to promote a national policy. In 2008, Thomas Friedman described the United States energy policy as "incoherent, ad hoc, and asymmetric."[91]

Regulatory efforts to control CO_2 emissions can take three approaches.[92]

1. *Subsidize Green Technologies.* From a governmental point of view, this approach tends to be relatively uncomplicated since the taxpayers tend not to notice the expenditures. On the other hand, governments must choose the technology to subsidize. Relative to greenhouse gas emissions, the general view is that competition in the private sector, with its freedom to range over all potential technologies, will lead to more innovation and technological advances. Once a government subsidy is in place, with public and private resources committed to a particular technology, it is difficult to abolish. Subsidization can actually discourage further innovation. Again, movement from one technology to another is an advantage of the private marketplace.

2. *Set Standards for Products and Processes.* For some polluting sectors, such as homes or automobiles, where large numbers of consumers are involved, this may well be the most effective approach. Requiring energy-efficient construction or banning incandescent lighting are examples. As with subsidization, these kinds of standards select the

products and processes to be controlled. This can foster rigidity and discourage technological innovation, like government subsidization.

3. *Establish a "Carbon Price."* This involves setting a price on pollution. The purpose of the carbon price is to establish a cost on emissions and a savings for conservation. The advantage of this approach is that it draws on the ingenuity of the private sector. The price can be determined in terms of a tax on emissions or in some kind of "cap and trade" system.

In general, taxation has the advantage of minimizing risk for the conserver or polluter, to the extent that it is anticipated to hold for the long term. On the other hand, once a tax is established at a specific level, it becomes rigid and difficult to change.

Cap and trade systems are more flexible than taxes from the macro point of view, although more risky for the participants. These systems are based on an officially determined overall cap for the level of carbon that is allowed to be emitted. Each company is then allocated a part of this cap through issuance or auction. This then becomes its individual cap, or allowed emission. Companies that can reduce their emissions below their cap can then sell their unused allowance to others who exceed their allowance, thus setting a market price on emissions. Over time the cap is reduced, thus influencing the cost of over-emission and the motive to reduce pollution. These are ingenious market systems. Markets are actually created for buying and selling things that do not yet exist; conservers are selling something that will not exist to polluters who will produce something that will exist. It is reminiscent of the commodities and futures markets at the Chicago Mercantile Exchange/Chicago Board of Trade Company. In order to function, the carbon markets need a standard unit of exchange, a means of verification or certification for the product (in this case, a prevented emission), and a structure to bring the buyer and seller together.

Under the Kyoto Protocol, Europe has developed its Emission-Trading Scheme (ETS). Those who reduce pollution below their allowance receive a certificate representing the amount that was not emitted. Many of these certificates come from the so-called "dirty" industries in Europe: electricity, oil, metals, building materials, and paper. In developing countries, certification is acquired through the United Nations under the Clean

Development Mechanism program. These U.N. "certified emission reductions" come from a variety of interesting sources. One example involves hogs, primarily in Brazil. Pigs emit methane, a hydrocarbon (CH_4), in their effluence. Amazingly, the average sow and her piglets emit nearly half a ton of methane yearly. Farmers can build lined and enclosed pools to collect the effluence and the methane emitted. They then use the captured gas to generate electricity and sell the nonemitted gas as a carbon credit on the European Trading System. Since methane is twenty-one times more potent as a greenhouse gas than CO_2, this can be a major source of revenue. Another example is that of Chinese refrigeration chemicals. Well over half of the certified emissions come from China. Carbon dioxide is a by-product of a chemical, trifluoromethane, used in refrigeration that has been banned in developed countries for some time. It is relatively cheap to capture and burn off the CO_2 from these refrigeration chemicals. Rather than ban their use, China has imposed a large tax on the emission of these chemicals and plans to establish its own market for certified emissions reductions.

The demand side of this market is easier to measure than the supply side. Polluters are given a target and need a permit to emit carbon beyond that limit. These targets are regulated in Europe's ETS. They exist in the form of voluntary limits in Japan. They may be demanded by corporations in the United States seeking reputational capital. Again, the ability to measure greenhouse gas emissions makes this system practical.

As with other assets, someone will create a market if there are buyers or sellers. An important early market channel for these pollution certificates is a London-based investment bank, Climate Change Capital. Although this market is small by the standards of financial markets, there were $30 billion in such certificates traded in 2006. The price was volatile, generally ranging from fifteen to thirty euros/ton. Trading of European certificates more than doubled in 2007, with the U.N. certificates increasing by almost a fourth.[93]

Another market, in fact the first carbon-trading market in the world, is the Chicago Climate Exchange (CCX). All six major greenhouse gases are traded on the CCX. For this exchange, companies set voluntary annual gas-emission-reduction targets, which then become legally binding. Member companies who reduce emissions below their targets earn surplus allowances. These carbon credits can then be sold on the CCX or banked for future years. Members who produce emissions above their targets must purchase these CCX "carbon financial instrument credits."[94] Other similar markets are evolving.[95]

As noted, cap and trade models can be risky for the participants, and free markets have a way of making regulators uneasy. Uncertainty about supply and demand is a given; prices can vary greatly; and these markets easily can be flooded with certificates. With the 2008 global recession, the price of carbon credits plummeted on Europe's ETS.

The underlying purpose of these types of efforts extends beyond the control of pollution to the stimulation of new, less-polluting alternatives. The higher the cost of overpollution, the greater the stimulus for alternatives.

The recognition of the problem of greenhouse gas emissions by programs such as those outlined above is triggering a plethora of technical innovations. A major effort is devoted to electricity produced from coal.[96] One approach to emission reduction is that of carbon sequestration from coal gasification plants. An example is a coal gasification plant in North Dakota, where CO_2 is separated from other gases, piped to oil fields in Saskatchewan, Canada, and injected into partially depleted oil fields, where it penetrates sand deposits and increases recovery of oil. There are about seventy of these kinds of CO_2 injection operations around the world. Some of the CO_2 remains in the partially depleted fields. What returns to the surface is recaptured and stored underground, often in fully depleted oil or gas fields.[97]

The use of nuclear power is also being reevaluated. Renewable sources of energy are being pursued. There is a great deal of technological advancement and innovation in solar and wind sources. The use of solar power has increased dramatically in recent years—41 percent per year from 2004 to 2007.[98] Photovoltaic cells are becoming increasingly sophisticated. In 1970 these cells created electricity at $20 per watt. By 2004 the cost was below $2.00 per watt. Solar thermal installations using mirrors to gather heat from the sun and convert it to electricity are coming on line. The ability to harness energy from wind is growing at 18 percent per year. In 1970 wind energy cost $2 per kilowatt hour. It has decreased to 5 to 8 cents per kilowatt hour. This compares to a cost per kilowatt hour from coal of 2 to 4 cents.[99] The boom in wind and solar production and installation collapsed with the 2008 economic turbulence, but these industries are still vibrant and will recover with the overall economy, resuming their previous healthy growth.

Creative new environmental technologies are surfacing. One company has proposed seeding the ocean with iron particles as a means of stimulating growth of plankton, which would enhance the ocean's ability to absorb carbon dioxide. This effort would be sold on the carbon offset market.[100] Hydrogen fuel cells are becoming a reality. Other exotic approaches are receiving consideration: capturing solar power in space and transmitting it via laser beams to earth; creating "solar sunshades" consisting of millions of small spacecraft; or sending engineered particles into the atmosphere to reflect sunlight.

Debate rages over how dependent we are on new technology to solve our global warming predicament. One group, focusing on global determination, concludes that the increase in CO_2 can be solved with present technology combined with a worldwide determination to use it.[101] Others, focusing on the expanding global economy, call for a fundamentally new set of low-carbon technologies.[102]

In summary, regulation is the key to environmental responsibility. Effective regulation concentrates on prevention rather than clean-up; sets standards that will create opportunities for companies to determine how to solve their own problems, often by new technology and innovation in their own production process or in new market opportunities; sets reasonable compliance deadlines, with flexible enforcement; and ensures that a company cannot gain by avoiding environmental investments. A measure of the success of environmental regulation is whether it fosters continual improvement.[103] The broader the governmental span of this regulation, the better—at state, regional, and national levels, and through international treaties or global governance networks.[104]

With respect to the individual corporation, Stuart Hart suggests a three-stage approach: First, shift from pollution control to pollution prevention. Second, consider the full life cycle of the firm's product. Third, develop clean technologies.[105] Clean technologies can have a major payoff in terms of reducing production costs, enhancing reputation capital, or finding new markets. Even in the absence of regulation, some management teams are successful in exercising environmental responsibility. Interface, Inc., outlined above as an example of an environmental normative departure from the market model, is actively working with its full product life cycle as part of its determination to leave a zero-carbon footprint.

In its environmental response, multinational management must push for effective, geographically broad regulation—truly a challenging task given the differences in national views and the political disagreements to be expected. Managers must begin by strategically positioning their own firms. Compared to other dimensions of corporate social responsibility, at least environmental concerns have one advantage; the issues are, by comparison, fairly clearly defined, and measurements of failure or success can be quantified.

Management Surveys

In its annual survey of business executives regarding issues of business and society, McKinsey continues to find a recognition of the need for social response.[106] The business executives acknowledge the risk to reputational capital if they miss a shift in social expectations, but they have reservations about which specific social concerns will affect their firms. In the survey, executives are asked to rank a list of specific issues expected to have an impact on their companies and industries by importance, from more to less important. The combined ranking for 2007, along with the changes in rank order from 2005, is indicated in Table 3.2.

Environmental issues moved from third place in 2005 to first place in 2007 (as reflected in a +2 difference). The category "human rights standards" continues to rank last. This reflects the problem that business executives have with the term. It is noteworthy, however, that the issues marked with an asterisk are specific human rights categories, and they register much higher, both in terms of their 2007 rank and the increase over the previous two years.

McKinsey identifies two institutions integrally involved with this evolving trend: the office of the United Nations Global Compact (UNGC) and the Global Reporting Initiative (GRI). The United Nations Global Compact was initiated by Kofi Annan in 1999. As outlined in chapter 7, it consists of ten principles for companies to incorporate into their operation on a voluntary basis. The Global Reporting Initiative, formalized in 1997, grows out of a partnership between an NGO, namely, the Coalition for Environmentally Responsible Economies, and the United Nations Environmental Program. The GRI publishes "Sustainability Reporting Guidelines"—a remarkably extensive and detailed set of indices—to assist

Table 3.2

Issues Ranked in Order of Importance, 2007	Change in Rank since 2005
Environmental issues, including climate change*	+2
Privacy, data security	+3
Job loss and offshoring*	−2
Demand for healthier or safer products	+4
Healthcare benefits, other employee benefits*	+1
Political influence/political involvement of companies	−4
Workplace conditions, safety*	+5
Pension and retirement benefits	−4
Ethical standards for advertising and marketing	+2
Pay inequality between senior executives and other employees	+1
Affordability of products for poorer consumers*	−2
Demand for more ethically produced products	+1
Demand for more investment in poor developing countries	+4
Opposition to foreign investment and freer trade	−1
Human rights standards	0

Source: Bonini, Hintz, and Mendonca, p. 55.

corporations in analyzing and reporting social, environmental, and economic impacts, beyond the required financial reports. Companies are increasingly using these guidelines as a framework for their corporate responsibility reports. The UNGC office and the GRI are closely collaborating to assist those companies who sign the Global Compact to effectively report their results, with guidance from the GRI.[107]

Another recent survey reflects a continuing acknowledgment of the need for social action with an increasing recognition of the importance for the firm to establish social policies and, further, to implement these policies. As mentioned earlier in this chapter, in 2008 the Economist Intelligence Unit surveyed 1,254 international executives on their view concerning "sustainability efforts." The definition of sustainability was broad: "This study has called sustainability those policies and processes which enhance the financial, environmental, societal, human, and other resources on which the company involved depends for its long-term health. Sustainability is a result of having such sustainable politics and processes, and aligning them so goals in one area are not compromised in favour of those in another."[108]

Executive priorities in the survey and the percentage of respondents agreeing that these were priorities included the following:

- improving environmental footprint of products (57%)
- improving energy efficiency (52%)
- developing new products to help reduce social or environmental problems (51%)
- reducing greenhouse gas emissions (40%)
- including environmental concerns in the supply chain (35%)
- addressing human rights issues in the supply chain (34%)
- communicating this performance to investors and stakeholders (61%)[109]

Although just 22 percent of survey respondents indicated that their companies issue formal reports on their environmental impact, 40 percent stated that their companies planned to publish such reports in the next five years."

These findings clearly demonstrate that surveyed executives have "gotten the message" from their societies. However, given the growing publicity on greenhouse gas emissions, this response seems low. Undoubtedly it will increase. The novelty of driving environmental change down the supply chain is also reflected in the data. Environmental change in the supply chain of multinationals may well be the next activist focus, following the human rights push in the apparel industry a decade ago. As noted, Nike and Wal-Mart have clearly received this signal.

Along with this enhanced recognition, *The Economist* noted, "Companies are still trying to figure out what sustainability means for their business and how to implement it."[110] Only 53 percent of respondees indicated that their firm had a coherent policy.

Costs were clear in the executives' minds (40 percent were concerned about costs); they tended to believe that gains would outweigh the costs (57 percent) but only modestly. Many executives regarded the source of these gains as the product markets.

In addition to costs savings through environmental efforts, respondents expected gains through reputational capital:

> Another oft-cited benefit of sustainability policies is enhanced reputation, with knock-on effects for brand value and reduced reputational risk. Respondents to our survey consider their leading objective: 79% ranked enhanced brand reputation as a 'very important goal' for their programmes. Among the benefits they expect from these policies, they put first an opportunity to attract and retain customers (cited by 37%), and fourth the ability to manage reputational risk (29%). Similarly, 18% of firms thought most of the customers would pay extra for "a brand renowned for its commitment to sustainable development," and a further 37% thought a "significant minority of customers would pay more."[111]

Respondents regarded implementation as a major hurdle. In addition to costs as the most formidable reported barrier, 36 percent of respondents were concerned over the difficulty in devising useful measures, controls, and targets.[112] As for the organizational process of integration, *The Economist* quoted respondents as follows: "Sustainability needs to be integrated into corporate structures and processes," and "until it affects someone's compensation and performance reviews, it won't appear as a serious priority for middle management."[113] In short, amid this enhanced appreciation of the importance of contributing to sustainability through social and environmental action, there remains great uncertainty as to how to go about it. Together the two surveys discussed above reflect a transition among business executives from "What is it?" to "How do we do it?"

III. MANAGERIAL DECISION MAKING

Each management team finds its own balance among the three modes of corporate responsibility, as shown in the above examples. The boundary between optimizing productivity in the basic market model and extending that model to achieve long-term enterprise sustainability is clear. Meeting the demands of the basic market model as the necessary condition became starkly evident with the 2008 economic meltdown. As the effects of the crisis work their way through the system and productivity is assured, however, alert management will keep an eye on the opportunity for a strategy to enhance enterprise sustainability, to the extent possible. The boundary between enterprise sustainability and normative departures from the market model is not as clear. While many social (including environmental) programs initiated with a sense of moral commitment have a wealth-enhancing effect, sustainability is not necessarily the core impetus. Nevertheless, the distinction is analytically important for managerial decision making. The key is to acknowledge these three distinct kinds of responsibility and then proactively pursue sustainability and moral corporate behavior where possible. In analyzing the firm's possibilities to pursue these roles, management must first assess the extent to which departures from the basic market model are available to it. Beyond that, given discretion, the notion of imputed costs will help management in deciding how to use that discretion.

As discussed above, the freedom of action to move beyond basic market pressures is the "managerial area of discretion." For sustainable enterprise development, redirecting resources to meet social expectations in their formative stages as judged by management requires the ability to compete in the product markets and freedom from dominance by the financial markets. To further divert resources to stakeholders beyond their direct contribution to wealth through reputational capital, or to environmental protection beyond cost savings, requires even greater freedom.

Assessing the managerial area of discretion is a key analytical consideration. Overall, this area is increasing with the digital revolution, as multinational enterprises gain power in the milieu of the global economic system.[114] There are two forces at work. First, markets are becoming increasingly competitive, which has an impact on multinational input costs and output prices, while at the same time the regulatory power of national governments is decreasing. Competition affects the cost of subcontracted products and services as well as labor, thus offsetting much of the price competition for output. Social regulatory costs decreased globally with the encroachment of competitive Anglo-American economies on the relational, community, and employee orientation of social market economies.[115] Moving forward, the increased involvement of governments in the marketplace and the interim confusion of regulatory structures will push all costs up.

The second force, as described in chapter 2, is the remarkable ability of multinational enterprises as a group to adapt to the rate of change associated with the digital revolution, thus gaining power relative to national governments as well as to other institutions, such as organized labor. With the macroeconomic collapse, this adaptability was again in evidence. On balance, within the constraints of global product or labor markets and governmental regulation, multinational enterprises have been able to maintain a substantial area of discretion.

Still, within the managerial area of discretion, managers are often reluctant to venture too far from the basic market model. Extending that model for sustainability involves an interpretation of social preferences that is not necessarily within the typical managerial comfort zone. As noted, for the multinational enterprise this is where a code such as the United Nations Global Compact can be critical in pursuing sustainability and where interaction with other firms and NGOs can be of value. Activists, on the opposite end of the attitudinal spectrum, believe that the business enterprise has unlimited freedom within the dictates of the product and financial markets and can readily undertake the activities espoused by the activist group. Their typical assumption is that corporate limits on social, including environmental, actions are self-imposed and that overcoming these limits is a matter of changing managerial behavior, not external market pressures.

Given discretion, management must decide whether it would be beneficial to move to a strategy of enterprise sustainability and what dimensions of the firm's operation should be involved in the new strategy. Further commitment of corporate assets on a moral basis to departures from the market model, an admirable and desirable goal, must be analyzed with care, since this could endanger the financial viability of the enterprise.

Figure 3.2 illustrates the financial relationship among the three roles. The basic market model is point zero. The horizontal axis represents resources committed for sustainability programs and/or those motivated by moral commitment. Resources can be any combination of financial, material, or human commitments. The vertical axis measures wealth as the reputational capital net of the cost or the net impact of ecological efforts. The "sustainability" area on the left half of the graph represents those investments expected to generate a positive long-term wealth effect through reputational capital or environmental savings. Conceptually, the

Figure 3.2   The Sustainability Moral Behavior Boundary

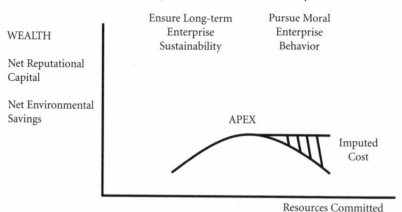

idea of wealth as a measure of long-term benefits set against short-term investments is very useful. There are alternative metrics for the measurement of this wealth, none of them fully satisfactory.[116]

As the amount of resources committed to a program increases, a point will be reached where the net positive returns will be maximized and no more net benefits can be achieved. When these activities reach their apex, the boundary between enterprise sustainability and moral corporate behavior is crossed, and net-positive wealth benefits become negative. Further commitment of resources amounts to a normative departure from the market model. Beginning at the apex, a useful metric is the imputed cost as a measure of the negative benefits incurred for the continued pursuit of a moral objective. This cost then becomes a measurable index against which managerial determination to "do the right thing" can be compared.

This model was conceptualized as the result of a visit to the Johnson & Johnson facility in Recife, Brazil, a city in northeastern Brazil with pockets of extreme poverty. The Johnson & Johnson facility in the Recife Industrial Park draws workers from the nearby Tieta Favella (slum). The daily corporate lunch program is the only substantial meal for most workers, since their families cannot afford a full dinner and seldom have breakfast. J&J initiated a program to provide breakfast for the workers. This proved to be a very good investment. Morning accident rates dropped, and worker motivation was enhanced. Workers then began to bring their wives and children to breakfast. Initially, because of the added motivational effect, the rate of return on the investment declined but was still positive. As the program continued, however, workers began to bring their extended families, often large, to breakfast, at which point the breakfast program passed the apex, net benefits were negative, and the program became a moral commitment for the company.[117]

The risk of moving beyond the basic market model and toward the right in Figure 3.2 is reflected in the experience of our earlier case examples. Note that at the time these cases were selected, they were all financially viable enterprises. In the example of Malden Mills, the financial commitment, although large, was relatively short-term and known. This case, indeed, tested the firm's financial viability in a competitive textile market. Following the almost heroic decision of Aaron Feuerstein to keep his plant in the Northeast, competition gradually eroded his Polartec competitive advantage. As his product line was pushed back toward a commodity basis, combined with the loss of customers during plant reconstruction, Malden Mills found it more difficult to compete with the lower-cost production sites outside the Northeast and was forced into bankruptcy.[118]

Changes in a firm's competitive position can push the firm toward the left in Figure 3.2 and lead to the departure of its normatively determined leader. This occurred in the case of Anita Roddick's Body Shop. Its success in natural cosmetics drew others into the sector. There was a substantial increase in competition from supermarkets and retailers offering similar and cheaper products. Combined with problems with distribution and the supply chain, financial performance faltered, whereupon Roddick resigned as CEO and left the board. The Body Shop experience is a reminder that sustainability is an extension of the basic market model and not a replacement for it. As noted in *The Economist* (with what appears to be satisfaction), "Capitalism has at last caught up with Ms Roddick."[119]

The opportunity for financial returns also applies on the upside when a technology finally becomes implementable. When a productive opportunity finally materialized for Energy Conservation Devices in the form of leadership and valuable patents, the investors narrowed their focus to patented Ovonic rechargeable nickel-metal hybrid batteries and solar panels. Over founder Stan Ovshinsky's objection, the board deemphasized other environmental projects, such as fuel cells and the associated large energy storage devices. At that point, Ovshinsky was asked to resign as chairman.[120]

In other cases, both the firm and the environmentally determined leader continue to prosper. The ecological commitment of Interface, Inc., is a long-term policy in a highly competitive industry. Its financial performance as of 2007 was strong. Even with larger, well-funded competitors being drawn into the modular carpet market, Interface continued its leadership. The determination of Roy Anderson to take responsibility for the full life-cycle of its products by recycling used carpet will be financially tested.[121]

In the precommitment stage, the notion of imputed costs is analytically useful. It provides a concrete measure against which moral judgments can be compared. As shown in these examples, the imputed cost can be great. Of course, this arbitrary set of cases is neither random nor extensive. The conclusion to draw is one of caution. While market participants may be moral, the product market itself is amoral. Owners can be a determined lot and may not be willing to wait for the distant returns of strategic positioning or normative departures.

A second issue is the lag between the strategic decision and the effects of implementing it. When a firm positions itself today, based on its anticipation of the future impact of its environmental progress and the distant future reputational capital or internal social capital, the market may be unaware of those plans and cannot include that future value today. The long-term effects will be captured only later, in the stock price, as the firm's performance unfolds over time.

IV. THE MOST APPROPRIATE ROLE

This chapter has identified three views of corporate responsibility, drawn from a spectrum between externally determined market models and normatively motivated enterprise behavior. The somewhat arbitrary division into three categories is an attempt to compare and contrast the basic market model with its extension into a longer-term focus on evolving social judgments, and to distinguish the normative model from these two. The basic market model is crisp and clear. Ensuring long-term sustainability as outlined here continues an opportunistic, enterprise focus. Long-term sustainability is not achieved in isolation from the basic market model (nor in normative departures from that model). Indeed, market pressures and moral judgments are central for long-term sustainability. Each enterprise must meet the efficiency demands of the marketplace if it is to survive. Long-term sustainability is approachable only when some area of managerial discretion—some managerial freedom beyond the efficiency demands of the markets—is obtained.

In some cases, a management team is forced into acting purely for the sake of market survival. In other cases, it achieves a balance among responsibilities through an astute use of the managerial area of discretion. The managerial key is to acknowledge the three distinct kinds of responsibility and proactively pursue sustainability and moral corporate behavior where possible.

From the side of normative departures, internally determined moral judgments and the resulting decisions must fit external social values over the long term. The key to successful normative departures from the market model is to gain recognition from the broader society for these departures and, perhaps more importantly, to motivate internal stakeholders through their inclusion in these judgments.

The determining values in the sustainability option are those reflected in the revealed preferences of society—the most appropriate ones for the company, as an artificially created corporate citizen. These are descriptive values that can be measured empirically. Social values go well beyond values reflected in minimum legal requirements. Indeed, in the case of strategically positioning the firm for enterprise sustainability, the social preferences in the future are the ones that really count. It takes time to carry out today's strategic decisions—time for the development of technologies, commitment of physical and human resources, policy determination, and organizational motivation.

The managerial determination of the appropriate strategic role for an enterprise and the implementation of that strategy are the themes underlying the discussion in the rest of this volume. Social values as part of the firm's environment have been stressed in the basic market model (values as reflected in governmental laws and regulation) and in the sustainable enterprise extension of the basic model (social preferences that will hold in the future), while morality as determined among the people within the firm guides the normative departures. This distinction between general social values and the morality of particular individuals or a small group within the firm does not hold in the implementation of the enterprise strategies. As individuals and small groups put these strategies into action, they are accountable for the moral judgments underlying these decisions. In this sense, ethics is central to the analysis as outlined in Part V of this volume.

We have argued that in interpreting social preferences and implementing socially oriented policies, it is often advantageous for a firm to work with NGOs, as reflected in many of the above cases. Chapter 4 examines such interactions from both business and NGO perspectives.

CHAPTER FOUR

Partnering with Nongovernmental Organizations

Both corporations and nongovernmental organizations must collaborate if each is to achieve its objectives in today's information-rich, integrated world. Corporate managers are increasingly aware of the need to position their firms to serve social preferences well beyond what the basic market model requires. This awareness is reflected in burgeoning corporate social responsibility efforts. Many of the examples in chapter 3 of implementing an enterprise sustainability strategy involved interactions with nongovernmental organizations. As we move from rule-based to principles-based corporate behavior, the role of nongovernmental organizations as a key component of civil society is becoming central. Effective corporate social action is increasingly a function of NGO partnering. For their part, NGO managers see increased opportunities to leverage the extensive human and material resources of the business enterprise in order to achieve their desired social impact.

101

These partnering opportunities will be assessed, first from the point of view of the business enterprise, and then from that of the nongovernmental organization.[1]

I. POSITIONING THE ENTERPRISE

The driving force for corporate involvement with nongovernmental organizations can be analyzed in terms of uniform enterprise standards set against the nuances of local circumstances, managerial operating interactions with local communities, outreach beyond the firm's operating environment, and donation programs.

Enterprise Standards and Local Exceptions

The business units of a multinational enterprise are located in diverse economic, political, social, and cultural environments. The importance of uniform societal and ethical standards for all of these business units has been emphasized. Just as each multinational establishes global product and production standards, with specific exceptions to fit unique local conditions, similarly, it must establish uniform social and ethical standards, with acknowledgment of local exceptions. Social and ethical standards are, of course, far more complicated than product standards due to the subtleties of cultural differences, the judgments involved, and problems of measurement. Still, each firm must have some set of rules that governs behavior across the enterprise network.

Management must identify some universally accepted set of values to avoid being pulled in disparate directions by the many conflicting local demands. This is the critical step in implementing principles that define multinational sustainability. The firm must then establish a set of standards, drawn from the universal precepts, that fit the specific details of the firm. These standards are then applied to all business units across the multinational enterprise network as a form of corporate law, requiring adherence by all internal decision makers. Specific exceptions are submitted to corporate compliance management.

On the other hand, reputational capital is not only a matter of determining which global concerns are most critical for legitimacy, but also a matter of local judgments, including how to minimize countervailing pressures at the local level. For the multinational enterprise, which operates on a cross-country and cross-cultural scale, the conceptual problem of relativism versus universalism becomes the pragmatic problem of local social judgments versus broadly communicated global legitimacy. (The distinction between relativism and universalism has been the topic of philosophical and theological debate over the centuries. In some respects, each culture and religion is unique, while in others, there is commonality across all belief systems. We will return to this issue in later chapters.)

The linkage of multiple societies in different cultures creates a challenge for the multinational enterprise as an organization. The good of the person within his or her own culture can easily conflict with uniform standards of behavior established for all business units of the enterprise network. The issue is this: Which cultural characteristics of which society should be established as the standard for the multinational network, and which should be part of local managerial discretion for the individual business unit?

Thus, a central task of global management is to identify a set of standards and translate these standards into policies that apply across the firm's enterprise network. The role of the local business unit is to implement the spirit of these policies applied to local situations.

Interpreting Local Communities

From a grassroots, conflict-resolution perspective, Mary Anderson provides great insight into the importance of local exceptions to uniform standards.[2] She makes a distinction between context and conflict: "context" involves a comprehensive review of issues, while "conflict" focuses on key driving factors in a specific situation. Contextual analysis can be related to corporate policy formulation; conflict analysis can be related to the implementation of these policies. Her comments, although directed "to destructive, often violent, intergroup conflict," apply in a less physically dangerous degree to all situations of multinational corporate presence, particularly in developing countries.

Anderson emphasizes that the blind application of network-wide policies may be highly destructive. Such effects do not mean that a particular policy is inappropriate as a uniform enterprise-wide guideline. They do mean that it may be totally inappropriate for local circumstances. As an example, standard corporate-wide policies to hire personnel based on merit, to invest in infrastructure, or to pay premium wages in developing communities as a means of contributing to their development may create local tensions and conflict.[3] Again, this does not mean that the enterprise policies are invalid. It does indicate that these policies must be modified or set aside in specific local situations.

How does the manager know when to depart from a corporate policy? This involves an understanding of local nuances and intercultural management competencies. The larger the firm as a presence in a community, the more critical this understanding becomes. Local communities are always complex. This is abundantly clear in situations such as the informal sectors across Latin America, in slums everywhere, or when local people are under oppression, as was the case under South African apartheid. This caveat applies to a manager from the local community as well as to one promoted into that position from another assignment in the enterprise network. The local individual is a member of a specific relational group and is influenced by its viewpoint. The outsider may simply miss the point.

Interpreting local uniqueness as a basis for applying enterprise standards is a role for the local NGO in an NGO/business partnership. In fact, the NGO's role often extends beyond interpretation to representation, in that it serves as (or at least presents itself as) a voice for the interests of the local community. (This may lead to collaboration as the local business unit and the NGO join their efforts to benefit the community, or to conflict as they dispute which entity more fully advances the community's interests.) The responsibility of the business unit manager is to represent the interests of the firm. From that viewpoint, contributing to the local geographic community is an opportunistic part of the basic market model. Local contributions build the local economy and contribute to trust, both of which will lead to stability and positive returns.

The experience of the Freeport-McMoRan mine in Irian Jaya (West Papua) Indonesia, described in detail in the book *Peace through Commerce*, demonstrates the difficulties in understanding local communities, the interweaving of issues, the unanticipated and unintended consequences of local economic and social actions, the short-term disruption while awaiting long-term benefits, the differences between perception and fact, and the potential for the same action to be viewed as beneficial or disastrous through different lenses.[4]

Another example covered in *Peace through Commerce* of a challenging local situation is the case described as "Promoting Sustainable Livelihoods and Grassroots Enterprise Development in Darfur and Southern Sudan." Given the fluidity and uncertainty in the area, a coalition of organizations chose the anthropological approach of participative action research. Field staff were involved in developmental conflict research, as well as in reacting to specific local needs. The focus was on entrepreneurial capacity, particularly for women. As it turns out, "Women often emerge as entrepreneurs in turmoil. . . . They may play an initial trigger role in stimulating positive cycles of change." Details of the struggle of internally displaced persons in Southern Sudan are unnerving. Still, researchers found resilient enterprise models in the confusion and conflict of this area, reminding one of the importance of bottom-up, grassroots development even in areas of conflict. The partnership network consisted of Sudanese and Canadian universities, Sudanese governmental agencies and NGOs, and other bilateral and multilateral institutions.[5]

Operational Involvement in Local Communities

Local operations are more productive in an environment of favorable local interactions than unfavorable ones. Employees, as well as many contractors and suppliers, are members of the surrounding communities. Employees want to be proud of their employer, and the firm needs dependable local contractors and suppliers. If properly organized, employee community programs can have an important positive influence on corporate culture. Most of the programs that involve employees in local volunteer work are motivated by the desire to enhance this local appreciation and employee pride.

For example, across the world, often in conjunction with NGOs, IBM has formed learning centers with donated computers. The goal as of 2006 was to support fifteen hundred such centers. IBM recognizes the contribution of these kinds of programs to reputational capital through the value of the brand.[6] As another example, IBM employees and retirees rely on an Internet site with technology tools, lectures, online tutorials, and best practices to support contributions to on-demand computing in local communities.

As another example, an extensive Nestlé program promotes dairy operations in ways that contribute directly to the firm's economic performance, as well as addressing local needs. Operating in two countries prone to violence, Colombia and Pakistan, Nestlé focuses on milk production. In Colombia, supporting the transition of demobilized militia members to dairy farming assures Nestlé access to a reliable source of quality inputs, while keeping the militia members demobilized. In Pakistan, Nestlé also establishes farmers in business and supports their milk production efforts. To reach the scattered farmers in the Punjab, Nestlé trains female agricultural extension workers. Nestlé deals in these cases with what it knows well—the production of milk.[7]

In Nigeria, Nestlé has focused on sustainable farming methods, here to support its food distribution. Confronted with the impact of HIV/AIDS on worker productivity, Nestlé created an education program in partnership with the International Red Cross and a film production program to promote peace and partnership with an NGO (Search for Common Ground). In these latter two cases, Nestlé is involved in outreach programs.

Outreach Programs

In addition to interactions between business and NGOs involving an extension of operations into local communities, there is a good deal of collaboration where the enterprise reaches beyond its local operating environment. Some of this is based on pure humanitarian concerns. Much of it comes from management's understanding of the changing social preferences and judgments in our increasingly integrated, information-rich world, as discussed in chapter 3.

Partnering with NGOs, particularly international NGOs, is a key dimension in conceptualizing and implementing outreach programs. The engagement with NGOs and other institutions, such as agencies of the United Nations, provides knowledge and insight from those whose worldviews may be substantially different from the worldviews of business managers. Moreover, these trusted institutions bring legitimacy to outreach activities, which then translates into reputational capital for the enterprise.

General Electric, for example, has made a major commitment to outreach in Ghana in terms of technology, products, and experience, although it explicitly does not donate cash. The initial phase consisted of hospital upgrades. During this phase, GE modified the technical products it donated and the nature of its planning processes to fit local needs. In Phase II, the lessons from the hospital upgrades were incorporated into a broader participation with Ghanian Millennium Village Projects. GE is involved in planning synergies (among regional hospitals, district hospitals, and village cluster clinics), as well as equipment donations and training. It works in a number of partnerships, from interaction with hospitals in the initial phase to the numerous governmental agencies, businesses, and entities of civil society participating in Millennium Village Projects.[8]

Donations

In other cases, the business enterprise may provide funds or products to institutions, usually NGOs or governments, allowing them to manage community or humanitarian development with little or no control over their allocations and actions. Here, the corporation is depending on the other institution to make a positive contribution to society. A second consideration is that the firm is not contributing managerial skills, as in the case of operations or outreach programs where management is involved in the long-term development of the specific project. In some situations, where the social need is far removed from corporate expertise, available corporate management is limited, the local community is not well understood by the donor, or the risk of direct involvement is high, donations may be the best option for contribution. In these cases, corporate management is well advised to choose the donor recipient with great care.

The Secure the Future Program of Bristol-Myers Squibb outlined in chapter 3 is an example of a carefully monitored donation program, in which more than two hundred recipient groups are followed with care in an evolving donor strategy.

The Angola Enterprise Program (AEP) is directed to economic development through the support of micro-, small-, and medium-sized entrepreneurs. Under the guidance of the United Nations Development Program, AEP implements the overall UNDP mission of "poverty reduction for sustainable human development."[9] Angola is a difficult entrepreneurial environment. In addition to the economic marginalization and health issues of Africa, Angola is emerging from three decades of civil war and is rated by the World Bank as one of the most difficult countries

in which to establish a business. In addition, as in all developing countries, micro- and small-business development is contained within its own
distinct culture.[10] AEP focuses on enhancing microfinance structures,
starting Business Development Services Centers, studying the micro/
small/medium business environment, and working toward appropriate
governmental policy and legislative reforms. It creates and participates in
a broad range of partnership networks. Given the complexities of these
circumstances, ChevronTexaco's partnership with AEP has been in the
form of funding ($3 million) as part of the company's broader $25 million
program, The Angola Partnership Initiative.

The Business View

There is a distinction in business strategy between operations sensitivity,
outreach programs, and donations. In the current environment, strategies are selected by management within an informed global society that
is reevaluating its preferences relative to corporate behavior as noted in
chapter 3.

Involvement in local communities has a direct payoff in terms of enhancing the firm's productivity as a part of the basic market model. Effectively channeling corporate, human, technical, and material resources to
social objectives as counseled by an NGO enhances a firm's local productivity and its competitive position.

With respect to outreach programs and donations, partnerships can be
motivated by (1) the long-term benefits that accrue to the firm through
external stakeholders, or (2) the existence of a humanitarian need which
the company is in a position to mitigate. These motives map onto, respectively, extensions of the basic market model to achieve sustainability and
normative departures from the market model. As noted, partnering with
NGOs can be a central component in the achievement of these objectives.
As argued earlier, the distinction between pursuing long-term enterprise
sustainability and normative departures from the market model is important for planning purposes, even though it is difficult to judge, even for
management, at the beginning of a venture. Put another way, it is often
difficult to predict the apex of the curve when the firm begins moving to
the right in Figure 3.2.

The above cases indicate that these strategies tend to be accomplished
successfully when undertaken in a close interaction with NGOs. Klaus

Leisinger calls for the involvement of NGOs in a broad range of human rights corporate decisions:

> Since intra-institutional analyses always involve the risk of being self-referential and therefore leaving out important aspects from the analysis, external consultations provide a better basis for decision-making. This is especially true in the case of complex political judgments, such as those required in connection with company-specific human rights issues. Not only is it wise to use the knowledge and experience of specialized NGOs in a company's own decision-making processes, society's pluralism of interests also creates opportunities. Potentially fatal deficits of perception arise when people or institutions confuse their view of things with the things themselves. Sustainable solutions to complex problems normally transcend the initial preferences of corporate management, taking into account differing life experiences, value premises, and constellation of interests to improve the quality of the eventual decision. Specialized interest groups are best able to present the relevant portfolio of values, to articulate special interests, and to show ways to preserve them.[11]

II. NGO/BUSINESS JOINT VENTURE PARTNERING

Just as the operating purpose of the firm is to meet the demands of the basic market model and to ensure long-term sustainability, similarly, the goal of the NGO is to efficiently and effectively meet the needs of its clients and to mature into a sustainable organization capable of innovating and expanding its client services. NGOs have become the formal, although varied, voice of civil society.[12]

NGOs—more precisely defined as nonprofit, nongovernmental entities—have flourished in the industrialized world for a long time. They have become a force in developing countries since the 1960s, paralleling the process of industrialization. Organizationally, NGOs cover a broad spectrum, including development nongovernmental organizations, professional associations, producers' organizations, social movements, labor unions, religious groups—congregations, religious orders, or base communities—and even the mass media.[13] The diversity of NGOs is captured by the Commission on Global Governance: "Some are issue-oriented or task-oriented; others are driven by ideology. Some have a broad public-interest perspective; others have a more private, narrow focus. They range from small, poorly funded, grassroots entities to large, well-supported, professionally staffed bodies. Some operate individually; others have formed networks to share information and tasks and to enhance their impact."[14]

There is a distinction between indigenous and international NGOs. Most indigenous groups are grassroots organizations. Firmly based in the local communities, they are created to serve the specific interests of their members or for general community support. Julie Fisher estimated as of 1998 that there were over 200,000 indigenous NGOs in the developing world alone, although their diversity makes exact figures elusive.[15]

Other NGOs operate on an international level. These groups generally seek legitimization through association with indigenous NGOs and are often the source of financial, informational, and strategic support for their grassroots associates, although indigenous NGOs in the Southern Hemisphere are increasingly going directly to donors in Northern industrialized countries for support. International NGOs provide more aid than the entire United Nations.[16] In 2001 the Centre for the Study of Global Governance estimated that there were 40,000 internationally operating NGOs.[17]

Accountability

The accountability issues of the NGO are similar to those of the business enterprise even though their structures differ. Since both kinds of institutions are part of civil society, the similarity is to be expected. In the United States, for example, NGOs are subject to requirements contained in state nonprofit corporation law and in federal tax exemption law.[18] These laws and regulations, and similar ones in other jurisdictions, set minimum standards and oblige the NGO to meet these standards, and to disclose information about their activities even in the absence of prescribed standards.[19]

The board (directors or trustees) of the NGO plays a more central role than in the case of corporations. Laura Chisholm summarized the fiduciary duties of the NGO board in an important 1995 article as loyalty, care, and obedience. Alnoor Ebrahim has elaborated on the challenges these duties present to boards:

Each of these standards of care, loyalty, and obedience is itself subject to varying degrees of ambiguity, but each generally attempts to hold board members responsible for seeking out and considering adequate information on which to base decisions (care), disclosing conflicts of interest and placing the organization's interests over personal ones (loyalty), and acting within the organization's mission while also adhering to internal organizational protocols for decision making (obedience, especially to members).[20]

Fiduciary duties in a corporation focus on the shareholders, but for NGOs there is a stronger stakeholder emphasis. NGO management must find a balance between a narrow focus on its institutional mission, the benefits to its clients and their communities, its donors, and boards as independent principals.[21] This balance is a matter of substantial debate in the NGO community.

The rules of the game are not as well established for NGOs as they are for the private business sector, where the acceptance of market competition as the driving force within legitimate regulatory constraints is a given; uniform, legally required transparency and accountability are enforced; accounting standards are consistent and uniformly applied; and financial analysts constantly evaluate this data and judge the performance of the firm.

Currently, two factors are changing the governance structures of NGOs. First, legal requirements are moving toward those applied to business firms. Second, donors are becoming more involved with NGO operations. They seek businesslike efficiency and monitor how their philanthropy is used.

In the United States, the Sarbanes-Oxley Act increased the federal scrutiny of all organizations, including nonprofits as well as publicly traded companies. For NGOs, "while regulation of nonprofit governance is generally seen as a state law matter, overseen by various state Attorneys General, the federal government has in recent years issued voluntary recommendations for governance practices and, on the annual information return filed by nonprofits with the IRS (Form 990), required increased reporting of such practices."[22] In addition to the increasing regulatory scrutiny, watchdog organizations such as the American Institute of Philanthropy are propagating.[23] Similar increases in regulatory scrutiny are occurring elsewhere.[24]

The dramatic increase in philanthropy in the United States and Europe (reflecting the creation of wealth in recent years and its uneven distribution) brings with it a determination on the part of business donors to be involved in the distribution. This has led to new demands relative to NGO organizational structures and management. This concern is articulated by Michael Porter, a crusader on the topic of NGO mismanagement, as described in an *Economist* article in 2006: "'Billions are wasted on ineffective philanthropy,' says Michael Porter, a management guru at the Harvard Business School. 'Philanthropy is decades behind business in applying rigorous thinking to the use of money.' Mr. Porter believes the whole of giving can be transformed by learning from the world of business. Many of the leaders of the new generation of philanthropists agree with him, so 'there is a big opportunity over the next 20 years to figure out how to make philanthropy effective.'"[25] A group of consultants, research firms, and bankers are assisting in this process. *The Economist* author observed, "The new approach to philanthropy is 'strategic,' 'market-conscious,' 'knowledge-based,' and often 'high engagement.'"[26]

A new kind of institution called the "social entrepreneur" is emerging. These are a combination of for-profit and not-for-profit institutions. They consist of partnerships and corporations formed to serve a social purpose, while earning an adequate return on investment. In addition, these kinds of entrepreneurs include management consultants, research firms, and philanthropic investment banks.[27]

NGOs are also developing voluntary codes. A recent example is the International NGO Accountability Charter, initiated by a group of eleven leading international NGOs. The theme is responsible advocacy as a way to assure public trust. The Charter members commit to a series of principles, including the maintenance of financial and political independence, responsiveness to local needs, an annual financial report, and advocacy consistent with their mission. The Charter also calls on its members to be responsible in their public criticism of individuals and organizations, and to encourage input by people whose interests may be directly affected by their activities.[28]

Strategy

NGO/business partnerships cover a wide spectrum, as reflected in the above case studies. From the NGO point of view, strategy has to do with the choice of issues that they will embrace and the balance between collaboration and confrontation. Some NGOs view themselves as "Advocacy Network Organizations," relying on lobbying, litigation, and protest to pursue their mission.[29] Ideology can be a determining factor in such cases. Frank Den Hond and Frank De Bakker argue that the ideological bonds of radical activist groups (as distinct from bonds of common interest and identity) lead them to less participatory tactics, and to the proclivity to challenge proactive firms more vigorously than they challenge firms that are laggards with respect to the NGO's mission. Radical activists stress moral as distinct from pragmatic legitimacy.[30] And ideologies, like cultures, change slowly. Another type of NGO is service based, focusing on assisting clients.[31] These reformist groups are more participatory in nature.[32]

The culture of the corporation can also influence the strategy selected by the NGO. Timothy Fort and Michelle Westermann-Behaylo identify three corporate cultures in terms of trust. For firms pursuing the neoclassical economic model and thus paying little attention to social issues, they propose a "hard trust," activist, confrontational approach. For firms pursuing a long-term strategy of social involvement as a means of enhancing brand image and reputational capital, they suggest a partnering, "real trust" collaboration. For corporations committed to social enhancement as a worthwhile end in itself, they recommend "good trust" partnerships—"built on inspiration and common commitments."[33] Long-term successful partnerships can evolve from "real trust" to "good trust."

Overall, there seems to be an increasing willingness to collaborate on the part of NGOs. As one article put it in 2005, "While a number of NGOs continue to exert direct pressure on the business community to accelerate change, a majority of NGOs have shifted from the pre-Seattle anti-globalisation movement (polarisers) to a more constructive alter-globalisation movement (integrators), which seeks change through alliances and partnerships built upon the complementary competencies, objectives and resources of NGOs and business. The WTO Summit in Seattle in 1999 was a major shifting point in the NGO movement, which was urged to make constructive alternative proposals to those issues which they denounce."[34]

Two case examples from Ford demonstrate both confrontational and collaborative approaches by NGOs. After Ford pledged to increase the fuel economy by 25 percent for its pick-up trucks and SUVs by 2005, a group of environmental NGOs placed a full-page ad in the *New York Times* charging that "Ford's fleet continues to produce more global warming pollution than any other major automaker." On the other hand, NGOs were part of a "summit" group at Ford in 2000 that "identified human rights as a key issue for multinational corporations," a conclusion that came as a surprise to Ford management. NGOs then participated in the preparation of Ford's "code of business working conditions," which upon completion was reviewed by human rights experts from other NGOs.[35]

An example reported in 2007 shows how confrontation can turn to collaboration. Two NGOs (Environmental Defense and The National Resource Defense Council) challenged the plans of a utility company (the Texas utility firm TXU) to construct eleven coal-fired generating plants. Broadcasting their plans through a website, these NGOs built a national coalition to oppose the construction. During the period of confrontation, a leveraged buyout group proposed to purchase TXU. At this point, through negotiations with the takeover group, the NGOs gained a number of environmental concessions in return for supporting the buyout.[36]

The Promise of Collaboration

Based on his experience in situations of conflict, John Lederach outlines the great promise of interrelationships and the potential contribution of business to conflict resolution. He defines the challenge of peacebuilding as follows:

> Peacebuilding represents the intentional confluence—the flowing together—of improbable processes and people to sustain constructive change that reduces violence and increases the potential and practice of justice in human relationships. . . .
>
> "Improbable processes and people" suggests that people and activities that would not likely come together on their own volition and connection are encouraged to do so with intentionality. This means that people who are not like minded and not like situated within the conflict context find themselves in relationship—flowing together—with a purpose of finding greater understanding and con-

structive engagement. In a word, this kind of confluence points toward the idea of creating space for meaningful though very unusual interaction.

Constructive change provides a goal and a direction for this flowing. In more specific terms it suggests that transformation is needed that reduces violence and increases justice in human relationships.[37]

As a strategic approach, Lederach identifies three types of conflict-creating gaps—the vertical gap (between higher-level leaders and grassroots participants); the justice gap (between negative peace as the mere absence of violence and positive peace as the experience of a viable quality of life); and the interdependence gap (between a focus on one's own needs and goals as central and the recognition that these are part of a larger, interdependent web of relationships that requires cooperation among diverse groups, who may neither like nor trust each other, in order to achieve their common and individual goals). In dealing with Lederach's vertical gap, we are reminded of Anderson's caution about the difficulty of grasping local situations and the need for local managers to "tie into the forces that locally support peace, connect to the processes that enable people to solve problems without violence, and reinforce the systems and structures that make intergroup relations positive."[38] Lederach points to the potential of business in bridging all three of these gaps. He frames that contribution in terms of pursuing what has been outlined above as the basic market model (the need for business to build relationships among a wide group of constituencies), as well as the extension of that model into longer-term sustainability strategies. Business builds relationships: "On the one hand, good business practices often have developed an unusual knack to understand and build on relational spaces where very diverse sets of people must interact, understand each other, and move in common directions. Second, business entrepreneurs, generally, are less concerned with the polarizing demands of conflict than with what they need to do good business. By virtue of this adventurous spirit they frequently find themselves as forerunners moving across lines of polarization, sometimes to the chagrin of their corresponding politicians."[39]

In managing these relationships, business has the "power of the convenor." The common interest in economic benefits among the diverse groups gives business the opportunity to serve as a "magnet," as reflected in the following partnership cases.[40]

Two NGOs are examples of initiating public/private partnerships. The Business Humanitarian Forum (BHF) promotes partnerships among the public sector, business, and NGOs in the conviction that "comprehensive and widespread cross-sector collaboration is essential to ensure sustainable development initiatives that are imaginative, coherent, and integrated enough to tackle the most intractable problems." Their nine phases of the partnering process—from identifying opportunities and partners, to building sustainability or agreeing on appropriate conclusions—provide solid guidance. This process has been demonstrated in a project to produce generic medicine in the challenging environment of Afghanistan. The hurdles were substantial, including the difficulty of overcoming the Afghan "brain drain" of technical people and the hesitancy of Western technicians to travel to Afghanistan. A key lesson that has been learned is to approach the project as a business case, not a humanitarian effort, and to select partners based on what they can deliver. Brigitte Scherrer has traced the phases of the partnering process from groundbreaking through production in 2007.[41]

As a second example, the Global Business Coalition on HIV/AIDS (GBC) works with business to take action on this worldwide health crisis. Economically, HIV/AIDS is a "potential threat to the creation of value" in terms of damage to economies, threats to security, diminishing workforces, and cuts in productivity and profits. In addition to these effects, consumers are changing their attitudes toward business, as discussed at length in preceding chapters. Among the many companies participating with GBC, two demonstrate this approach—Unilever and M·A·C Cosmetics. On its Kenyan tea plantations, Unilever partners with a number of local groups from the Kenya HIV/AIDS Business Council to support local schools. The fashion cosmetic producer M·A·C works with retailers in its cause-related marketing, contributing portions of its earnings and raising external funds for its M·A·C AIDS Fund.[42]

As these examples show, NGOs bring valuable expertise and different worldviews to partnerships with business. They are an integral part of the joint venture's potential social and environmental contribution, in spite of the fact that the partners come from very different kinds of institutions and cultures.

III. SUSTAINABLE LONG-TERM PARTNERSHIPS

The goal of both the business enterprise and the engaged NGO is to ensure the sustainability of the joint venture or counseling interaction—a true challenge, given that NGO/business partnerships are unions across diverse cultural lines. For NGOs, consisting of unusually bright, committed, and determined people, the institutional organization tends to be more like a university than a business enterprise. Compounding this cultural difference, many NGO members are in the nonprofit sector due to a disdain for business. From the NGO viewpoint, as outlined by Leisinger, "NGOs engaged in joint projects with companies must . . . tread a fine line in their dealings with the corporate world if they want to avoid 'capture' and minimize the risk of being smothered in a corporate public relations embrace. As self-appointed corporate watchdogs and whistleblowers, NGOs run a risk of their own credibility by appearing to be too close to the very institutions they set out to monitor and hold accountable." Partnership tensions can be magnified by the media. "It is a fact that the media prefer scandal, controversy, and accusations over reports on corporate good deeds."[43] And positive media coverage is central to the NGO in its fund-raising efforts, as well as its reputational capital.

From the perspective of business, interaction with NGOs is generally well beyond management's comfort zone. Partnerships involve relinquishing control to others outside the business, who, managers believe, may turn from collaboration to confrontation when things go wrong and who are in a position to use shared information against the firm.

For these reasons, Leisinger stresses the role of a written contract:

> You need to create an atmosphere of trust and encourage open dialogue on the issues, but you should also make a written contract with the rights and duties of all partners and the way they should interact. Make the contract waterproof, not to give work to lawyers, but to shed light on all the implications. You must do that at the beginning, when everybody wants the project to succeed, because once the problems start, it's too late. If your partners are heterogeneous, there can be a lack of mutual understanding because of different institutional cultures or perceptions of problems. . . . Writing a contract

and discussing every paragraph allows you to evaluate the potential weaknesses and strengths, the opportunities and the threats. You can create a contingency plan if something goes wrong—and if the problem you are tackling is complex, something will. The plan should designate credible third parties to help in the event of trouble. You must also ensure you can cope with institutional-capacity issues, a lack of mutual understanding, and the cultural differences. People with a business background, delegates from NGOs, governmental employees, and social workers may have totally different perceptions of the world.[44]

However managed, the key to successful partnerships is trust, as demonstrated by the following three cases.

The first is the Botswana Comprehensive HIV/AIDS Partnership (BCHAP), an interesting example of initial distrust developing into a sustained, effective partnership. The process was initiated by Merck's search for ways to address the HIV/AIDS pandemic in Africa. Beginning in 1996, Guy McDonald, a Merck executive, initiated a strategy that became known as the Enhancing Care Initiative. Based on the observation that HIV/AIDS initiatives in Africa each tended to focus on only a part of the pandemic, McDonald developed a comprehensive plan. Through 1999 and 2000 he met with groups working with HIV/AIDS in Africa, including a number of sessions with The Gates Foundation. The first test of trust occurred when The Gates Foundation organized a meeting of major foundations and international organizations to discuss collaborative approaches to HIV/AIDS in developing countries. McDonald flew to the meeting in Seattle. As the meeting convened, the head of The Merck Company Foundation was included but McDonald was not, even though he had met repeatedly with The Gates Foundation, a foundation closely associated with its business founder. At the meeting, "people were saying that they did not want Merck to present. They didn't trust the private sector and they openly questioned why Merck should be allowed in."[45] After several hours of discussion, McDonald was invited to participate. As trust evolved, this partnership became the Botswana Comprehensive HIV/AIDS Partnership.

A second example of building partnership trust across extreme ideological barriers is the Middelburg Forum. South African apartheid put all businesses in the untenable position of trying to operate under unjust laws. In the late 1980s, Middelburg Steel and Alloys (MSA), a subsidiary of Barloworld, found itself in the middle of a major local political issue as well. The town of Middelburg had turned off the lights and water to the local black township for nonpayment of bills. Daniel Malan outlines the situation: "The white council was in financial trouble as a result of nonpayment for services, the black councilors from the township did not have any legitimacy in their own community, the comrades (a term for activists within the Mass Democratic Movement) were facing intimidation and threats from the security forces, and the trade union leaders were branded as sell-outs by many comrades as a result of their participation in the Forum." Assuming the role of political activist, MSA assembled the parties as the Middelburg Forum, which, over time, transformed the town.[46]

Third, the interaction among two multinational extractive companies (Occidental Petroleum and Cerrejón, the largest open pit coal mine in Latin America), a London-based NGO (International Alert), and a Colombian think tank (Fundación Ideas para la Paz, or FIP) provides a strong example of building trust among the partners as a way of avoiding inadvertent contributions to the Colombian conflict and moving ahead positively. Against a history of confrontation between NGOs and business over the conflict in Colombia, Alexandra Guáqueta outlines how FIP worked with the partners. "The presence of FIP as an interface between Alert and the companies helped to build trust. Intermediation was more than just facilitating preliminary meetings; it was about bridging two worlds: one more technical, dominated by engineers, result-oriented, and used to dealing with hard facts and quantitative indicators, and the other more centered on discourse, used to the fuzziness of social themes, and process-oriented. There also was bridging to do between local understandings about Colombia's reality and foreign perceptions as well as local and international interpretations of human rights."[47]

Partnership tensions are exacerbated when the NGO is asked to undertake a formal assessment of a business enterprise's social or environmental performance. The firm's concern is articulated by Leisinger:

> Independent, outside audits are important for the credibility of a company with regard to its efforts at compliance; they are even a prerequisite for such credibility. . . . It is true to say that those who have nothing to hide have no need to fear in an external audit: on

the contrary, success stories reinforce both the motivation within the company and the reputation of the company in the public eye. But a credible audit must also reveal the gaps and deficits that exist in any large company. The concern of the company is that outside auditors will concentrate on these gaps—not least in order to strengthen their own reputation as an incorruptible authority—and construct out of them a report that could provide fodder for scandalmongers. In such a case, the performance of the weakest link in the company would become the deciding factor for the standing of the company as a whole. Unfair accusations would rapidly destroy the internal acceptance of outside audits. But it is clear that even the most serious-minded and selfless auditing organisation cannot prevent the problematical parts of its finding arousing far more public excitement and interest than success stories. And this is also bearable. Sulkily retreating into a corner, on the other hand, does not win any friends.[48]

The case of the giant Freeport-McMoRan mining venture in Indonesia and the audit of its full social, political, and economic impact by the International Center for Corporate Assessment (ICCA) exemplifies the challenge in these kinds of assessment partnerships.[49]

A survey from the business perspective undertaken by Global Corporate Citizenship Initiative led to the following "seven success factors of effective partnerships."[50]

1. Openness, transparency and clear communication to build trust and mutual understanding;
2. Clarity of roles, responsibilities, goals, and "ground rules";
3. Commitment of core organizational competencies;
4. Application of the same professional rigor and discipline focused on achieving targets and deliverables that would be applied to governing, managing, and evaluating other types of business alliances;
5. Respect for differences in approach, competence, timeframes, and objectives for different partners;
6. Focus on achieving mutual benefit in a manner that enables the partners to meet their own objectives as well as common goals;

7. Understanding the needs of local partners and beneficiaries, with a focus on building their own capacity and capability rather than creating dependence.

From an extractive industry viewpoint relating to large projects, Donal O'Neill would add the need for a thorough impact assessment before undertaking the project. He also emphasizes the importance of the involvement of "business development departments with profit-generating responsibility" and clear identification of the person or group who represents the enterprise. For the partnership, he counsels that the relationship needs to be formalized, input should be roughly equal, trust is built on shared achievement with early successes important, and that it is an advantage to involve third parties including government.[51]

NGOs would agree with most of these guidelines. Of particular interest is the Business Humanitarian Forum lesson from Afghanistan. As Scherrer commented, "probably the most striking lesson learned is to try to move away from a purely humanitarian approach of wanting to help the local population and toward adopting a real business approach instead."[52]

In its work with Occidental and Cerrejón, International Alert and FIP noted the need for sensitivity on the part of each partner. Guáqueta comments, "The parties had to work constantly to build trust and to adjust to each others' worlds. For the companies, one component of trust was FIP's and Alert's interpretation of local realities. The companies were not seeking either organization to echo their own views but rather to demonstrate the ability to understand local culture and be objective. . . . FIP and Alert had to adjust social science jargon to simple terms that nonspecialists could grasp easily."[53]

In summary,

Partnerships where participants have the ability to continuously revise their knowledge, together with process-oriented approaches where participants allow the dynamics of interaction to inform and influence their perception of what matters, stand the best chance of success. Under such conditions it matters less who has the *a priori* "higher moral standing," than who is able to substantiate which demands can be met and which are unreasonable. Given stakeholder

consensus on, and common understanding of, the basic supporting pillars for solutions, reaching agreement on the details can be
facilitated on a case-by-case basis as the "us versus them" attitude
softens up.[54]

As supported so clearly in the above cases, NGO counsel on corporate
social efforts and partnering in joint projects can substantially improve
corporate performance. Beyond this contribution, the participation of
NGOs can sharpen the social judgment of the firm's legitimacy, thus increasing the firm's reputational capital and internal motivation. While the
NGO will want to be careful in its acknowledgment of positive enterprise
contributions so as to avoid the perception of being used by the firm, enhanced legitimacy will move the apex of the curve in Figure 3.2 up and
to the right. For the firm, this means lower imputed costs and a motive
for more action. For the NGO, it means leveraging enterprise assets and
power to achieve the NGO mission. And collaboration rather than confrontation can encourage managers to move beyond the new apex into
normative departures from the market model.[55]

Based on these examples, it is clear that business needs the insight and
the networks of NGOs if it is to compete in the basic market model, to
successfully gain long-term sustainability by responding to changing social preferences, or to venture into normative departures from the market
model. In turn, NGOs need the resources of the business enterprise if they
are to achieve the social contribution for which they exist. These are not
easy partnerships; both sides find themselves on strange ground. Yet in
today's world, confrontation, while sometimes inevitable, can be destructive for both institutions.

PART III

FOUNDATIONS OF HUMAN RIGHTS

The pursuit of enterprise sustainability requires identifying a social standard. A wealth of social counsel is available in the writings of numerous religious traditions over the centuries. The Abrahamic traditions (Judaism, Islam, and Christianity) are broadly known. Less recognized and available (at least in the Western context) are the nontheistic social teachings of Confucianism and Buddhism and the various traditions of India.

One perspective, which can be traced through a number of traditions, has evolved in the Christian context as "Catholic social thought." The human rights element in Catholic social thought is of interest in that it has changed dramatically over the last century and a quarter. Catholic social thought has become one of the most richly elaborated, religiously-based bodies of coherent thinking on social policy to emerge in the second half of the twentieth century. It will serve here as an example of all such systems.

The Universal Declaration of Human Rights, considered as a set of social values and forged in the aftermath of the Second World War, reflects a detailed statement of these rights conceived from a secular perspective. The activities of the United Nations since the Declaration continue to refine these rights in their contemporary context and extend their reach to embrace cultural uniqueness.

Part III thus addresses human rights as a set of social values as well as moral principles. Chapter 5 traces the historical development of human rights in Catholic social thought and poses the question of its universality. Chapter 6 reviews the Universal Declaration of Human Rights together with its continuing interpretation by the United Nations and considers its global legitimacy.

CHAPTER FIVE

The Nature of Human Rights

Contemporary views of human rights have deep roots in the philosophy of natural law and liberal rights theory. Catholic tradition has been intimately involved with both: as an integral component of natural law philosophy over the centuries, and as a tradition at odds with liberal philosophy, including the liberal theory of human rights. In all of these, there is a tension between universalism and relativism.

I. NATURAL LAW

The idea of a natural law dates back to the pre-Socratics of ancient Greece, who focused on the orderliness of the universe.[1] Although they introduced the idea of laws in nature, these Greek philosophers did not extend their ideas to define or consider rights.[2] Augustine tied the law of nature to God's will and the "natural light" in humanity, thus providing the basis for the concept of obligation.[3] In the twelfth century, following the Christian discovery of Muslim writings on Aristotle,[4] Thomas Aquinas produced a synthesis of Aristotelian thought and Christian theology, presenting a world ordered by the laws of nature in which God has created a special place for human life.

Among the many contributions of Aquinas to the natural law tradition, two have particular relevance to the practice of management.

First, Aquinas formulated natural law theory as a form of principled reasoning, thus indicating that morality itself has a basis in rationality. He held that reason is independent of theological beliefs, but since human nature and reasoning are the creations of God, human reasoning can identify God's will through the study of human nature. As Manuel Velasquez and F. Neil Brady state: "This remarkable claim—unaided reasoning reflecting on human nature can attain a revelation of God's commands—is perhaps the most profound theological insight embedded in natural law theory."[5]

Second, Aquinas combined an ethic of principle—involving the idea of basic goods toward which human nature is oriented—with habits of a person's character, the possession of which enables the person to achieve these goods. As Velasquez and Brady explain, "Catholic morality became both an ethic of principle and an ethic of virtues, the two being integrated together by a teleological account of basic human goods."[6]

Although natural law theory clearly lays the foundation for a theory of rights, particularly in its focus on obligations, individual human rights have not been an explicit part of this tradition. In fact, Lloyd Weinreb goes so far as to argue,

> The philosophy of natural law has, on the whole, not been much concerned with the matter of rights. Greek sources from which natural law emerged scarcely noticed the subject at all. . . . Christian theology, which achieved its classic expression in the philosophy of Thomas Aquinas, likewise did not in the first instance uphold rights of the individual; rather, it confirmed his personal responsibility while still within and subject to the Providence of an omnipotent God. . . . In contemporary philosophy, although they are frequently joined for rhetorical effect, there is scarcely any connection, substantive or formal, between natural law and rights.[7]

Others find an evolutionary relationship. As Tom Campbell states, "This [medieval natural law] tradition is carried forward by contemporary followers of Thomas Aquinas such as John Finnis and has echoes in the more secular theories of Amartya Sen (1999) and Martha Nussbaum, according to whom human beings have certain capabilities on the basis of which we can ascribe to them rights."[8]

Right vs duties

II. LIBERAL RIGHTS THEORY

The evolution of human rights theory draws heavily on the liberal theory of the seventeenth through the nineteenth century. Liberal theory bases human rights on a common foundation of individual freedom.

A sequence of philosophical ideas—beginning with Thomas Hobbes's focus on the good of the individuals who make up the commonwealth, to John Locke's "state of perfect freedom" of the individual to order his or her actions, and to Immanuel Kant's "self-legislating autonomous will"—explains the great value that is placed on individual freedom in Western cultures. These thinkers were not devoid of communal concerns. Kant's concept of practical reason contains a communal dimension. Locke's concept of the social contract includes the fact that it must be exercised "within the bounds of the natural law,"[9] and he also argues for the right of the poor to possess the surplus of the rich.[10] However, their overarching emphasis is on the freedom of the individual. The impact of this liberal thought is clearly evident in eighteenth-century documents such as the United States Bill of Rights and the French Declaration of the Rights of Man and Citizen.

In an elegant theory, John Rawls reconstructs the liberal tradition in the form of a general conception of justice, which includes a set of basic rights. He posits a social contract that is entered into by free, equal, and rational individuals, each of whom starts from an "original position" of a veil of ignorance regarding his or her own circumstances but with complete and accurate information about the condition of the larger group. From such a starting position, Rawls believes that such individuals will agree on a set of rules for social cooperation and develop a structure of institutions and processes for the distribution of benefits and burdens.

Rawls argues in *A Theory of Justice* that two principles would be agreed upon in this original position. First, each person is to have an equal right to the most extensive total system of basic liberties compatible with a similar system of liberty for all. Second, social and economic inequalities are to be arranged so they are both (a) to the greatest benefit of the least advantaged and (b) attached to offices and positions open to all under conditions of fair equality of opportunity.[11]

Note that these two principles are ordered in that the first principle has absolute weight—basic liberties will be secured for each person before structuring society to provide for the greatest benefit to the least advantaged.[12] These procedures reflect what Rawls terms a "pure procedural justice" since the outcome is judged by the fairness of the procedures.[13]

David Hollenbach outlines liberal theory in the following terms:

> Freedom to be a self-legislating source of one's own morality, freedom to be a self-governing citizen in political society, and freedom of exchange and initiative in the economic sphere have been clustered together in an identifiable cultural tradition. Philosophically, the rights to freedom of conscience, religion, thought, and expression must be guaranteed because they are preconditions for a self-legislated or freely chosen vision of the good life. In turn, rights to suffrage, free exchange, and private property are prerequisites for the protection of autonomy in the political and economic domains.[14]

Thus, in liberal theory the individual has claims for herself or himself, whereas in the theory of natural law, the focus is on the duties of the person to the common good.[15]

III. CATHOLIC SOCIAL THOUGHT

The Catholic Church has been an integral part of the history of natural law theory. Its negative reaction to liberalism has been both political and philosophical. The political reaction was aimed at those who directed their liberal convictions toward the institutional church as well as toward governments. Philosophically, the liberal emphasis on individualism and the general lack of interest in the common good were seen as contrary to the natural law tradition of the church.

Peter Steinfels summarizes the political dimension in the eighteenth and nineteenth centuries in Europe:

> The drama begins when the French Revolution tries first to tailor the church to a revolutionary pattern and then, having fallen short in the effort, attempts to replace Christianity altogether. The church casts its lot with counter-revolution. During the restoration, the papacy renews and reinforces the bonds between the throne and altar with a series of concordats and with support for Metternich's Holy Alliance.
>
> For the rest of the century, this post-revolutionary settlement is repeatedly challenged and gradually dismantled—by revolutionary forces in 1830 and 1848; by the loss of the papal states to a unified Italy in 1870; by Bismarck's 1873–78 *Kulturkampf* against the church in a unified Germany; by the French Third Republic's turn to Giambetta's anticlericalism in 1877.[16]

This tension continues when, "at the [nineteenth] century's end, the pope has sentenced himself to becoming a 'prisoner in the Vatican' and the church is forced to the margins of cultural and political life."[17] In the twentieth century, with its two world wars and the experience of the Cold War, the political tension between the church and European governments has eased, even as the church has played a more active role in political advocacy.[18]

Throughout this period, philosophically and theologically, the church has rejected individualism as conceptualized in liberal rights theory as being too naturalistic and materialistic but has since come to embrace the idea of human rights on its own communitarian terms. As Hollenbach notes, "During the last century and a half, the Roman Catholic Church has moved from strong opposition to the rights championed by liberal thinkers of the eighteenth and nineteenth centuries to the position of one of the leading institutional advocates for human rights on the world stage today. . . . This shift is one of the most dramatic reversals in the long history of the Catholic tradition."[19]

exploitation & marginalization

Toward the end of the nineteenth century, in the midst of political conflict, Pope Leo XIII broke with the Catholic Church's resistance to Western political and social developments and initiated a policy of participation through his encyclical *Rerum Novarum* (1891).[20] This document introduced a new direction in Catholic social thought.[21] Leo XIII established the importance of the dignity of the human being as the basis of Catholic social thought, a concept that has been a continuing tenet of that tradition. This claim of dignity led to the claim of economic and social rights for workers. "The first thing of all to serve is to save unfortunate working people from the cruelty of men of greed, who use human beings as mere instruments for moneymaking."[22] Affirming the existence of a right to adequate food, clothing, and shelter as a component of the right to a just wage, Leo XIII introduced the idea of a "preferential option for the poor," which remains today as the overarching principle of Catholic social thought.

As a challenge to the secular liberal theory and events of the time, however, Leo XIII remained opposed to what he saw as the absolutism of majority rule in democracy. He strongly supported hierarchical social structures rather than democratic ones.

Following Leo's pontificate, human rights concerns lay dormant in the Catholic tradition until the pontificate of Pius XI (1922–39). To the centrality of human dignity and rights for the poor, he added the notions of social justice and of the rights of the person in relation to the state. He spoke out against fascism, Nazism, and communism.[23] He also introduced the idea that institutions can be consciously changed.

During his papacy, Pius XII (1939–58) clearly articulated the thesis that human rights include both social interactions and personal rights. He held a negative view of technological change as reducing persons to "mere cogs in the various social organizations,"[24] and proposed instead a "community of morally responsible citizens."[25] However, Pius XII never formally acknowledged the United Nations Universal Declaration of Human Rights, although it was formulated during his pontificate.

It remained for John XXIII in *Pacem in Terris* (1963) to "boldly set forward the most powerful and thorough statement of the Roman Catholic understanding of human rights in modern times."[26] He drew on language from the Universal Declaration, outlining a set of rights similar to those in the Declaration. Praising the Universal Declaration, he stressed the need for a supranational authority to ensure global peace. His respect for the Declaration began much earlier, when, as Cardinal Roncalli, the papal nuncio in Paris, he was in close touch with those drafting the Declaration.[27] At the time, Angelo Roncalli was "a popular mediator between conservative churchmen and a younger, more socially active, clergy."[28] René Cassin, a central figure in the Commission on Human Rights, wrote in his memoirs, "I received discreet personal encouragements from the Papal Nuncio Roncalli."[29]

In *Pacem in Terris*, John XXIII added a communitarian dimension to the Declaration. Sandi Cornish describes these additions as follows: "Pope John built on the secular Declaration to produce a 'Christian Charter of Human Rights,' which saw human rights as based on the dignity of the human person created in the image and likeness of God, and giving emphasis to the social nature of the person and the reciprocal nature of rights and duties."[30] Pope John stressed that, while each person has moral claims as a function of his or her dignity, there is also a corresponding duty and responsibility to society.

Pacem in Terris is similar to the Universal Declaration. The list of rights in the encyclical (paragraphs 11–27) essentially maps onto the articles in the Declaration. The encyclical summarizes the Catholic human rights tradition as consisting of personal rights, social rights, and instrumental rights. Drawing from the eight basic categories in the encyclical—Bodily, Political, Movement, Associational, Economic, Sexual and Familial, Religious, and Communication—three are selected here to amplify the categories of personal, social, and instrumental rights.[31]

- Personal Rights: The dignity of the human being remains at the center of the teaching. Personal rights are the condition necessary to ensure this dignity. Drawing from the eight basic categories of rights, personal rights include
  - bodily rights: right to life and bodily integrity
  - economic rights: right to work
  - political rights: right to self-determination
- Social Rights: Recognizing that human and social interaction is necessary for the provision of personal rights, social rights are positive obligations of society toward its members. Examples include:
  - bodily rights: right to food, clothing, shelter, rest, medical care

- – economic rights: right to adequate working conditions and a just wage
- – political rights: right to political participation
- Instrumental Rights: This is the institutional component of social rights. Macro institutional organizations such as the law, the economy, or health care must be structured to ensure social rights. Instrumental rights would include:
  - – bodily rights: right to security in sickness, inability to work, old age and unemployment
  - – economic rights: right to organize unions and right to property
  - – political rights: right to juridical protection of public participation

An important contribution of the Second Vatican Council, convened by John XXIII, was the conclusion that human rights at any point of time are historically conditioned. Hollenbach summarizes this point: "from the perspective of the Council, social, economic, and cultural rights, defined in relation to historical conditions, assume a new place of importance in the Catholic Human Rights Tradition."[32]

During his papacy, Paul VI (1963–78) was particularly conscious of the historical setting of social institutions and the issues related to transnational patterns of interdependence. The institutional sensitivity introduced in *Pacem in Terris* and developed in Vatican II and by Paul VI moved Catholic human rights concerns closer to issues of both application and the uniqueness of institutions in different settings.

John Paul II (1978–2005) subtly extended the political reach of the Catholic Church and championed human rights. He supported the Universal Declaration and was involved in activities of the United Nations. In his global travels he called attention to the abuse of human rights across the world. In *Laborem Exercens* (1981) he argued for the dignity of work. In *Sollicitudo Rei Socialis* (1987) he criticized liberal capitalism for its superdevelopment and submission to consumerism.[33] *Centesimus Annus* (1991) addressed market economies. It emphasizes their efficiency (as a reaction to the experience of Eastern Europe).[34] Here, the pope again levels against capitalism (he distinguishes capitalism from market economies) the charge that it results in an emphasis on "having rather than being." In this encyclical, John Paul II makes a distinction between systemic exploitation and marginalization. This distinction has important connotations for the United Nation's Global Compact, as will be noted later.

In summary, Catholic social thought reconceptualizes the individual with rights as conceived in liberal theory as a person who is the subject of both rights and obligations, by virtue of her nature as a participant in the social interactions that compose the broader systems and institutions of her time. This redefinition draws on Catholic social thought in natural law theory.

Jean Elshtain captures well this balance between the individual and society:

> The modern social encyclicals of Leo XIII, Pius XI, John XXIII, Paul VI, and John Paul II "affirm much more strongly the importance of the individual and, as Thomas [Aquinas] never did, of his or her rights." But these rights are not "spoken of primarily as individual claims against other individuals or society. They are woven into a concept of community that envisions the person as a part, a sacred part, of the whole. Rights exist within and are relative to a historical and social context and are intelligible only in terms of the obligations of individuals to other persons." This understanding of persons steers clear of the strong antinomies of individualism versus collectivism. Catholic social thought does *not* offer a "third way," as if it were simply a matter of hacking off bits and pieces of the individualist-collectivist options and melding them into a palatable compromise. Rather, it begins from a fundamentally different ontology from that assumed and required by individualism, on the one hand, and statist collectivism, on the other. The assumptions of Catholic social thought provide for individuality and rights as the goods of persons in community, together with the claims of social obligation.[35]

IV. THE UNIVERSALITY OF HUMAN RIGHTS

Universality is an important component of any discussion of standards that apply to human beings. Is there a single set of moral principles that is both universally binding and captures all issues of ethical significance? Or, as the relativists argue, is no ethical view, regardless of its source, better than any other? Any discussion of a moral issue must place itself somewhere on this universalist/relativist spectrum.[36]

This issue is important to our discussion in at least three respects:

1. Universalism/relativism is an issue central to the idea of human rights and how they affect precepts in the law or civil society. It is debated philosophically and theologically.
2. The manifest principles in the Universal Declaration of Human Rights are intended to be just that.
3. A challenge for multinational management is to determine a set of standards based on universal principles that will hold across its enterprise network while, at the same time, allowing for the uniqueness of local business units in different cultural settings.

Arguments about the issue in general will be presented in this section, with specific application to the Universal Declaration and multinational management in the chapters that follow.

Traditions of Universalism

Universality is an explicit claim in both natural law and Catholic social thought. It underlies liberal theory.

The emphasis on individual freedom in Locke, Kant, and Rawls does not make them relativists. Rather, their reasoned contractarianism makes claims that transcend history and culture. As noted earlier, the freedom of liberal theory abstracts from a person's historical or communal context.[37] Campbell supports this view and argues that the theory articulated in Rawl's original "theory of justice" was intended to be universal. (Later, he points out, Rawls in his book *Political Realism* restricted his theory to apply only to liberal democracies, a less-than-universalist claim.)[38] Elshtain comments, "Contractarianism of an atomistic sort posits the self as given prior to any social order—ahistorical, unsituated, a bearer of abstract rights, an untrammeled chooser in which choices lie his freedom and autonomy."[39]

In the natural law tradition, the universalist tradition begins with the classical emphasis on the unity and orderliness of the cosmos. Since that time (as noted earlier), there have been numerous strands of natural law theory. Michael Perry summarizes the central universalist position: "The 'natural law' that the idea of human rights presupposes is simply that all (or virtually all) human beings share some significant characteristics, in that sense they share a 'nature,' in virtue of which some things are good for every human being—some things are valuable for (and, so, should be valued by) every human being—and some things are bad for every human being—some things are harmful to (and, so, should be disvalued by) every human being."[40]

The natural law is pluralistic as well as universal. Although these two terms are sometimes used synonymously, there is a subtle but distinct difference between them. The natural law is universal because of the underlying sameness of each person. It is pluralistic in the acknowledgment that all human beings are not alike in some respects, and that there are cultural differences. In contrast to universalism, pluralism as described by Perry recognized that "there are many important respects in which human beings are not all alike; some things good for some human beings, including a concrete way of life, might not be good for every human being, and some things bad for some human beings might not be bad for every human being."[41]

The commonality of human dignity in Catholic social thought as the core of its human rights stance is a universalist statement. The political, economic, and social rights that flow from this core principle are thus universal as well. They are intended to apply to all people in all cultures.

The Relativist Challenge

There are at least three ways of looking at the relativist challenge to universalism. One is anthropological relativism—the claim that, other than some physical characteristics, all needs, especially social needs, are a function of a person's culture.[42] A second relativist challenge is that it is impossible to come to a common understanding or agreement over cultural differences.[43] A third relativist position is that the cultural context should have a critical part in determining the specific shape of universal principles.

Anthropological Relativism

The anthropological challenge is directed to the claims of liberal rights theory and, particularly, to the notion of natural law. The relativist denies commonality, arguing that an individual's nature is strictly a function of her personal history in her own unique culture. The natural law position counters with an acknowledgment that there are differences drawn from the uniqueness of each person's historical circumstances with his or her own relationships and social identities, but argues that there is something beneath socialization that defines human nature.

Pope John Paul II states this natural law position as follows:

> The great concern of our contemporaries for historicity and for culture has led some to call into question . . . the existence of "objective norms of morality" valid for all peoples of the present and the future, as for those of the past. . . . It must certainly be admitted that man always exists in a particular culture, but it must also be admitted that man is not exhaustively defined by the same culture. . . . [T]he very progress of cultures demonstrates that there is something in man which transcends those cultures. This "something" is precisely human nature: This nature is itself the measure of culture and the condition ensuring that man does not become the prisoner of any of his culture, but asserts his personal dignity by living in accordance with the profound truth of this being.[44]

Another counter to anthropological relativism as it relates to human rights is an empirical analysis of the "existential roots" of these rights.[45] This approach, acknowledging that the language of human rights is not a part of many cultures, studies the traditional roots of these cultures in search of a core respect due to human beings. For example, Amartya Sen challenges the thesis that "Asian values are less supportive of freedom and more concerned with order and discipline, and that the claims of human rights in the areas of political and civil liberties, therefore, are less relevant and less appropriate in Asia than in the West."[46] Following a careful study of Confucianism, Buddhism, and the various traditions of India, he concludes, "It is hard to make sense of the view that the basic ideas underlying freedom and rights in a tolerant society are 'Western' notions, and somehow alien to Asia."[47] In a broader study, UNESCO has sponsored a number of projects to study the existential roots of human rights across cultures. Their general conclusion is that a respect due to human beings exists across the world.[48]

Kofi Annan put it more bluntly, "You don't need to explain the meaning of human rights to an Asian mother or an African father whose son or daughter has been tortured and killed. They understand it—tragically— far better than we ever will."[49]

Epistemological Relativism

The second relativist challenge is of a different character. It questions the possibility of overcoming transcultural disagreements. This epistemological relativism maintains that persons are so entrenched in their own history and culture that they are incapable of dialogue with, or understanding of, other cultures.

This challenge views a culture as a cohesive whole. It misses the fact that numerous subcultures and cultural outliers constantly interact to change attitudes or modify behavior. Indeed, in many situations intercultural dialogue can be more productive than intracultural dialogue.[50] This is not to deny the difficulty of trying to understand the position of a colleague or challenger steeped in another culture. That difficulty holds for a manager of a multinational enterprise network as well as in political debate.

Alasdair MacIntyre's views are informative here. For MacIntyre, all moral thinking takes place within a historically contingent context. Our reflections are shaped by cultural factors such as certain beliefs, motivations, and practices—the profound and formative influences of which we are largely unaware.[51] This position has led MacIntyre to a strong rejection of the universality of human rights. In *After Virtue* he states, "there are no such rights, and belief in them is one with belief in witches and in unicorns."[52]

Against this historicist, anti-universalist claim, however, MacIntyre proposes a tradition of inquiry. This is a "living tradition" that can assimilate ideas "generated elsewhere" through a "method of dialogue and mutual inquiry."[53] It is MacIntyre's emphasis on inquiry that moves his objection from an anti-universalist or epistemological stance to one of cultural relativism in the narrow sense defined below, which is compatible with universalism.

Cultural Relativism

The concept of cultural relativism used here is a very narrow definition of a term that tends to be broadly applied to any cultural challenge in the literature. Its focus is on the context of the application of universal principles. As Perry states, "The embodiment of the value that makes the most sense in any context inevitably depends on the particularities of the context in which the value is to be achieved. . . . [P]articularities of context, especially cultural particularities, do and should play a role in determining the specific shape—for example, the specific institutional embodiment—one or another culture gives to a value (e.g., freedom of the press) represented by a human rights provision."[54]

The narrow definition of cultural relativism is similar to the Thomistic distinction between fundamental principles and secondary precepts. Velasquez and Brady describe this distinction as follows:

> A third significant characteristic that Aquinas' analysis imparted to the natural law tradition was a surprising willingness to countenance moral diversity. As we have seen, the most general precepts of natural law . . . are held to be universally evident and universally binding on everyone. These fundamental principles provide an "unchanging" and so absolutist component of natural law. But the more detailed normative conclusions that reason derives as "secondary precepts" from the "primary" injunctions to pursue these fundamental goods . . . are neither universally known nor universally valid but have a relativistic dependence on local realities. Consequently, while some moral norms are so immediately related to the fundamental goods (e.g., the norm that innocent life is not to be destroyed) that they are universally binding, other moral norms are derivative and subject to cultural and historical variability.[55]

As they note, quoting Aquinas, "practical reasoning is concerned with what our actions can bring about and such things can be brought about in more than one way. . . . [Consequently,] in practical reasoning different people may correctly draw different conclusions from the same general premises."[56]

In this sense, the fact of cultural relativism is a component of any political, economic, or social application of human rights.

Managerial Implications

The multinational firm, as we have discussed in previous chapters, needs to find a set of principles with which to implement its strategy for long-term enterprise sustainability. The first step is to determine standards that apply across the enterprise network. The foundation for these principles, as we argue, is the Universal Declaration of Human Rights as delineated in chapter 6, extended to the United Nations Global Compact in chapter 7.

Once network-wide standards have been established, the second step is to implement these standards in the local business units. In this sense, managerial decision making must strike a balance between universality and cultural relativism, narrowly defined: that is, management must make the Thomistic distinction between (1) universal principles based on fundamental goals and (2) secondary precepts based on the local reality as a function of its unique history and culture.

CHAPTER SIX

The Universal Declaration of Human Rights

The problem of divergent or even conflicting human rights values came into focus with the initial discussions for the United Nations in 1945 in reaction to the brutality of World War II. Still, amid the political posturing as the war approached its conclusion, human rights issues surfaced only sporadically in the initial deliberations.[1] In an early draft proposal for the U.N. Charter, human rights were mentioned once.[2] In the final draft, however, the principle of human rights appeared several times in the text, which affirmed the "faith in fundamental human rights" and the promotion of "universal respect for and observance of human rights and fundamental freedoms for all without distinction as to race, sex, language, or religion."[3] A definition in terms of specific rights remained for the appointment of the Commission on Human Rights in June 1946. The Commission was assigned the responsibility of proposing an international bill of rights as well as a plan for implementation[4]—a daunting task once the

clash between the Soviet Union and the West had been openly acknowledged by both Churchill and Stalin.[5]

I. THE COMMISSION ON HUMAN RIGHTS

The Commission held its first meeting in January 1947. The final draft
of its declaration was submitted to the General Assembly of the United
Nations in December 1948. As one would expect, there were many approaches advocated by different commissioners. Following the liberal
rights tradition, the delegates from the West championed civil and political rights. The Soviets, critical of the liberal stress on civil and political
rights, pushed for economic and social rights since these rights are at the
core of Marxism and have been present in all constitutions of the Soviet
Union since 1918. Marx had held that individual rights in liberal theory
were overemphasized and that genuine individual freedom could only be
achieved in solidarity with others. He regarded liberal rights as egotistic,
arguing that human liberation depends upon a transformation of the entire economic and social system.

The inclusion of economic and social rights also enjoyed support well
beyond the Soviet Union. According to Mary Ann Glendon, "the Declaration's articles dealing with rights to work, unionization, education, and
so on were not included as concessions to the Soviets. They enjoyed wide
support from the liberal democracies, a fact that is hardly surprising in
view of their resemblance to the 'second bill of rights' proposed in Franklin Delano Roosevelt's 1944 State of the Union message, and to the social
rights and obligations that were becoming standard features of most post-
war constitutions."[6] Agreement on the precise content of these articles,
however, was extremely difficult to achieve. England, in particular, wanted
these rights to be handled in a separate document. The Soviet Union, for
its part, opposed any language that would appear to relegate such rights to
an inferior rank.[7] In general, reflecting the political events of the day, the
Soviets remained obstructionists throughout most of the discussion in the
Commission on Human Rights.

As the articles were being drafted, wording became an issue. For example, the Islamic delegates voiced concern over the rights to marry in

Article 16 and the declaration of freedom of religion in Article 18. Saudi Arabia's spokesperson charged that the terms "equal rights" for men and women "ignored more ancient civilizations."[8] Other Muslim countries, however, accepted the term "equal rights" with the understanding that it did not mean "identical rights."[9] Saudi Arabia later accepted the idea of freedom of conscience and religion but expressed concerns that this would encourage proselytization, which has historically caused so much bloodshed. Again, the position of the Muslim countries was mixed.

After almost two years of intense interaction, the third committee of the Commission on Human Rights voted on each article. Twenty-three of the thirty articles gained unanimous approval.[10] For the full draft, seven countries abstained—the six members of the Soviet bloc (including Yugoslavia) and Canada, although Canada quickly reversed her position.[11]

The draft was submitted to the U.N. General Assembly on December 9, 1948. In the General Assembly, the vote to accept the Universal Declaration was 45 in favor, 8 abstentions, and none opposed.[12] Saudi Arabia abstained over the article on religious freedom. The Soviet bloc abstentions were judged by Eleanor Roosevelt to be based on Article 13, affirming the right of anyone to leave his country.[13]

II. THE UNIVERSAL DECLARATION

The Declaration is an impressive statement, particularly in the context of the political tensions of the time. For the purpose of our discussion, the document is separated into six parts.[14]

Overview Statements: Preamble and Articles 1 and 2

PREAMBLE
WHEREAS recognition of the inherent dignity and of the equal and inalienable rights of all members of the human family is the foundation of freedom, justice, and peace in the world,
WHEREAS disregard and contempt for human rights have resulted in barbarous acts which have outraged the conscience of mankind, and the advent of a world in which human beings shall enjoy free-

dom of speech and belief and freedom from fear and want has been proclaimed as the highest aspiration of the common people,

WHEREAS it is essential, if man is not to be compelled to have recourse, as a last resort, to rebellion against tyranny and oppression, that human rights should be protected by the rule of law,

WHEREAS it is essential to promote the development of friendly relations between nations,

WHEREAS the peoples of the United Nations have in the Charter reaffirmed their faith in fundamental human rights, in the dignity and worth of the human person and in the equal rights of men and women and have determined to promote social progress and better standards of life in larger freedom,

WHEREAS Member States have pledged themselves to achieve, in cooperation with the United Nations, the promotion of universal respect for and observance of human rights and fundamental freedoms,

WHEREAS a common understanding of these rights and freedoms is of the greatest importance for the full realization of this pledge,

Now, Therefore, The General Assembly Proclaims

This universal declaration of human rights as a common standard of achievement for all peoples and all nations, to the end that every individual and every organ of society, keeping this Declaration constantly in mind, shall strive by teaching and education to promote respect for these rights and freedoms and by progressive measures, national and international, to secure their universal and effective recognition and observance, both among the peoples of Member States themselves and among the peoples of territories under their jurisdiction.

ARTICLE 1. All human beings are born free and equal in dignity and rights. They are endowed with reason and conscience and should act towards one another in a spirit of brotherhood.

ARTICLE 2. Everyone is entitled to all the rights and freedoms set forth in this Declaration, without distinction of any kind, such as race, colour, sex, language, religion, political or other opinion,

national or social origin, property, birth or other status. Further-
more, no distinction shall be made on the basis of the political,
jurisdictional or international status of the country or territory to
which a person belongs, whether it be independent, trust, non-self-
governing or under any other limitation of sovereignty.

Together these initial statements present "the general principles of dignity, liberty, equality, and brotherhood" and their application to "all members of the human family." They affirm that the responsibility for rights
extends beyond the relationship between a sovereign state and its citizens
to a universal concern. The first two articles set forth the dual nature of
universality: All human beings are included (Article 1) and no one can be
excluded (Article 2).

Individual Rights: Articles 3 through 11

ARTICLE 3. Everyone has the right to life, liberty and security of
person.
ARTICLE 4. No one shall be held in slavery or servitude; slavery and
the slave trade shall be prohibited in all their forms.
ARTICLE 5. No one shall be subjected to torture or to cruel, in-
human or degrading treatment or punishment.
ARTICLE 6. Everyone has the right to recognition everywhere as a
person before the law.
ARTICLE 7. All are equal before the law and are entitled without
any discrimination to equal protection of the law. All are entitled
to equal protection against any discrimination in violation of this
Declaration and against any incitement to such discrimination.
ARTICLE 8. Everyone has the right to an effective remedy by the
competent national tribunals for acts violating the fundamental
rights granted him by the constitution or by law.
ARTICLE 9. No one shall be subjected to arbitrary arrest, detention
or exile.
ARTICLE 10. Everyone is entitled in full equality to a fair and public hearing by an independent and impartial tribunal, in the determination of his rights and obligations and of any criminal charge
against him.

ARTICLE 11. (1) Everyone charged with a penal offense has the right to be presumed innocent until proved guilty according to law in a public trial at which he has had all the guarantees necessary for his defense. (2) No one shall be held guilty of any penal offense or of any act or omission which did not constitute a penal offense, under national or international law, at the time when it was committed. Nor shall a heavier penalty be imposed than the one that was applicable at the time the penal offense was committed.

These are the individual rights that are broadly included in national constitutions. The series of rights specified in Articles 4 through 11 can be viewed as enlarging the principles of Article 3.[15]

Rights in Civil Society: Articles 12 through 17

ARTICLE 12. No one shall be subject to arbitrary interference with his privacy, family, home or correspondence, or to attacks upon his honour and reputation. Everyone has the right to the protection of the law against such interference or attacks.

ARTICLE 13. (1) Everyone has the right to freedom of movement and residence within the borders of each state. (2) Everyone has the right to leave any country, including his own, and to return to his country.

ARTICLE 14. (1) Everyone has the right to seek and to enjoy in other countries asylum from persecution. (2) This right may not be invoked in the case of prosecutions genuinely arising from non-political crimes or from acts contrary to the purposes and principles of the United Nations.

ARTICLE 15. (1) Everyone has the right to a nationality. (2) No one shall be arbitrarily deprived of his nationality nor denied the right to change his nationality.

ARTICLE 16. (1) Men and women of full age, without any limitation due to race, nationality or religion, have the right to marry and to found a family. They are entitled to equal rights as to marriage, during marriage, and at its dissolution. (2) Marriage shall be entered into only with the free and full consent of the intending spouses. (3) The family is the natural and fundamental group unit of society and is entitled to protection by society and the State.

ARTICLE 17. (1) Everyone has the right to own property alone as well as in association with others. (2) No one shall be arbitrarily deprived of his property.

The statements on freedom of movement, asylum, and nationality include an international dimension involving freedoms of citizens toward their countries.[16]

Note that Article 17 does not refer to "private" property. Caught between the United Kingdom's position that the concept of private property is so broadly, legally assumed that it is not necessary to include it, the Soviet position that acceptable subsistence should not be grounded in private property, and the Latin American position that private property should be tied to a decent existence, the Commission decided to drop the word "private."

Rights in the Polity: Articles 18 through 21

ARTICLE 18. Everyone has the right to freedom of thought, conscience and religion; this right includes freedom to change his religion or belief, and freedom, either alone or in community with others and in public or private, to manifest his religion or belief in teaching, practice, worship and observance.

ARTICLE 19. Everyone has the right to freedom of opinion and expression; this right includes freedom to hold opinions without interference and to seek, receive and impart information and ideas through any media and regardless of frontiers.

ARTICLE 20. (1) Everyone has the right to freedom of peaceful assembly and association. (2) No one may be compelled to belong to an association.

ARTICLE 21. (1) Everyone has the right to take part in the government of his country, directly or through freely chosen representatives. (2) Everyone has the right of equal access to public service in his country. (3) The will of the people shall be the basis of the authority of government; this will shall be expressed in periodic and genuine elections which shall be by universal and equal suffrage and shall be held by secret vote or by equivalent free voting procedures.

These articles, in particular, reflect the liberal theory as outlined earlier. As part of the Declaration, they expand the umbrella of personal and group rights. And, as Glendon points out, "Communist regimes, colonial powers, and monarchies alike joined in the overwhelming vote of approval for the principles of Article 21 that would one day transform their world."[17]

Together, Articles 3 through 21 affirm civil and political rights. These are often referred to as "first-generation rights." Beginning with the specificity of individual rights, they expand to the more general political rights. First-generation rights are the rights of the individual to noninterference by the state. These rights are relatively easy to define and, with clear thresholds of violations, can be ensured by legislation. By and large, ensuring these rights is not financially expensive.

Economic, Social and Cultural Rights: Articles 22 through 27

ARTICLE 22. Everyone, as a member of society, has the right to social security and is entitled to realization, through national effort and international cooperation and in accordance with the organization and resources of each State, of the economic, social and cultural rights indispensable for his dignity and the free development of his personality.

ARTICLE 23. (1) Everyone has the right to work, to free choice of employment, to just and favourable conditions of work and to protection against unemployment. (2) Everyone, without any discrimination, has the right to equal pay for equal work. (3) Everyone who works has the right to just and favourable remuneration ensuring for himself and his family an existence worthy of human dignity, and supplemented, if necessary, by other means of social protection. (4) Everyone has the right to form and to join trade unions for protection of his interests.

ARTICLE 24. Everyone has the right to rest and leisure, including reasonable limitation of working hours and periodic holidays with pay.

ARTICLE 25. (1) Everyone has the right to a standard of living adequate for the health and well-being of himself and of his family, including food, clothing, housing and medical care and necessary social services, and the right to security in the event of unemployment, sickness, disability, widowhood, old age or other lack of livelihood in circumstances beyond his control. (2) Motherhood and childhood are entitled to special care and assistance. All children, whether born in or out of wedlock, shall enjoy the same social protection.

ARTICLE 26. (1) Everyone has the right to education. Education shall be free, at least in the elementary and fundamental stages. Elementary education shall be compulsory. Technical and professional education shall be made generally available and higher education shall be equally accessible to all on the basis of merit. (2) Education shall be directed to the full development of the human personality and to the strengthening of respect for human rights and fundamental freedoms. It shall promote understanding, tolerance and friendship among all nations, racial or religious groups, and shall further the activities of the United Nations for the maintenance of peace. (3) Parents shall have a prior right to choose the kind of education that shall be given to their children.

ARTICLE 27. (1) Everyone has the right freely to participate in the cultural life of the community, to enjoy the arts and to share in scientific advancement and its benefits. (2) Everyone has the right to the protection of the moral and material interests resulting from any scientific, literary or artistic production of which he is the author.

As noted, these rights did not appear suddenly on the scene at the insistence of the Soviet Union. They have deep roots in national constitutions and were sponsored in the Declaration by social democratic and Christian political parties as well as Socialist parties.[18]

Article 22 introduces these rights as a group which supports the dignity of each individual as a member of society, with economic, social, and cultural rights to be assured by national governments and international cooperation.

Article 23, Part 4 endorses a right that has proved to be particularly problematic, namely, "Everyone has the right to form and to join trade unions for protection of his interests." While this clause is included in most legal regimes across the world, it is seldom enforced in developing countries, particularly those attempting to attract foreign investment or subcontracted production, as in the case of the apparel industry. In a handful of countries, including China, the legal right to join an independent trade union is not recognized.[19]

As a set, these Articles call for a different approach on the part of the state. Often referred to as "second-generation rights," or "programme rights," these are positive obligations of society as distinct from the independent entitlements of Articles 3 through 21. The promotion of economic, social, and cultural rights involves long-range commitment and planning on the part of the state. They are expensive; specific thresholds can be difficult to define; and financial tradeoffs are required among the specific rights.

Necessary Conditions: Articles 28 through 30

ARTICLE 28. Everyone is entitled to a social and international order in which the rights and freedoms set forth in this Declaration can be fully realized.

ARTICLE 29. (1) Everyone has duties to the community in which alone the free and full development of his personality is possible. (2) In the exercise of his rights and freedoms, everyone shall be subject only to such limitations as are determined by law solely for the purpose of securing due recognition and respect for the rights and freedoms of others and of meeting the just requirements of morality, public order and the general welfare in a democratic society. (3) These rights and freedoms may in no case be exercised contrary to the purposes and principles of the United Nations.

ARTICLE 30. Nothing in this Declaration may be interpreted as implying for any State, group or person any right to engage in any activity or to perform any act aimed at the destruction of any of the rights and freedoms set forth herein.

Article 28 provides the overview for this set. "Its affirmation of the need for social and international order echoes the main Preamble's insistence on the rule of law and friendly relations among nations."[20] The duties and limits of Article 29 describe the two essential features of this order, while Article 30 looks to the future.

Even the casual reader is struck by the demanding nature of the Universal Declaration. The Declaration has initiated a remarkably broad-based effort on the part of many countries and institutions to enhance human rights.

III. UNIVERSAL LEGITIMACY

From a normative standpoint, the manifest human rights as outlined in the Declaration are universal because they are declared as such by the framers. The Declaration affirms universality in a dual sense: the declared rights apply worldwide, and they are inclusive because they apply without distinction of any kind. In 1948 this was, indeed, a radical breakthrough at the theoretical level.[21]

A Western Document?

As the Declaration was being prepared, the American Anthropological Association leveled against it the charge of cultural imperialism, based on a form of anthropological relativism. In its words, "The rights of Man in the twentieth century cannot be circumscribed by the standards of any single culture or be dictated by the aspirations of any single people. Such a document will lead to frustration, not realisation of the personalities of vast numbers of human beings."[22]

Indeed, at the time of the Declaration, much of the world's population was not represented in the United Nations. The defeated Axis powers were explicitly excluded. Large parts of Africa and some countries in Asia were still under colonial rule. Within these constraints, however, the committee that drafted the final Declaration was a global representation of the United Nations itself: "besides Europeans and North Americans, there were six members from Asia—giants such as China, India, and Pakistan, plus Burma, the Philippines, and Siam. Islamic culture was predominant in nine nations—Afghanistan, Egypt, Iran, Iraq, Pakistan, Saudi Arabia, Syria, Turkey, Yemen—and strong in India and Lebanon. Three countries had large Buddhist populations—Burma, China, and Siam. Only four were from the African continent—Ethiopia and Liberia, plus two that would not count as representative of black Africa—Egypt and South Africa. In addition, there was the numerous and outspoken Latin American contingent. Six of the European members belonged to the Communist bloc."[23]

A number of non-Westerners were prominent in committee deliberations. Two later served as president of the U.N. General Assembly: Carlos Romulo from the Philippines and Charles Malik from Lebanon. Pengchun Chang, head of the U.N. Chinese delegation, was a highly respected philosopher.[24] Another member, Hermañ Santa Cruz from Chile, had participated in drafting Latin American statements on human rights. Hansa Mehta, who chaired the working group on implementation, later became one of the women advisors on drafting the rights provision of the Indian constitution.

Thus, to the extent possible within the makeup of the United Nations at that time, this was an experienced, articulate, representative group. In addition to the committee, there was input from many other sources. "Before the whole two-year process from drafting and deliberation to adoption reached its end, literally hundreds of individuals from diverse backgrounds had participated. Thus, Malik (Third Committee Chairman) could fairly say, 'The genesis of each article, and each part of each article, was a dynamic process in which many minds, interests, backgrounds, legal systems and ideological persuasions played their respective determining roles.'"[25]

The critics' response was that the committee members (perhaps with the exception of Chang) had been heavily involved with Western thought and hence did not fully represent the national cultures of their delegation. Ironically, however, this very claim supports the importance of dialogue and refutes the epistemological relativist argument that transcultural understanding and agreement are inherently impossible (as noted in chapter 5).

Universality in the Processes of Application

The Declaration has been effective in initiating dialogue, modifying ideas, and expanding applications. The Declaration itself was a statement of intent. Application was intended to take place through international treaties as well as national constitutions and legal systems. Two conventions transformed the Declaration into international treaties: the 1966 International Covenant on Civil and Political Rights and the 1966 International Covenant on Economic, Social and Cultural Rights. These conventions resulted in formal treaties that each member nation was invited to sign. The initial level of support for these covenants was substantially less than for the Declaration; consensus on the documents was not reached until 1966, eighteen years after the Declaration itself, and they did not take effect until 1976, when they had been ratified by 35 member nations.[26] Support has grown substantially over time: as of April 3, 2009, 69 member nations had signed the Covenant on Economic, Social and Cultural Rights and 160 were parties to it, while 72 member nations had signed the Covenant on Civil and Political Rights and 164 were parties to it.[27] The Declaration and these two covenants together are generally referred to as the International Bill of Human Rights.

Progress to narrow the gap between universality in theory as all-inclusive and the application of these principles in practice continues on two fronts: conventions for the rights of groups such as women and children; and the establishment of regional systems for human rights protection.[28]

In the process of applying the Declaration, numerous non-Western voices have been involved. "This dynamic has been greatly influenced by the participation and the initiatives of non-Western states. Indeed, one of the stereotypical representations of international human rights shows a composite picture of 'Western' civil and political rights, 'socialist' economic and social rights, and 'third world' rights such as the right to self-determination and the right to development."[29]

The Catholic Church has been active in supporting human rights, theologically and in practice. As noted earlier, all of the human rights in the Declaration are now supported in Catholic social thought. Associated with these formal advances in human rights, a plethora of vigorous NGOs motivated by this tradition have had a direct impact on the implementation of human rights in civil society, as well as substantial influence on government policy as well.[30] Scholars in other traditions, including Buddhism and Hinduism, have responded with vigorous discussions regarding the concept of rights in those traditions. "Engaged Buddhism" is one interesting example of human rights in a non-Christian context.[31]

Continuing Cultural and Geographical Tensions

Criticisms of the Declaration's formulation of human rights continue to be expressed as part of the implementation process. Eva Brems notes that "mainly, the perceived threat to the universality principle is coming from outside the Western world. From around the globe, but in particular from East Asia, Africa, and the Muslim world, voices are heard claiming that human rights are Western-made and for that reason make a less-than-perfect instrument for use outside the West. Partly, this contains criticism of the Western-dominated mainstream international human rights protection system and its concepts. Partly it expresses alternative, contextually shaped human rights views."[32]

Brems has carefully followed these issues in an analysis of the human rights discourse in non-Western areas of the world.[33] Her overall assessment is that "the very large majority of the examined texts either implicitly or explicitly accept the general and worldwide applicability of international human rights. This widespread acceptance of the universality principle testifies in the first place to the authority of the discourse of international human rights, and is partly the result of the strong pressure exercised in this field by the international community."[34]

Relative to Africa and Asia, she notes that "particularist human rights discourse has three dimensions: political, economic, and cultural. Yet the political dimension is stressed more in Asia than in Africa and the cultural dimension is more central in Africa than in Asia."[35] Taken together, the argument is that "we, Asians (or Africans) want the freedom to attach more importance to economic and social rights than to civil and political rights in our human rights policy." Moreover, "when our human rights performance is assessed by the international community, we want our score in the field of social and economic rights to be taken at least as seriously as our score on civil and political rights. This implies an upgrading of economic and social rights at the world level, i.e. a transformation."[36]

Brems's view is that the Islamic discourse is a religious response and addresses only issues of culture:

> The 'culture' that is the central element in this type of human-rights discourse, is a particular type of culture, i.e. religion. What is more, Islam is considered to be a religion with a set of rules governing all types of human behaviour, written down in a holy book and collected sayings of the Prophet, to which divine authority is attached. This has an influence on the debate and on the possibilities of reaching a solution, both from the human-rights side and from the culture side. . . . the claims based on religion seem to be more radical than those based on other cultural grounds. Once the content of the religious rule is established in an authoritative manner, there is very little flexibility: it has to remain intact, because theoretically at least human beings cannot alter divine commandments.[37]

Overall Assessment

In spite of these continuing tensions, it is fair to say that the Declaration has changed the world. With the move from principles to action, the idea of a set of principles and the recognition of their importance have spread dramatically, along with the conflict over specific applications. In this sense, the Declaration has grown in recognition and legitimacy.

John Humphrey, a Canadian member of the Commission on Human Rights and director of the U.N. Division of Human Rights from 1946 to 1966, summarized the importance of these principles well on the Declaration's twenty-fifth anniversary:

> The Declaration and the principles enunciated in it have been officially invoked on so many occasions both within and outside the United Nations that it can be said that it is the juridical conscience of the international community, that the rules enunciated by it are normatively binding, and this whether they are in fact respected or not. It can be said that the Universal Declaration of Human Rights authentically defines those human rights and fundamental freedoms which the member states of the United Nations undertook to respect and observe by the Charter but which the Charter does not itself define. In retrospect after a quarter of a century, the adoption of the Declaration appears as a much greater achievement than anyone could have imagined in 1948.[38]

Thus, it can be argued that the Declaration along with the dialogue and applications it has triggered is the most legitimate international social norm in history, and one that any firm looking for a strategy of enterprise sustainability should emulate. Even though business enterprises are not entirely free of international political relationships or formulations of domestic national policy, their operating decisions have a large impact on global human rights. The United Nations Global Compact, discussed in the next chapters, provides the transition from the concepts in the Declaration as extended through the International Bill of Rights and various conventions, and as politically applied through regional systems and international legal structures, to the business enterprise.

PART IV

IMPLEMENTING A
HUMAN RIGHTS STANDARD

Against the general theological, moral, social, and political background of human rights, as discussed in Part III, we turn to their implementation in the enterprise: developing and carrying out a plan of action. A social standard for the multinational firm, we have argued, is an essential starting point for a strategy of long-term sustainability and, for that matter, provides a guide to normative departures from the market model.

Human rights can provide the basis of socially effective uniform network standards. Required are principles specifically targeted to business and an action plan to apply them to the specific firm. Chapter 7 outlines a human rights business standard, in the form of the United Nations Global Compact. Chapter 8 outlines the implementation of this standard at Novartis, a large Swiss pharmaceutical company.

CHAPTER SEVEN

The United Nations Global Compact

The United Nations Global Compact (UNGC) initiative evolved from a challenge posed by Secretary-General Kofi Annan to the business community at the Davos World Economic Forum in January 1999. "I call on you—individually through your firms, and collectively through your business associations—to embrace, support, and enact a set of core values in the areas of human rights, labor standards, and environmental practices." His vision was to "give a human face to the global market."[1] Annan has also stated, "It is not enough to say—though it is true—that without business the poor would have no hope of escaping their poverty. Too many of them have no hope as it is. Those who have the power and means, governments *and* business, must *show* that economics, properly applied, and profits, wisely invested, can bring social benefits within reach not only for the few but for the many, and eventually for all."[2] Intense interactions among business chief executive officers and associations, nongovernmental organizations, labor unions, and four U.N. agencies for over a year led to the formulation of nine principles. Businesses were invited to embrace these principles and to incorporate them in their strategies and decisions.

From the managerial viewpoint, the UNGC is a set of social principles, broadly perceived as legitimate, that are useful in implementing the goal of long-term enterprise sustainability. The necessary process is to translate these principles into a set of standards that become general rules reflecting the uniqueness of the firm in its environment, which are then applied across the multinational enterprise network. Given the uniqueness of the operating environment of each of a firm's business units, in contrast to the uniform network standards, the tension of universality versus cultural relativity moves from philosophical debate to decisions about specific actions. This is the challenge of implementing the UNGC.

This chapter outlines the nature of the Compact principles and the extent of their acceptance by NGOs and the business communities.

I. COMPACT REQUIREMENTS

Initially there were nine principles in the Compact adopted in 2000. A tenth was added in 2004 after extensive discussion and analysis. These principles can be summarized as follows:

General Human Rights Principles
1. Support and respect the protection of internationally proclaimed human rights within their sphere of influence.
2. Make sure they are not complicit in human rights abuses.

Labor
3. Uphold the freedom of association and the effective recognition of the right to collective bargaining.
4. Promote the elimination of all forms of forced and compulsory labour.
5. Promote the effective abolition of child labour.
6. Uphold the elimination of discrimination in respect of employment and occupation.

Environment
7. Support a precautionary approach to environmental challenges.
8. Undertake initiatives to promote greater environmental responsibility.
9. Encourage the development and diffusion of environmentally friendly technologies.

Corruption
10. Business should work against corruption in all its forms, including extortion and bribery.

Note that Principles 1 and 2 differ in nature from Principles 3–10 in that these first two are the fundamental core of the others. The first two principles call for the overall defense of human rights, which can include a broad range of human rights concerns in local situations, whereas the other eight define and particularize the basic tenets of Principles 1 and 2 to the rights of labor, the environment, and dealing with corruption. Principles 3 through 10 are so-called hypernorms.[3] They specify the precepts that will be uniform across the multinational network in all operating locations (business units).

General Human Rights Principles

Principles 1 and 2 address the duties of the corporation relative to the rights of its stakeholders. They capture the full reach of the Universal Declaration of Human Rights. In specifying these duties, there is a distinction between the duty not to deprive and the duty to protect.[4] This is drawn from the philosophical identification of three levels of correlative duties associated with the deprivation of any right:

1. Duties to avoid depriving. These duties are limited. "Duties to avoid depriving require merely that one refrain from making an unnecessary gain for oneself by a means that is destructive for others."[5]
2. Duties to protect from deprivation. Duties to protect usually arise because others have failed in their duties to avoid. "If everyone who ought to fulfill duties to avoid did so, performance of duties to protect might

not be necessary."[6] This set of duties includes a responsibility to assist in the development of social institutions in order to help avoid the creation of incentives to deprive. Since it is generally the responsibility of government to ensure that members or institutions of society do not deprive citizens of their rights, duties to protect on the part of the nongovernmental organizations or business organizations in a society are often a reflection of governmental failure.

3. Duties to aid the deprived. The duties to aid generally come into force because of the failure of the first two sets of duties in the broad society, often as a function of past abuses. "If the fulfilment of duties to protect is sufficiently inadequate, duties to assist may be overwhelming."[7]

These sets of duties are interrelated since virtually all rights involve correlative duties at all three levels, although, for civil society, they are not generally the responsibility of the same institution or kinds of institutions.

The UNGC principles address the first two levels of duties. In Principle 2, the call for businesses "to make sure they are not complicit in human rights abuses" fits the duty to avoid. Principle 1 extends the corporate duty to the second level of duties—"to support and respect the protection of internationally protected human rights within their sphere of influence." The requirement to protect is more demanding than the requirement to avoid deprivation. It involves cooperation with other institutions of government or civil society, necessitating a proactive effort on the part of enterprise management.

There are two correlative duty limitations in the statement of Principles 1 and 2. First, there is no stated duty to aid the deprived. Second, Principle 1 calls for protection within the firm's "sphere of influence." Although some managers see this principle as extending their stakeholder boundaries to include the stakeholders of firms to whom they subcontract, the "sphere of influence" limitation does not hold the enterprise accountable for the human rights of those with whom it does not have some kind of linkage. This means, for example, that a multinational with operations in Rio de Janeiro does not have a responsibility for the poor in the favelas beyond the families and local communities of their employees. In this way, Principle 1 distinguishes between exploitation and marginalization—the distinction made by John Paul II in *Centesimus Annus*. The enterprise is directed not to deprive but to protect the human rights of its stakeholders (those people and institutions with whom it has a linkage), but it is not held responsible for the marginalized—those with whom there is no linkage. The other principles are more specific.

Labor

The principles related to labor are drawn primarily from the group of economic, social, and cultural rights in the Universal Declaration, as refined in the progress toward applicability by the International Labour Organization's Declaration on Fundamental Principles and Rights at Work (1998).

Principle 3: Uphold the freedom of association and the effective recognition of the right to collective bargaining.

The origin of this principle is Article 23 in the Universal Declaration. The challenge in applying Principle 3 is the difference between national law and its enforcement. The gap is particularly glaring in the free trade zones of developing countries. Many National Ministries of Labor are concerned that a full enforcement of laws on the right to collective bargaining will discourage foreign direct investment. This was clearly the case in El Salvador's apparel industry.[8] In addition to enforcement issues, a small group of countries, including China, do not allow free trade unions. Unions in China are all controlled by the government. Again, in the apparel industry, most manufacturers accept the Chinese arrangement. A few institutions restrict the licensing of their logos and do not allow products made in China to bear their logo. (This is the case with the University of Notre Dame, which interprets the legal prohibition of free trade unions as not in accordance with the principles of Catholic social thought.)[9]

Principle 4: Promote the elimination of all forms of forced compulsory labor.

This principle finds its origin in the civil and political rights section of the Universal Declaration, Article 4.

Principle 5: Promote the effective abolition of child labor.

This principle is implied in Article 25 of the Universal Declaration and made explicit by the International Labour Organization. The ILO requirement is as follows: "The minimum age for admission to employment or work should, in principle, not be less than the age for completing compulsory schooling and in no event less than the age of 15 years. The worst form of child labour, including hazardous work, should be prohibited for those under 18."[10]

Given the specific age limits, the multinational enterprise has no alternative but to ensure this requirement. In some cases, this is unfortunate. The underlying assumption is that the child has an educational alternative, which is surely not the case in many developing countries. Frequently, a clean working environment with a nutritious lunch is far better than the circumstances a child under age 15 can find elsewhere.

Principle 6: Uphold the elimination of discrimination in respect of employment and occupation.

Principle 6 is drawn from the Universal Declaration, Article 23.

Environmental Protection

Although the Universal Declaration is silent on the protection of the environment as a human right, the nature of that document clearly embraces protection of the environment. The principles in the UNGC are drawn from the United Nations Conference on Environment and Development (1992), whose report is referred to as the "Rio Declaration on Environment and Development." Agenda 21 was adopted at that conference as a plan for achieving sustainable environmental development in the twenty-first century.

Principle 7: Support a precautionary approach to environmental challenges.

The Rio Declaration states the underlying principle: "Where there are threats of serious or irreversible damage, lack of full scientific certainty shall not be used as a reason for postponing cost-effective measures to prevent environmental degradation." The UNGC identifies the key elements of an approach based on this principle as "prevention rather than cure—it is more cost-effective to take early actions to ensure that the irreversible environmental damage does not occur. This requires developing a life-cycle approach to business activities to: manage the uncertainty; ensure transparency."[11] The precautionary principle is a very controversial issue. Some business scientists claim it inhibits any technical development, since there is always uncertainty as to the outcome. Others take a more balanced approach.

There is a subtle distinction between prevention and precaution. Prevention applies when there is a scientifically known cause and effect. Cost is an issue. Precaution applies when there is scientific uncertainty as to cause and effect.[12]

Principle 8: Undertake initiatives to promote greater environmental responsibility.

Agenda 21 defines environmental responsibility as the "responsible and ethical management of products and processes from the point of view of health, safety, and environmental aspects. Toward this end, business and industry should increase self regulation, guided by appropriate codes, charters and initiatives integrated into all elements of business planning and decision making, and foster openness and dialogue with employees and the public."[13]

In implementing this principle, collaboration is absolutely necessary if the individual firm is not to be at a competitive disadvantage.

Principle 9: Encourage the development and diffusion of environmentally friendly technologies.

Agenda 21 defines environmentally friendly technologies (EFTs) as those that "protect the environment, are less polluting, use all resources in a more sustainable manner, recycle more of their wastes and products, and handle residual wastes in a more acceptable manner than the technologies for which they were substituted. [EFTs] are not just individual technologies, but total systems which include know-how, procedures, goods and services, and equipment as well as organizational and managerial procedures."[14] This is a tall order.

Corruption

Principle 10: Business should work against corruption in all its forms, including extortion and bribery.

Corruption is a recognized plague in social, political, and economic development. It is estimated that corruption adds 10 percent or more to the cost of business worldwide, with bribery estimated as a $1 trillion industry.[15] Actions to block these practices have been more determined in recent years through the efforts of NGOs such as Transparency International, national governments, regional groups (for example, the Organization for

Economic Co-operation and Development), and the United Nations Convention against Corruption, signed by 140 nations as of 2008. The UNGC worked closely with Transparency International to incorporate this new global consensus into the Compact.

Principle 10 has a broad reach. Global Compact participants commit "not only to avoid bribery, extortion, and other forms of corruption, but also to develop policies and concrete programs to address corruption. Companies are challenged to join governments, U.N. agencies, and civil society to realize a more transparent global economy."[16]

Requirements for Business to Join the Compact

The Global Compact is a voluntary initiative; there is no framework for legal enforcement. The decision to embrace the principles is left to the individual enterprise. There is no screening of the firms that join the Compact and no endorsement by the United Nations. Member companies become participants in a set of embedded networks working toward the consideration of human rights in business activities.

Joining the Compact involves a letter of commitment from a firm's CEO. Companies are then asked to issue a clear statement of support for the Global Compact; to describe in their annual financial reports or other prominent corporate reports (such as sustainability reports) the actions they are undertaking in support of the Global Compact's principles through the engagement mechanisms of Learning, Dialogue, Local Networks, and Projects; and to provide a "concrete example of progress made or lessons learned in implementing the Principles, for posting on the Global Compact's website."[17]

II. REACTIONS TO THE COMPACT

The Compact was a bold move on the part of U.N. Secretary-General Annan, given the historical relationship between the United Nations and business. Efforts to control the activities of transnational corporations have been widespread among U.N. agencies. Before the Compact, many U.N. groups understood their role as a defense of U.N. developing-country members from exploitation by the multinational enterprise. The developing-country activism of the mid-1970s, with its calls for a "New International Economic Order," was intended to assure more favorable global treatment for development-oriented goals through a broad restructuring of the global system. The "Charter of Economic Rights and Duties of States" and a reinvigorated United Nations Conference on Trade and Development sought to increase the share of global wealth flowing to the developing world.[18]

The broadest and most concentrated attempt to exert U.N. control over the international business community was undertaken by the U.N. Commission on Transnational Corporations, with its U.N. Code of Conduct for Transnational Corporations. The process was controlled by U.N. members in conflict with, rather than in collaboration with, multinational executives. By the mid-1980s this effort had floundered. Prakash Sethi described the outcome as follows: "After an effort of more than ten years, millions of dollars in expenditures, and thousands of hours in negotiations and deliberations, the resultant document could best be described as full of empty rhetoric and devoid of any practical usefulness, with the result that everyone involved is only too willing to forget its very existence."[19]

Exceptions to this overall tension between the United Nations and business are a number of successful U.N. humanitarian collaboration efforts with business, such as those by UNICEF or UNAID.[20] Other examples in the health field include collaboration between Novartis and the World Health Organization on leprosy, as mentioned in chapter 8.

As for the Global Compact, acceptance has been mixed. There has been continued resistance by some U.N. agencies, condemnation by a number of NGOs, acceptance by the international business community, but few U.S. corporate ratifications.

Skepticism of U.N. Agencies and Some Developments

Many U.N. agencies remain skeptical of the Compact. Sethi attributes their continued resistance to "reasons of turf and out of concern about compromising their mission. These agencies also saw the Global Compact as the Secretary-General's attempt to cozy up to the private sector."[21] The Commission on Human Rights Sub-Commission on the Promotion and Protection of Human Rights passed a resolution in 2003 entitled "Norms on the Responsibilities of Transnational Corporations and Other Business Enterprises with Regard to Human Rights."

This resolution includes a series of norms with clear roots in the Universal Declaration and the addition of environmental requirements that become the responsibilities of multinational corporations. The preamble recognizes that states have the primary human rights responsibilities and that corporations have the "obligation to promote, secure the fulfillment of, ensure respect of, and protect human rights recognized in international as well as national laws." Fifteen norms are stated in terms of what corporations "shall" do—shall ensure, shall observe, shall not engage.

Two of the last five norms demonstrate the determination to enforce these norms. Norm 16 states, "Transnational corporations and other business enterprises shall be subject to periodic monitoring and verification by United Nations, other international and national mechanisms already in existence or yet to be created, regarding application of the norms." Norm 18 calls on an enterprise to provide reparations to those adversely affected by its failure to comply with the norms.

While the norms of this document cover essentially the same ground as the ten principles of the UNGC, the Sub-Commission included legal obligations on the part of the multinational enterprise, in contrast to the voluntary compliance assumed by the Compact. The proposed legality of the norms has been an issue. After a careful evaluation, Douglass Cassel and Sean O'Brien concluded: "Viewed as horatory guidelines, the norms are expansive, ambitious, and generally laudatory. Viewed as law, however, they are open to serious question."[22] The Sub-Commission's draft norms have not been accepted by the parent body, the Commission on Human Rights as a document with legal standing.

The seven corporate members of the Business Leaders Initiative on Human Rights attempted to "road test" the norms. The chairwoman, Mary Robinson, delicately pointed out that "a number of important questions still require answers not provided by the draft norms and there is a recognition that the debate must now move on."[23]

In an attempt to find common ground between these draft norms, the work of Mary Robinson and the Business Leaders Initiative on Human Rights, and the first two principles of the UNGC, Kofi Annan appointed John Ruggie as a "Special Representative on the Issue of Human Rights and Transnational Corporations and Other Businesses" in 2005. Three years later, after extensive meetings with all interested parties, Ruggie issued a report entitled "Promotion and Protection of All Human Rights,

Civil, Political, Economic, Social and Cultural Rights, Including the Right to Development."[24] Klaus Leisinger regards this report as "a new benchmark against which companies will be assessed in the 'court of public opinion.'"[25]

Ruggie presented his findings in a three-part framework. First, the state has a duty to protect human rights. This includes protection against human rights abuses by non-state actors. There are policy as well as legal dimensions to this duty.

Second, corporations have a responsibility to respect human rights. In describing this responsibility, Ruggie notes, "To respect rights essentially means not to infringe on the rights of others—put simply, to do no harm."[26] In analyzing the notion of responsibility to respect, Ruggie addresses two terms from the UNGC: "sphere of influence" in the first principle and "complicit" in the second.

He considers the sphere of influence in terms of impact (damage caused by the company) and leverage (company influence over other institutions that are causing harm). With respect to leverage, he cautions, "Asking companies to support human rights voluntarily when they have influence is one thing: but attributing responsibility to them on that basis alone is quite another."[27]

As noted earlier, complicity can draw the firm into an involvement with those state and non-state actors that have abused human rights. Here, Ruggie emphasizes the importance of corporate "due diligence" as a means of identifying and avoiding indirect involvement in abuses. This is the same idea as "reflexive law" outlined in chapter 3.

The third component of Ruggie's framework is access to remedies. The associated responsibility applies to both state and non-state actors. With respect to the state, this includes judicial processes as well as non-judicial mechanisms. With respect to corporations, Ruggie cautions against mechanisms where the firm can act as both a defendant and judge.

The Ruggie mandate has been extended for three more years, in coordination with the human rights working group of the UNGC. Leisinger anticipates "that the debate will become less general, more sector-specific, and more focused on economic, social, and cultural human rights. Whereas governments will continue to define the scope of legal compliance, the broader scope of the responsibility to respect human rights will continue to be defined by public expectations."

Overall, Ruggie's notion of responsibility to respect has a more limited scope than the position espoused throughout this volume, or that practiced by many multinationals such as Novartis, as outlined in the next chapter. In our view, responsible respect is less likely to produce benefits for long-lasting corporate sustainability than a more proactive approach.

NGO Reticence

The reception of the Global Compact among NGOs was generally negative. A group of NGOs, along with a number of prominent scholars, sent two stinging letters to Secretary-General Kofi Annan shortly after the publication of the Compact.[28] These critics objected to the basic premise of the Compact, arguing that the relatively free trade and investment environment of economic globalization endorsed by the Compact is not capable of improving the plight of the global poor. As the initial letter stated, "First, the text implies a universal consensus that open markets are the primary force for development. As you are aware, there is intense debate over the benefits and harms of free trade and market liberalization as currently promoted by the WTO [World Trade Organization] and other institutions."[29]

A second concern was the voluntary nature of the Compact and the lack of monitoring and enforcement provisions. "Without monitoring, the public will be no better able to assess the behavior, as opposed to the rhetoric, of corporations. Without independent assessment, the interpretation of whether a company is abiding by the Global Compact's principles or not will be left largely to the company itself."[30] The writers contended that corporate performance must be associated with regulation. Once corporations began to ratify the Compact, the group forwarded a second letter specifically assaulting the human rights records of five of the early ratifying companies. Other NGO reactions included that of Amnesty International, which forwarded a similar critique calling for independent monitoring, reporting, and a system of sanctions.[31] However, Amnesty International has since joined the Compact.

Among the numerous other reactions, Felicity Hill of the Women's International League for Peace and Freedom, speaking at a U.N. Global Policy Forum, stated similar reservations and added: "We worry that the rhetoric and verbal overtures to the NGO community are becoming more profuse and flowery, but our access to the U.N. is becoming more and more limited."[32]

In spite of the reticence of some concerning the Compact, a number of well-respected international NGOs have joined the Compact and are actively participating in its activities: Amnesty International (as noted above), Conservation International, Business and Human Rights Resource Centre, Global Witness, and Transparency International. Other members of civil society, including the International Trade Union Confederation, as well as a number of academic and policy institutions, have also joined. As of June 2009, there were 1,776 nonbusiness participants, of which over six hundred were NGOs.[33] Nevertheless, the contention over the Compact highlights the deep distrust of many NGOs toward the business sector and the difficulty of dialogue between business and NGOs.

Credos and Codes

Aside from philosophical differences concerning the role of business in the world, most of the criticism of the Compact results from attempting to make what is formulated as a credo into a code of conduct. The intent is clearly that of a credo: "it is meant to serve as a reference to stimulate best practices and to bring about convergence around universally shared values."[34]

Monitoring performance, validating results, and imposing sanctions, while appropriate for codes, do not fit a credo such as the UNGC.[35] For those scholars and NGOs who would treat the Compact as an enforceable code, there are three practical questions concerning monitoring and sanctions: (1) What institution will monitor and at what transaction costs? (2) Who will verify these reports? (3) How will legal regulations be enforced?

The first two questions are amenable to solution, but at a high financial cost.[36] Given the corporate numbers and diversity of Global Compact membership, a monitoring and assessment program would be an enormous undertaking. The experience of financial reporting with its long history illustrates the challenge.[37] Over time, measurements have been refined and designated by professional accounting associations and governmental regulators. The process of internal controls through which the numbers are generated is increasingly regulated, with, for example, a governmental requirement in the United States that corporate CEOs certify the effectiveness of these controls. The notoriety of reporting failures attests to the overall quality of the accounting profession. In addition to financial reporting, the financial data are evaluated for users by another professional group—financial analysts.

Reporting, certification, and assessment for the principles of the U.N. Global Compact would be far more demanding than for financial performance. Metrics for social impacts are more controversial and often less precise than financial measurements. Environmental performance also raises issues such as those associated with the precautionary approach (UNGC Principle 7).

An initial step in measurement and reporting is provided by the Global Reporting Initiative. GRI has developed a set of guidelines for corporations to follow in reporting the so-called "triple bottom line" of economic, environmental, and social impacts. Initiated in 1997, the GRI grew out of the concern for environmental sustainability in a joint venture between the Coalition for Environmentally Responsible Economics (CERES, which is an NGO) and the United Nations Environmental Program. GRI states its vision and mission as follows: "The Global Reporting Initiative's (GRI) vision is that disclosure on economic, environmental, and social performance is as commonplace and comparable as financial reporting, and important to organizational success. GRI's mission is to create conditions for the transparent and reliable exchange of sustainability information through the development and a continuous improvement of the GRI Sustainability Reporting Framework."[38]

The GRI Sustainable Reporting Guidelines are developed through a multi-stakeholder process joining together a range of participants drawn from business, NGOs, labor, accountants, investors, academics, and governmental agencies. The breadth of this consensus building network and the number of organizations who follow the guidelines (more than fifteen hundred as of January 2009) assures its legitimacy.[39]

The reporting framework outlines a set of principles as well as indicators that an organization can rely upon to measure and report their performance. Historically, the guidelines have focused on the organization's "impacts" through a remarkably broad range of measures: direct and indirect economic impacts on the stakeholders of the organization and economic systems; living and nonliving natural systems; the organization's interaction with social systems.

There have been three sets of guidelines—the initial set in 2000, a revision in 2002, and another in 2006, each following an exhaustive interaction of the participants indicated above. The third version of the guidelines (G3) in 2006 shifted the reporting focus from a concentration on impacts to include a greater emphasis on managerial procedures. Moving forward, changing the guidelines will be an incremental process of continual adjustment as distinct from major revisions.

The UNGC and GRI work closely together. The Sustainability Reporting Guidelines can provide an effective framework through which an organization can measure and report its performance in their required annual Communications on Progress (COP) report to the UNGC. "The G3 Guidelines provide Principles, Disclosure on Management Approach, and Performance Indicators—all organized in a framework that clearly responds to each of the Global Compact's disclosure requests and can enhance the quality of the COP."[40]

Thus, the GRI is making significant progress in extending corporate reporting beyond financial data to broader economic as well as social and environmental impacts. Its work demonstrates what is involved in social and environmental reporting. The reach of its metrics is far greater than those in standard financial reporting. While certification of these data is yet to develop, assessment is being conducted by the financial analyst community, in the form of socially responsible investment funds. As reported in 2006, about two hundred of these funds now manage one out of every nine dollars under professional management in the United States.[41]

In addition to measurement concerns, legal regulation, as advocated by many scholars, holds little promise. As argued in chapter 1, we are currently in a period of "regulatory void." National governments are losing their policy freedom, and global governance networks are slow to develop. The questions of who will enforce such credos, and how, are not easily answered at this point. We remain in a regulatory void.

Corporate Response

As of June 2009, there were 5,206 business participants from 130 countries. The difference in acceptance of the Compact between European and U.S. enterprises was marked. There were about 1,500 Global Compact companies in Europe, compared to 125 in the United States. Most of the U.S. firms who have joined the Compact are medium-size or small enterprises, including less than ten in the Fortune 500.[42]

Much of the hesitancy of U.S. firms can be traced to the litigious environment of the United States.[43] U.S. corporate lawyers advise their firms that by signing the Compact, they are committing to general principles that expose the firm to litigation if their activities do not meet the specific standards as interpreted by others. The precautionary approach (Principle 7) is particularly sensitive. In 2004, the American Bar Association addressed this legal concern by drafting a letter intended to preclude litigious claims for use by companies when they join the Compact.[44]

A second source of reticence by U.S. firms is the requirement to "uphold the freedom of association and effective recognition of the right to collective bargaining" (Principle 3). The language of the principle itself is not a threat. However, legal staffs and managers in the United States are concerned that the U.N. will use this principle as a lever to pressure for an increase in pro-union as opposed to union-neutral policies.[45]

In continental Europe, the response of business firms to the Compact is conditioned by different legal environments and regulatory regimes. Litigation is not considered a major problem. And much of the protection of employees and the environment supported in the Compact is already embedded in regulatory requirements. Overall, European managers are more amenable to these requirements than American ones, and have a lower sense of threat associated with labor and NGO interactions.

III. IMPLEMENTING THE UNGC PRINCIPLES: UNIVERSALISM AND RELATIVISM ONE MORE TIME

The key to strategic positioning for long-term enterprise sustainability, as noted in chapter 3, is to achieve legitimacy in the eyes of society. This translates into reputational capital through external stakeholders (those who can influence the activities of the firm), such as consumers, the media, communities, and finally, regulators. External legitimacy then motivates internal stakeholders.

Taking human rights as the social standard, legitimacy requires the acceptance by global society of the principles of the Universal Declaration of Human Rights and the United Nations Global Compact. It behooves the individual firm to work for this overall acceptance. This calls for Compact members to collaborate with the other elements of civil society—especially, other businesses and a broad range of NGOs. A starting point is participation in the UNGC learning forums.[46] Firms are also encouraged to join regional or industrial groupings of multinationals, NGOs, and other actors to apply the principles in regional contexts. Over forty active networks were reported in 2007.[47]

Enterprise Network Standards

Broad social acceptance of the UNGC and a firm's membership in the UNGC, however, are not enough; the individual firm must achieve its own legitimacy. Transparency of corporate activities and accountability are the first necessary requirements for achieving firm legitimacy.

As noted, the Compact encourages participating companies to follow GRI guidelines. In order to establish a record of positive activities demonstrating transparency and accountability, management must successfully implement the UNGC principles within its organization. The first step is the conversion of general principles to standards (guidelines, rules) for corporate behavior that uniformly apply across the multinational enterprise network. This translation is an application of the Universal Declaration as targeted to the principles of the UNGC. Specific standards for Principles 3 through 10 must be established in the form of corporate rules.

From Standards to Action

The second step is to reach a balance between the application of the top-down network rules and a sensitive response to unique local conditions. The success of the UNGC depends on the decisions and action of local management. The local managers are the ones who must allocate resources based on their judgment as to the flexibility contained within the rules. In addition, they must recognize and react to human rights issues unique to the local business unit. As argued in chapter 4, in many cases this grass-roots sensitivity is best achieved in partnership with a local NGO.

The tension between uniform network-wide standards and sensitivity to extenuating local human rights issues is a reflection of the distinction between universality and plurality, and an example of the tension, discussed earlier, between universality and cultural relativism. In the multinational case, this issue is best solved in each circumstance by sensitive, informed management of local business units. Principles 1 and 2 depend on local responses. The threshold of human rights abuses is a function of local economic circumstances. The definition of rights thresholds can vary in different locations, depending on specific features of that environment. For example, the threshold at which a person would be considered to be deprived of her rights to participation may vary significantly from one socioeconomic context to another.

The sphere of influence in Principle 1 needs to fit local institutional structures. In the absence of effective local governance, management may be challenged to reach beyond the usual stakeholder boundaries toward people who are not closely linked to the firm, or to extend the firm's response beyond the duty to avoid and protect from deprivation, to a duty to aid the deprived.[48] The requirement to protect (Principle 1) involves collaboration, again, that recognizes the uniqueness of local institutional structures. An inadequate local or national determination and capability to protect can broaden the multinational firm's duty in that the firm may find it necessary to assume the slack from governmental agencies, nongovernmental organizations, and other business enterprises. Protection calls for collaboration, often with the same local institutions that were among the violators. Note that the necessary dialogue is generally very difficult at this local level.

The importance of bottom-up action is reflected in multinational organizational structures when firms adapt to their changing environments, as outlined in chapter 2. In what McKinsey describes as a "multilocal" organization, the importance of country managers is stressed: "Companies need country managers who are neither all-powerful (as they might be in a purely national organization) nor largely divorced from the running of the business and focused solely on providing shared services, as happens in many multinationals. The required qualities include a willingness to reach out to many parts of the organization and the ability to resolve problems across networks of people from different units and to cope with greater ambiguity than traditional country heads face."[49]

In the final analysis, a corporate culture sensitive to the dignity of local stakeholders and their communities is the key to the corporate protection of human rights. Sensitivity to human rights and determination must be embedded throughout the organization, penetrating all the way to the local decision maker. Nothing really happens until it happens at the grassroots. This is probably the greatest challenge of the Global Compact.

Within the corporate organization, this challenge is complicated by very different attitudes, such as those of managers enculturated in European social market concepts as distinct from the more competitive Anglo-American approach.

The argument has been that the United Nations Global Compact offers the most legitimate social standard for a strategy of long-term enterprise sustainability. It is in the interest of each participating firm to enhance the legitimacy of the Compact through collaboration with other businesses, NGOs, developing countries, and communities. And as Oliver Williams points out, "because the Compact has the visibility, global reach, and the convening power that accrue to it as an instrument of the U.N., it is likely to be more effective than other credos with similar missions. Since the Compact is based on principles that were accepted by most governments of the world, it offers a vision of the global community accepted by all nations."[50] Although the lack of monitoring and verification remains a concern for many outside the business sector, one should not underestimate the importance of inclusion, structure, and example—including the major players in a structured interaction where their best performance becomes a challenge across the structure.

In implementing this standard, the distinction between top-down uniformity versus bottom-up flexibility is not a crisp one. In applying corporate standards to the decisions at the grassroots, there is always flexibility. Keeping this flexibility within acceptable limits takes judgment. Moreover, local situations will arise that call for a human rights response not covered by corporate standards. This takes determination. The problem of finding the correct balance is analyzed in the next chapter in the context of the pharmaceutical company Novartis, and in Part V in the context of managing the enterprise as a community.

CHAPTER EIGHT

Implementing the Global Compact at Novartis

The Novartis experience is reported in two main parts. The first part describes the initial implementation of the Global Compact principles, shortly after the company signed the Compact in 2000.[1] The second part reports the Novartis experience eight years later and assesses the successes and remaining challenges. The first part is based on extended interviews in 2002 with eighteen Novartis executives (listed at end of this chapter), who openly and frankly described their early experiences in implementation and what they anticipated. These interviews resulted from a UNGC program in which independent academic analysts were invited to assess the implementation of the Compact principles. This first part reports one of these initial studies, which analyzed the inclusion of the Compact as an integral part of a strategy for sustainable corporate development. The 2008 update in the second part is a summary of printed materials and discussions with Klaus Leisinger, a key individual in the UNGC process at Novartis and the special advisor on the Global Compact to U.N.

Secretary-General Kofi Annan in 2005 and 2006. Each of these parts describes a slice of the dynamic process. Six of the managers initially interviewed have retired; four have moved on, and their organizational roles have been assumed by others.

I. INITIAL IMPLEMENTATION

The spirit of the Global Compact found fertile ground at Novartis. It has become an integral part of Novartis corporate strategy since the enterprise was formed by the merger of the two large Swiss pharmaceutical companies, Sandoz and Ciba, in 1996. Following a four-year concentration on economic consolidation and performance, Daniel Vasella (Chairman and CEO) signed the Global Compact. Together, productivity-based economic performance and a proactive approach to the expectations of society are envisioned by Novartis as the key to long-term corporate success within the rapidly integrating global economic, political, and social environment of today's large multinational corporation.

The following discussion outlines the Novartis strategy and its initial implementation; reviews the process of extending corporate strategy to incorporate social concerns into the economic business model; assesses the process of implementing the strategy; and outlines specific examples of this strategic positioning.

Strategic Positioning

Post-Merger Economic Consolidation

Sandoz and Ciba approached the merger into Novartis ("new skills" in Latin) as an operating response to the growing competition, concentration, and institutional buying structure in the globally integrating life science industry. Both companies had roots in Basel dye production during the late nineteenth century, and had entered the merger after what the 1996 *Novartis Operational Review* called "their best year ever."[2] External observers, however, were less reassuring as to the past history of the two companies. According to *Forbes*, "Sandoz and Ciba-Geigy were plodding, risk averse and assiduously Swiss firms that often got trounced by faster, fiercer U.S. rivals. The research pipeline was dry, and marketers were slow on the draw."[3] On the other hand, financial analysts embraced enthusiastically the formation of Novartis. It was the largest industrial merger in history at that time, and thereby became the world's largest life science company (spanning health care, agribusiness, and nutrition) and the second largest pharmaceutical firm.

The postmerger period of intense performance-based consolidation included changes in the structure of the firm as well as its management system:

- At the time of the merger, Ciba's Dyestuffs, Additives, and Plastics divisions were spun off into a separate company, "Ciba Speciality Chemicals."
- Due to the lack of substantial synergies with other Novartis activities, the Agriculture division was divested in 2000 and merged with the agricultural division of Astra-Zeneca to form the Syngenta corporation. At that time, the agribusiness operation was the largest in the world. It represented 28 percent of Novartis revenue and 24 percent of operating income.
- In 2000, Novartis shares were listed on the U.S. stock exchange as American Depository Receipts, positioning Novartis as more attractive to U.S. investors.
- Merger personnel redundancies were reduced largely through natural attrition and early retirements. Some employees started their own businesses with financial support from the Novartis Venture Fund. In the first year following the merger, the workforce was reduced by 9,199, at which point 62 percent of the anticipated merger cost synergies and the targeted 12 percent workforce reduction were achieved. At the same time, 2,400 new people with necessary expertise were hired.
- During the consolidation phase, a third of the hundred most senior managers joined Novartis from other companies. In the United States, of the top thirteen executives in 1999, only two remain.
- Performance-based compensation was rigorously applied across the company. Total compensation targeted the fiftieth percentile of the compensation offered by a set of comparable competitors. Over six thousand employees now receive share options as part of their remuneration.

- The pharmaceutical business was split into worldwide strategic business units centered around therapeutic areas and customers, with some of its global management headquartered in the United States.
- The Novartis presence in the U.S. market was dramatically increased—the sales force grew from 3,100 to 4,600 in 1999 alone, probably the fastest expansion in pharmaceutical history. The *Wall Street Journal* in 2002 credited CEO Daniel Vasella with "transferring the firm into a bare-knuckled, American-style marketing powerhouse,"[4] by using direct-to-consumer advertising, upgrading sales training, and accepting the risk of comparing the firm's products with the best the industry has to offer in clinical trials and post-approval marketing.
- The process of drug discovery and development was reorganized and revitalized to get drugs to the market more quickly. At the time of the merger, over half of drug sales were from patent-expired products. Development time has been shortened from twelve to about eight years, with a sharper market-oriented focus.
- The financial performance reflects the synergistic value of the merger and the emphasis on managerial performance.

Strategic Expansion to Include Corporate Citizenship

By 2000, with the consolidation process becoming secure, Vasella believed Novartis had achieved the economic freedom to be more encompassing in its response to societal claims on business enterprises. In July, Novartis signed the United Nations Global Compact following a conversation between Secretary-General Kofi Annan and Daniel Vasella. The Global Compact served an important coalescing role, as Novartis moved to a sustainable long-term position in the market. Urs Baerlocher, the senior executive for implementing the policy, describes the role of the Global Compact as follows: "The Global Compact, its principles and requirement to demonstrate credible action, triggered a discussion within Novartis on the nature of human rights, access to medicines, and the existing Code of Conduct, which led to our Corporate Citizenship Policy as an encompassing view of Novartis responsibility." According to Karin Schmitt (Head, Foundation Affairs, Novartis Foundation), "The Global Compact was an opportunity to show the Novartis commitment to human rights values, and the determination to live up to them realizing that we are inviting public scrutiny."

As a first step in implementation, the general Global Compact principles had to be particularized for the specific Novartis environment. The Corporate Citizenship Policy translates these principles to fit Novartis as a global pharmaceutical company. During its year-long preparation, Novartis planners sought the counsel of nongovernmental organizations such as the World Resources Institute, SustainAbility Ltd., and the Stakeholder Forum for Our Common Future (formerly UNED Forum).

In introducing the Policy on Corporate Citizenship in October 2001, Vasella stated:

> The Policy was developed in response to our commitment to the Global Compact, which was set forth by the Secretary-General of the United Nations, Kofi Annan. Across geographies and throughout our organization we will, in all our business, social, and environmental activities, strive to be in line with the principles of the Global Compact. We believe that adhering to values is especially important for large organizations in times of rapid change and globalization, as they provide guiding principles. In our business, we are using innovative new technologies to search for novel lifesaving medical treatments. In some cases, these developments raise ethical challenges which must be carefully considered with the establishment of proper boundaries, but Novartis' ultimate goal is to contribute to helping patients in need.
>
> On a global level, Novartis is committed to sustainable development and its three principles of economic, social, and environmental progress. We want to be a leading corporate citizen, both technologically and economically, and achievement of that goal is closely linked to our ability to contribute to the benefit of people. Our Policy on Corporate Citizenship outlines our pledge, and it is both a strategic business initiative—and the right thing to do.[5]

At Novartis, corporate citizenship is not considered a socially responsive add-on. It is intended to be an integral, necessary component of a successful pharmaceutical company. Novartis is serious about this being a strategic business initiative. Martin Batzer (Head, Pharma Affairs) describes this initiative in terms of a "license to operate." "It is the third concentric circle in a strategy of economic maximization for shareholders; attention to other stakeholders including associates (the Novartis term for employees), customers, and communities; and the third part of continuing attention to the permission of society for the right of the corporation to exist. Integrating these three circles and ensuring that the third (license to operate) feeds back into the other two is the key to sustainable corporate development in the long term. If you don't have the license to operate, you can forget everything else." And, as noted by Terry Barnett (President and Chief Executive Officer, Novartis Corporation), "Right now, as a pharmaceutical company, that license seems to be up for renegotiation. At issue is the appropriate role of the pharmaceutical industry in the total healthcare environment." Baerlocher states, "If we want to be truly successful we need to achieve beyond products and services. We also need our stakeholders to recognize that we are a valuable part of society, a good corporate citizen." Johannes Frey (Head, Corporate Affairs) notes, "Often the pursuit of corporate citizenship can have a direct payoff. You follow a risk management approach as we have refined it in our Health, Safety, and Environment Practices of incurring an expense now to minimize great damage down the road. Corporate citizenship is an investment."

A Strategy of Corporate Citizenship

In its Policy on Corporate Citizenship, Novartis commits itself to the broad vision of human rights—the same base as the Global Compact principles: "The Novartis core values are based on the fundamental rights of every individual, such as the protection of privacy, freedom of opinion and expression, freedom of association, nondiscrimination, and the right to be heard. We seek to promote and protect the rights defined in the Universal Declaration of Human Rights of the United Nations within our sphere of influence. We do not tolerate human rights abuses within our own business operations."[6]

Focus on Process

This policy goes well beyond the political and civil rights that form the core of what are called the first generation of human rights. It also includes second-generation economic, social, and cultural rights. In most business activities, it is the second-generation rights that are to be promoted and protected "within our sphere of influence"; the related abuses are not to be tolerated "within our own business operation." These second-generation rights are far more difficult to specify than first-generation rights, since society is continually redefining its human rights concerns and acceptable thresholds; while national legislation supports these rights, they have received only modest recognition in the constitutions of modern Western cultures; they can easily become politicized; they can contradict one another; and protecting second-generation rights can be expensive.

Given the continuing advance of societal expectations for the private sector, and based on a foundation of valuable experience in responding to environmental and social needs, Novartis is focusing on the *process* of achieving corporate citizenship. The process begins with an articulation of one's ultimate vision as quoted above, supported by a strategy and a system that incrementally ratchet toward that vision through a steady process of setting, measuring, achieving, testing, and refining standards. The idea is to establish a transparent process relating to those inside as well as outside the firm, where objectives can be adapted as learning occurs and measurements are refined. There will be shortfalls, as Norman Walker (Head, Human Resources) observes: "I can't say we will meet all of our requirements today. It's a journey we have started with the purpose of seeing that our standards are achieved." In the final analysis, however, as Vasella states, "Don't make commitments you can't keep."

Focus on Experience

In its implementation efforts, Novartis draws on a valuable history of involvement with civil society in its environmental and social response through its Health, Safety, and Environment (HSE) initiative and the Novartis Foundation for Sustainable Development.

The HSE initiative began in the early, technologically driven, production-focused, and ecological era of the 1980s. Over time, HSE has become a part of line managerial responsibility. It is analyzed annually in the context of local legal requirements, relative impact, competitive performance, and available state-of-the-art technology. Targets are set for each sector, performance is measured (116 sites in 2001), and results are externally verified and published in detail. The development of this HSE process over the years has benefited substantially from dialogue with representatives from the other components of civil society.

The HSE experience has helped Novartis find a balance between precaution and innovation in applying the "precautionary approach." As discussed in chapter 7, this approach, more than any other clause of the Global Compact, has created hesitancy among firms in the United States. The Global Compact is not specific in its Principle 7, "Support a precautionary approach to environmental challenges." As quoted in previous chapters, Article 15 of the United Nations Rio Declaration states: "Where there are threats of serious or irreversible damage, lack of full scientific certainty shall not be used as a reason for postponing cost-effective measures to prevent environmental degradation." In applying the approach to human health as well as the environment, Novartis makes a distinction between prevention and precaution. Prevention applies when there is a scientifically known cause and effect. Prevention is an issue of cost. Precaution applies when there is scientific uncertainty as to cause and effect. As Kaspar Eigenmann (Head, Corporate Health, Safety, and Environment) points out: "When the activity could lead to grave consequences, even if there is no full scientific proof, one should take reasonable measures. The principle makes common sense. It's the application that creates controversy—how is the reasonable likelihood or the application of reasonable measures to be determined?" The Novartis position states: "We take a precautionary approach in the innovation and development of new products and technologies. To this end, we follow a step-by-step approach, we engage in scientific peer review, and we consider benefits and risks of innovation in a scientific and transparent manner,"[7] a position initially "challenged" by the U.S. legal staff. Alternatively, as Julie Kane (Vice President, Novartis Corporation) notes, "Lawyers are nervous, but their role is to advise about the risk so management can make the right decision."

The Novartis Foundation for Sustainable Development concentrates on sustainable development in the poor regions of the world. It pursues social development projects in partnership with local NGOs: work with AIDS orphans in Northern Tanzania and South and East Africa; conflict management and the empowerment of women in Palestine; community development in Brazil and Sri Lanka; and leprosy cure and rehabilitation in partnership with the World Health Organization (WHO), National Health authorities, and NGOs.[8] Other activities include a social research and publication program and stakeholder dialogue and networking. Stakeholder dialogue is stressed through conferences, symposia, workshops, and membership in social committees and boards.[9]

The twenty-some years of experience with each of these initiatives has helped Novartis recognize the value of access to the information and worldviews of civil society. There are many guiding principles about how best to undertake the dialogue between management and representatives from other segments of civil society. Two experiences, as reflected in the interviews, have been helpful in shaping Novartis policy. Kaspar Eigenmann describes one interaction that began in the late 1980s. At a casual dinner following a formal meeting on chemicals policy, a small group of participants from Ciba-Geigy and The Ecological Scientific Institutes in Vienna and Freiburg i.B. concluded that dialogue would be more productive than confrontation. They initiated a series of small informal meetings, often with neutral experts. Initially, neither side told their colleagues about these discussions, since both assumed their colleagues would judge this kind of interaction to be inappropriate. Over time, each side learned to appreciate the other's logic. Some discussion topics led to joint research and scientific publication, some only to more talk. In all, around five projects emerged from this contact. The periodic meetings continue, with new, younger people joining the process.

A second, stakeholder experience related by Klaus Leisinger (Executive Director, Novartis Foundation) illustrates the importance of including the decision makers in the process of dialogue. In a joint corporate/NGO attempt to assess the consequences of Green Gene Technology, senior corporate and NGO management assigned the task to staff specialists. In an effective dialogue over three years, the participants learned from each other in what Leisinger describes as a "discursive learning curve." They reached consensus on a series of recommendations. However, it was a consensus to which neither corporate nor NGO senior management would agree, since they had not participated in the learning curve and could not be convinced of the conclusions.

Based on these kinds of experiences, the Novartis stakeholder policy states: "We provide relevant information and actively listen to stakeholders. In assessing controversial products, processes and technology, we seek dialogue with all stakeholders."[10] This policy extends the business model of listening to the market to the sustainable corporate model of listening to the signals from civil society. As Andreas Seiter (Head, Stakeholder Relations) explains, "It's important that we tell them, but even more important that they tell us. When there is a developing issue which influences our future business strategy, we should be part of that debate, listening first before we make our point." The idea is to extract issues as they begin to form, long before they reach the media threshold, at which point perceptions tend to harden. If initiated early, discussions are interesting for both sides, particularly when there is scientific evidence to share. This window of discussion opportunity can last up to six years.

From Concept to Action

The idea of corporate citizenship is defined by headquarters as a component of long-term corporate sustainability. However, managers at the local levels, where the policy takes effect, face a plethora of immediate concerns and pressures to meet short-term performance targets. Dieter Wissler (Head, Corporate Communication) describes the challenge: "The deeper you go into the organization, the greater the pressure on short-term results, and the less a person thinks about corporate social responsibility. For local managers, corporate citizenship can be seen as a dictate from headquarters that drains energy from their operating focus." Complicating the distinction between headquarters and the field at Novartis are differences in the European and American views about the role of the Global Compact principles in corporate sustainability. What is clear in the European perception is not as clear in the U.S. environment.

Norman Walker sees corporate citizenship as a more difficult task than implementing the HSE Policy. "It poses a deep challenge to a company and the way it operates, it is much more about our collective behavior. This demands a specific attitude throughout the organization." Erwin Schillinger (Head, International Coordination) makes a similar comparison to the Novartis Code of Conduct, initiated on a global basis two years before the Global Compact. "The Global Compact added a whole new dimension. While the Code addresses individual rights and responsibilities, the Global Compact is an obligation of the company with the necessity of bringing managerial decisions in line with its provisions."

A senior management Steering Committee was formed with the charge of making corporate citizenship an integral part of line management, including the information system, performance measurement, and incentives. A campaign of awareness was initiated throughout the organization. Following a series of corporate announcements, the Corporate Citizenship Policy was the topic of one-fourth of the program at the annual retreat of the top Novartis executives at Interlaken in February 2002, as well as sectoral and regional management meetings. Discussions were initiated through the Novartis Intranet. According to Walker, "You need to allow people to understand why you are pursuing these changes. This is best accomplished by engaging people face-to-face in a young company like Novartis. The enthusiasm for corporate citizenship as a strategic initiative has been a pleasant surprise. We found that the purpose of the company is very important to our people, far more than just coming to the office day after day. This is something they can relate to." On the other hand, according to Barnett, "While our people in the United States are proud to have their company endorse the Principles, they are very much focused on the realities of the marketplace. They are somewhat detached from the Principles and do not see their relevance as a U.S. issue."

The next step was to formulate specific guidelines. In structuring the guidelines, the Steering Committee prepared an inventory of policy commitments that relate to the underlying themes of the corporate citizenship strategy and how this strategy unfolds into specific concerns to be addressed. Further preparation involved the analysis of a wide range of United Nations documents and various codes of business conduct. The Universal Declaration of Human Rights, the International Covenant on Civil and Political Rights, and the International Covenant on Economic, Cultural, and Social Rights provided the broad framework. More specific guidance on qualitative and quantitative standards was drawn from the International Labor Organization conventions, recommendations, and declaration, as well as other specific principles, such as the United Nations Code of Conduct for Law Enforcement Officials, the U.N. Human Rights Sub-Commission Draft on Universal Human Rights Guidance for Companies, and the OECD Guidelines for Multinational Enterprises. The Steering Committee's topics for consideration extended, for example, all the way to the possibility of credit schemes for microentrepreneurs in the supply chain. Checklists for core indicators of minimum requirements and best practices were prepared. In the end, however, there were surprisingly few specific standards in these documents.

Five guidelines were issued in 2002. These guidelines, in preparation for a year, were debated internally at all levels of the organization and circulated externally for comment. Each guideline addresses assignees' responsibilities, provides principles and standards, and outlines the management process and reporting criterion unique to the specific guideline.

Guideline 1: Management of Corporate Citizenship. This initial guideline regulates the scope and applicability for those that follow. It sets the structure for the "active management of corporate citizenship." Specific operating positions are created and responsibilities assigned within each division and country organization, along with managment processes. The broad reach of the document addresses priority conflicts that might arise between corporate citizenship and short-term operating objectives that need to be arbitrated; a safe complaint procedure for employees who report corporate citizenship deficiencies; application of the principles to Novartis partners; and reporting and audit procedures as well as the possibility of commissioning external auditors.

Guideline 2: Fair Working Conditions. This guideline is directed to human resources, including the related aspects of human rights. The creation of a reporting system is an important component of this guideline. Before the Global Compact, working conditions were considered a local responsibility. Early resistance to the reporting system was reminiscent of the early days of the HSE—people asked, Why do we have to do this? What's it really for?

The third Global Compact principle was discussed at length in the preparation of this guideline. Principle 3 asks world business "to uphold freedom of association and effective recognition of the right to collective bargaining." Jeff Benjamin (Vice President and Deputy General Counsel, Novartis Corporation) states, "Our existing policy is union neutral. Our companies make sui generis decisions." While the language of the principle itself is neither inflammatory nor risky, legal staffs and managers of many companies, particularly in the United States (as discussed in chapter 7), are concerned that the United Nations will interpret and measure the principle in ways that put pressure on firms to be pro-union.

The guideline clause on freedom of association recognizes the employee's right to choose whether to join a trade union or employee association, but establishes criteria for these associations in terms of democratic principles, the existence of written statutes, a history of legal compliance, and that they be free and independent associations not committed to violence. Additional criteria may be established by local Novartis companies. As in other Novartis policies, dialogue is included: "Each Country Service Officer shall establish a communication process that ensures a free exchange of opinion [with associates] and a constructive dialogue."

The guideline section on wages goes well beyond the Global Compact: "In each market, full-time wages must be set at or above a level that covers the market price of a basket of goods and services representing the subsistence level for an average worker in the town or region in question." Dependent children are included in this "living wage."

Guideline 3: Business Ethics—Bribes, Gifts, and Entertainment. This guideline covers a topic not initially included as a principle in the Global Compact (Principle 10 on corruption was added in 2004). In 2002, this guideline drew on the provisions of the Novartis Code of Conduct.

Governmental corruption, bribery, and marketing practices, along with access to medicines, were identified by Novartis top management at the introduction of the Corporate Citizenship Policy in Interlaken as the most important issues facing the industry.[11] Batzer sees marketing practices as the toughest part in all of the guidelines: "How does one find the balance between competing in what has become a very aggressive market set against the exposure to the damage of what are viewed as unethical practices, with guidelines that hold across cultures and legal regimes?" The Code of Conduct states, "No employee shall make any payment, or kickback, or offer improper financial advantage to an official of a government or a government-controlled entity for the purpose of obtaining business or other services, as set out in the OECD Convention on Combating Bribery of Foreign Public Officials."[12] This is a true challenge; Christian Seiwald (Sector Head, Generics) has said, "Corruption is a problem that all companies have to confront. Solutions can only be home grown." There are undoubtedly cases of corruption; the task of Novartis is to change that behavior.

Here, especially, senior management must convince everyone in the company of the seriousness of bribery. Johannes Frey notes, "What headquarters would regard as a corrupting action can make sense to a local associate focusing on a specific business transaction in a lenient community who does not internalize the great risk to the company in an environment where the company needs to prove every day that it lives by its statements."

This guideline defines and prohibits bribing of government officials directly or through intermediaries. It addresses the distinctions between, and provides guidance for, facilitating payments, gifts and entertainment, charitable donations and cultural contributions, political donations and contributions, and acceptable payments. Local managers must explicitly report on their large transactions and consult with the relevant Corporate Citizenship Officer for any payments exceeding $US 100. Acts of private bribery are particularly difficult to assess due to the complex of codes, regulations, and contractual provisions that apply.[13]

Guideline 4: Human Rights. The focus of this guideline is on Principles 1 and 2 of the Global Compact: to "support and respect the protection of internationally proclaimed human rights within their sphere of influence" and to "make sure that they are not complicit in human rights abuses." This guideline outlines civil and political rights in terms of the "right to equal opportunity and nondiscriminatory treatment; right to security of persons; rights of employees (tied to Guideline 2); respect for national sovereignty; respect of local communities and indigenous people; intellectual property rights and technology transfer."

In outlining the Novartis commitment to economic, social, and cultural human rights, this guideline acknowledges the importance of working with others. "Novartis cannot on its own implement economic, social, and cultural rights." The guideline gives preference to third parties who observe the U.N. Global Compact. It supports "private meetings with high-ranking (governmental) officials when human rights are at stake." For all human rights stakeholders, "Novartis sees dialogue with human rights stakeholders both as an opportunity to learn about other parties' points of view and as a chance to contribute to the debate from the corporation's point of view."

The guideline also outlines "special obligations" specific to a pharmaceutical company, in terms of patents and pricing policy for "life-saving medicines under conditions of individual and collective poverty." Outreach of the Novartis Foundation for Sustainable Development is included.

Assessment of the Novartis human rights impact is conducted annually by the Corporate Citizenship Steering Committee with the consultation of external stakeholders. Compliance is monitored at the country level as part of internal and external auditing. Implementation is the responsibility of "Corporate Management, global division, CPO-Heads (Pharma), and local BU-Heads (Consumer Health)."[14]

Johannes Frey believes that this will be the most difficult guideline to implement. The margin of judgment is great, as can be the cost of making a mistake. Managers must include governments and NGOs (groups with whom they tend to be uncomfortable) in their decisions, with the attendant loss of control.

Guideline 5 concentrates on third-party relationships. The Novartis Policy on Corporate Citizenship states, "We give priority to business partners, suppliers, and contractors who share our societal and environmental values, and we support their efforts to promote these values through their business activities." The questions to be addressed in translating the policy into guidelines, as outlined by Kaspar Eigenmann, include, "How do we assess those who share our values; how is giving preference different from imposing specific standards; how does one balance how far to press one's values on third parties and what legal liabilities are created; how does responsibility differ for subcontractors using Novartis technology, for suppliers where Novartis takes most of their output, or where national legal environments are weak? On a practical basis, where should initial efforts be concentrated—on the largest subcontractors in the most difficult countries?"

The guidelines are continually reviewed and revised in terms of new experience and refinement of measurements. Standards will be clarified as general principles become linked with concrete business activities.

Establishing Credibility

Implementing a long-term corporate citizenship strategy is a matter not only of actions but also of perceptions: of being perceived as doing a good job both by internal and external stakeholders and by the broader society. As an integral component of sustainable corporate development, corporate citizenship becomes a matter of pride for members of the Novartis organization, generates positive reputational effects among external stakeholders, and ensures continuation of the license to operate from the broader society. Taking the HSE and Foundation experience as a model, Novartis intends that NGOs will have input into its process, measurements, and targets, as well as certification of the results.

The active management of corporate citizenship means making it an integral part of Novartis line management and, to the extent possible, part of the practices of third parties. Each of the guidelines concludes with a section on "reporting criteria and measurement." The internal process of auditing compliance follows the procedures of the financial and HSE audits. Specific responsibilities have been created throughout the organization and assigned as collateral duties. Novartis concluded that making the compliance auditing responsibility a collateral duty at numerous levels throughout the organization was more effective in bringing about organizational change than creating a few staff positions whose exclusive responsibility was compliance. Most of these collateral duties are currently assigned to the human relations and legal staffs, although Eigenmann would like to include more line managers. The initial emphasis was on managerial processes and auditors serving in a consulting role, but the auditing function will increasingly include performance, as measures are refined and targets set—following the HSE experience. Given that transparency is a necessary precondition for credibility, these assessments became a component of the Novartis annual report, following a process initiated in 2002. At that time, the HSE data and verification, which had been published in a separate Operational Review since 1996, were also included in the annual report.

External monitoring is yet to be resolved. It is accepted in principle and included in the guidelines but not yet implemented. As Leisinger notes, "Independent external verification plays an important role for the credibility of a company's compliance effort—indeed, it is a precondition. . . . The search for consensus should therefore not focus on the question 'Yes or No' but on the 'How.'" As with all external monitoring systems, there are questions of appropriate expertise, the process and its cost, the protection of proprietary information, the external monitor's attitudes and organizational culture as well as their own credibility, and the public disclosure process and detail. An unusual problem with the idea of NGOs as monitors, as outlined by Peter Tobler (Compliance Officer), is the breadth of the Corporate Citizenship Policy compared to the typically more narrow focus of the individual NGO. An ideal external monitor is one with credibility who is willing to participate with Novartis as they both jointly work to improve a transparent process. As successful as the HSE external auditing process has become, it is still a public verification of technical data collected and reported by Novartis.

Examples of Implementation

Three examples of Novartis's application of the principles of the Global Compact and the Corporate Citizenship Policy follow. Two projects involve the issue of access to medicine, which is unique to the pharmaceutical industry. The third example is common across industries, particularly those relying on subcontracted production in developing countries.

It is estimated that over one-third of the world's population lacks access to essential health services, including drugs. Limitation of access to treatment is a multifaceted issue involving the absence of medical services, unreliable health and supply systems, lack of sustainable financing, irrational selection and use of drugs, and the availability and price of drugs.

Society is coming to the conclusion that medical care is a human right, and that the pharmaceutical industry has a unique responsibility to help sick people gain access to life-saving medicines. This is an extension of the Global Compact Principle 1, which asks businesses to "support and respect the protection of internationally proclaimed human rights within their sphere of influence." In outlining the specific requirements associated with that principle, the U.N. directs business responsibility toward an extension of the workplace, by ensuring the "rights to basic health, education, and housing (in areas where these are not provided)." Pharmaceutical programs to provide access to medicine reach well beyond the workplace and local communities to a broader "sphere of influence," embracing patients far beyond the traditional stakeholder boundaries. This breadth reflects Dr. Vasella's early experience in medical practice, as well as that of other physicians in Novartis and the industry generally. It also recognizes a view expressed by Vasella: "Unless the pharmaceutical industry achieves its objectives of being an accepted and valued player in society, we will be at a disadvantage in every new law and regulation that comes up."

Pharmaceutical companies are responding. They are networking with civil society, governmental agencies, and components of the United Nations in projects for developing countries. Novartis, for example, is part of the Global Alliance to Eliminate Leprosy. The firm donates a multidrug therapy that can cure the disease in six months or a year (depending on the form of the disease) for all patients in the world. The drug has been made available free of charge since 1995, and Novartis is committed to continue its donations until leprosy has been eliminated. Through the Novartis Foundation for Sustainable Development, in conjunction with governmental agencies, private foundations, the WHO, and the World Bank, the inadequacies of local health infrastructure as well as the fear and prejudice associated with leprosy are gradually being overcome. Another partnership with the WHO is for the treatment of malaria. In conjunction with the Chinese Academy of Military and Medical Science, Novartis discovered and developed the most potent antimalarial drug for noncomplicated cases of malaria caused by the parasite *Plasmodium falciparum*. By agreement with WHO, Novartis is providing the drug at cost. For Novartis employees and their nuclear families in developing countries, the firm is also involved in the diagnosis, treatment, and care of HIV/AIDS, tuberculosis, and malaria. If treatment is not available through other sources, Novartis pays for the cost of assuring this coverage.

Some pharmaceutical firms are directly involved in finding treatments for diseases for which there is no viable commercial market, thus posing a challenge to the wealth-maximizing business model. Merck, as described in chapter 3, developed MECTIZAN to treat river blindness, a disease which had devastated the populations of rich tropical river valleys for centuries. Novartis has created an Institute for Tropical Diseases in Singapore (discussed in example 1 below), which will concentrate on the discovery of treatments for these kinds of diseases.

The new research approach of searching for molecular targeting therapies is expensive, thus driving treatment costs beyond the reach of many patients. Here, broad patient assistance programs, such as the Novartis graduated assistance program for its new anti-cancer drug, Gleevec (discussed in example 2 below), are coming into use.

Research on Tropical Diseases: Example 1

The Novartis Institute for Tropical Diseases was established in 2002 in collaboration with the Singapore Economic Development Board. The purpose of this research institute is to discover treatments for diseases of poverty, beginning with tuberculosis and dengue fever. Only a small share (less than 10 percent) of the total pharmaceutical spending on research is directed toward tropical diseases, which comprise 90 percent of the world's health problems.

The Global Compact was an important stimulus in the firm's decision to emphasize drug discovery for tropical diseases. Paul Herrling (Head, Research) noted, "Within Novartis, the Global Compact stimulated the discussion of access to medicines which led to the idea of a tropical disease laboratory and to Singapore." On a broader basis, the kind of awareness reflected in the Global Compact has brought shareholders from resistance, to acceptance, and now to preference for these kinds of contributions. "Feedback at shareholder meetings about the Singapore project has been very positive."

The Singapore institute is one of many collaborative efforts of Novartis.[15] As a noncommercial effort, however, the open nature of its research environment is unique. Indeed, the intent of the institute is to become a center for developing-country scientists, with a major training component. Its initial focus on tuberculosis (a bacterial disease) and dengue fever (a viral infection from parasites) will be extended to other tropical diseases. Its contribution will be in drug discovery; it will seek other partners for the development of these drugs.

More important than the financial commitment by Novartis of $US 122 million to fund the working budget for the first ten years is access to Novartis laboratory management skills and experience in drug discovery. In addition, Novartis contributes specific compounds that may have potential for the treatment of tropical diseases. As Herrling comments, "In the drug discovery process, it repeatedly occurs during searches for a specific therapeutic profile that medicines are found to have additional beneficial effects in other diseases. One could imagine that while searching for drugs against the hepatitic C virus, something useful for dengue fever might be found, and vice versa. This occurs because evolution uses similar biological mechanisms in different contexts." Thus, a mechanism is being implemented to redirect compounds or small molecules that show potential for the treatment of tropical diseases from the Novartis commercial discovery laboratories to the Institute for Tropical Diseases. At the time of the interview, Herrling had two of these compounds on his desk for evaluation. One compound in particular, while ineffective against cancer, had been identified as a possible treatment for parasitic tropical infections, given the nature of the compound and its history.

Ensuring Access to a Viable Commercial Drug: Example 2

The second example involves an economically viable commercial drug. A breakthrough in drug discovery, Gleevec (known as Glivec outside the United States) has demonstrated unprecedented efficacy in treating a relatively small population of cancer patients.[16] It holds a virtual "efficacy and tolerability" monopoly in treating specific forms of leukemia and rare gastrointestinal tumors. The Novartis position is that no appropriate patient should be denied access to this expensive drug for financial reasons. As such, the company has initiated patient support programs around the world.

Gleevec is a young drug with stunning early success in treating chronic myelogenous leukemia (CML), a disease with a mortality rate of near 25,000 yearly across the world. Herrling describes Gleevec as "a new class of drugs based on understanding the pathway which leads from the gene to the disease and targeting the therapy to that specific abnormality." The results of the first clinical trials, begun in mid-1998 and initially reported in December 1999,[17] "took the oncology-hematology community by storm." Of the thirty-one patients in this Phase I trial, all experienced a significant decrease in the number of cancerous white blood cells (symptomatic of the disease), while a third experienced very significant reduction or disappearance of cancer cells with the diseased chromosome. Based on these early results, Novartis, in rapid fashion, began industrial-scale production in February 1999 (a complex process taking eight to nine months and requiring a dozen steps) and initiated its Phase II clinical trials. Application for approval by the United States Food and Drug Administration was completed in March 2001, just thirty-two months after the first human trials. This compares to the typical drug development time of six years.[18] As David Epstein (President, Novartis Oncology) described the process, "We believe this is the fastest from first dose in man to filing." Approval (a process that can take anywhere from twelve to eighteen months normally) was granted in seventy-two days. The product was at the wholesalers within twenty-four hours of approval. It is currently approved in most countries for treating certain forms of CML and now certain forms of gastrointestinal stromal tumors (GIST).

Thanks to the Internet, the news of Gleevec has spread rapidly across the world. At a worldwide price of between $2,000 and $2,500 per month, most patients would not be able to pay for the drug without insurance or reimbursement through their country's healthcare system. Novartis management firmly believes that a drug with such a dramatic potential should be available to all appropriate patients with CML. At the same time, as a breakthrough drug, Gleevec must provide a profit in order to support additional investment, not only in its further study but also for further research in oncology and other therapeutic areas. The Novartis solution is to make Gleevec available worldwide through special assistance programs.

A specific program was devised for the United States since the U.S. healthcare system is not a federally subsidized one, as is the case in most other industrialized countries. This is a graduated program with patient assistance offered at various levels based on income, assets, and household size—from receiving the drug free of charge if assets are below a certain amount and income less than $44,300 a year, to paying a graduated portion of the total cost. Assistance extends beyond five times the poverty level in some instances. (Most donation programs are limited to less than two times the poverty level.) The operation of this system in the United States is managed by a third party—Documedics—with specific expertise in reimbursement programs in oncology. In the United States, Gleevec is covered by virtually all private insurance policies, although it is not covered by Medicare (since Medicare only covers injectables or physician administered drugs, and Gleevec is an oral therapy). Patients contact the Gleevec Reimbursement Hotline to determine if they are eligible for assistance. Documedics then assesses the patient's income, assets, and household status based on the information provided by the patient, assists in the search for alternative reimbursement sources, and, if necessary, initiates the Patient Assistance Program. Gleevec is then shipped directly to the patient. The Gleevec Program is precedent-setting in the U.S. market. Many pharmaceutical companies, including Novartis, have made drugs available to those who could not afford them, but no one else to date has published a graduated support system based on a patient's ability to pay. This program works due to the dependability of medical diagnosis, the assistance of the physician's office staff and the Novartis sales force, access to Documedics, and the breadth and uniformity of private healthcare coverage.

A different kind of program exists outside the United States—the Glivec International Patient Assistance Program (GIPAP). This is not an additional reimbursement program but rather a donation program that follows specific criteria. Outside the United States, the nature of the healthcare systems and the quality of infrastructures varies dramatically. In many countries the government healthcare system subsidizes pharmaceuticals. However, a large number of countries do not have health insurance at all—private or government. For these countries, Novartis has initiated the GIPAP Program. Through GIPAP, the drug is made available in countries where it is approved for treating certain forms of CML and GIST. Qualified patients are those who are properly diagnosed, not insured, not reimbursed, and have no other financial recourse (they are unable to pay privately).

To ensure that appropriate patients are considered for this drug therapy, applications for GIPAP assistance must be initiated by physicians on behalf of their patients. The physician must be involved in all stages of the treatment (diagnosis, prescription, and follow-through). This regulation is in accordance with the World Health Organization (WHO), which provides global guidance on essential drugs and medicines and works with individual countries on implementation of national drug policies.

The Max Foundation, an international nonprofit organization dedicated to people with leukemia and other blood-related diseases, administers GIPAP (applications are available via the Internet, www.themax foundation.org). Most communication with the Max Foundation is through the Internet. The creativity of this approach is the reliance on the physician and the use of the Internet as the systemic vehicle. Together, these minimize the distributional infrastructure.

Ensuring the Rights of Workers: Example 3

An early step by Novartis in implementing the Global Compact was a baseline survey undertaken by the Steering Committee to assess issues relative to compliance with the principles and to identify areas of sensitivity to human rights abuses, where Novartis operations could be vulnerable. Of particular concern were third-party activities.

While Novartis has no legal liability for the stakeholders of subcontracting firms, it determined that this is a component of the human rights policy as indicated in the Global Compact, since the well-being of subcontractor stakeholders is affected by the activities of Novartis. This is particularly true when the stakeholders do not have adequate local background institutions to represent their interests. In Western Europe and the United States, society has decided that these third-party stakeholders are the responsibility of the multinational, a view which can conflict with those of the developing world.

This third example arose from the baseline vulnerability assessment based on the Global Compact Principle 6: "to uphold the elimination of discrimination in respect of employment and occupation." In addition, Principle 2 requires a business "to make sure they are not complicit in human rights abuses." The initial vulnerability questionnaire identified two examples of abuse. To the surprise of management, one was in Basel, Switzerland, where a janitorial contracting firm was paying less than the community standard. Another example was the practice of pregnancy testing at a subcontracting production facility in a developing-country free trade zone. The management of the plant was performing pregnancy tests on job applicants during a preemployment physical without the applicants' knowledge, and was denying employment to pregnant women. Before the Global Compact emphasis on human rights, pregnancy testing had never surfaced as a part of Novartis's anti-discrimination policy.

As with most human rights issues, there were a number of complicating factors. The production facility was owned and managed by the local government, as was the whole free trade zone; undisclosed pregnancy testing was not against the law; a condition of employment across the free trade zone, as a matter of official policy, was that the worker be unmarried and not pregnant. The senior plant management believed they were making an important contribution to the applicant by providing a physical examination—perhaps the first in her life. It was argued that since most of these applicants were migrant workers from distant, remote villages, they should know about their pregnancy in time to return home for the birth and for the nurturing environment of the extended family—an environment that could not be replicated at the plant site. The management of the plant and that of the free trade zone were convinced that their policy was the best for the applicant, for the free trade zone, and for their society.

The counterargument, based on the dignity of the applicant, was that pregnancy is such a central and unique component of a woman's identity that, even though others may treat the issue with great respect, the woman herself should decide whether to reveal her pregnancy and determine what would be best for herself and her child.

Pregnancy testing can be viewed both as a form of sex discrimination and a violation of a woman's right to privacy. While sex discrimination is prohibited by an International Labour Organization convention, it does not explicitly address pregnancy testing. The United Nations Human Rights Committee has called on member states to include the right to privacy in their legal codes, although few have.

Denying employment on the basis of pregnancy can, in many countries, pit local practice against global hypernorms. Is this an area where global society should, and has the right to, overrule local practice? Local Novartis management argued that pregnancy testing was an accepted practice in the country, as directly represented by the government-owned facility and management of the zone. They urged that a change would jeopardize the relationship with a plant that had demonstrated acceptable overall standards for labor practices over an extended period of time and was a model plant for its environment (as confirmed by an on-site monitoring visit). Beyond the pregnancy testing issue, insistence on a change of policy could have a negative effect across a broad range of other interactions between Novartis and the government.

This issue found its way to the Novartis Executive Committee, consisting of the top eight executives in the company. The committee, which Vasella chaired, judged that the practice was, indeed, discriminatory and would be stopped immediately. The current policy is that pregnancy testing is offered cost-free as part of the application physical, but is not a condition of employment.

Status as of 2002

In a pharmaceutical company, long-term performance depends upon the success of research and development, as well as the marketing of useful and safe pharmaceutical products, and on the managerial acumen to achieve the financial results needed to sustain that research and development. For Novartis, the spirit of the Global Compact has become a strategic component of sustainable corporate development. It is interwoven with the business model and cuts across the economic, social, and environmental aspects of decision making. The Compact principles, particularized in the Corporate Citizenship Policy, help the firm meet the expectations of society so critical for its long-term development. Implementation depends upon the ability to continually refine the process of measuring, setting, and achieving targets for the human rights dimension of Novartis and third-party operations, within an overall vision; the capability of line management to integrate corporate citizenship into the economic business model and to settle tensions between competing objectives as they arise; and the credibility of the process as perceived by internal and external stakeholders, as well as the broader society.

Novartis is midstride in bringing its strategy of long-term corporate sustainability to fruition. Top management has implemented the principles of the Global Compact, as evidenced by the above examples. These reflect Novartis's uniqueness as a pharmaceutical corporation in discovering and distributing drugs, and its more general role as a multinational subcontracting its production to third parties. These outcomes are measurable in terms of drugs discovered, patients served, and rights protected. Still, these are senior management initiatives. The goal of integrating the Corporate Citizenship Policy into the mindset of the operating manager remains a work in progress. The question is whether the process of implementation and compliance is up to the challenge. It promises to be a more daunting task than either the Health, Safety, and Environment (HSE) initiative or the Code of Conduct.

The vision is clear—as is the determination of senior management. The publication of guidelines in 2002 initiated the system of standards and accountability, a system that appears capable of evolving toward fulfillment of the vision. Credibility is an open question. Internal credibility will grow with the implementation process. Based on experience, Novartis management is convinced that their policy of early, open dialogue with external stakeholders will lead to improved decisions and to external credibility. Verification will be part of the social as well as the environmental process. Formal, external monitoring has yet to be introduced. This is a continuing process. As Vasella notes, "The policy incorporates our aspirations—recognizing that we still have some areas where we do not yet live up to the policy."

II. BUILDING MOMENTUM: 2008 ASSESSMENT

Since joining the Global Compact, Novartis has continued its efforts to be a leader in implementing the Compact.[19] The basic managerial structure for the implementation process initiated in 2001 is still in effect. This has called for substantial efforts in measuring, auditing, and reporting environmental impacts, as well as working toward the same kinds of standards in the less measurable and more diverse area of human rights. This section will report on these efforts. Following a summary of the environmental program, the focus will be on labor rights (Principles 3 through 6 of the Compact), with their extension to a living wage and third-party relationships as examples of network-wide involvement. The assessment then turns to human rights from the bottom up—programs initiated at national business units. Together these demonstrate the necessary intensity required in managing and sensitizing a company to the notion of including human rights principles in its decision making.

Environmental Programs

Novartis and its predecessor companies have a long history of measuring, controlling, and reporting their environmental emissions. (See references to HSE in the first part of this chapter.) In 2005, Novartis extended that effort by voluntarily committing to the emission standards of the Kyoto Protocol as a part of a general energy-saving, waste reduction, water conserving, and inclusive emission program.[20]

The Kyoto Protocol calls for the level of greenhouse gas emissions by 2012 to be 5 percent below the level in 1990. Novartis emissions are targeted in two categories. Emissions from combustion and manufacturing processes were reduced from 401 thousand tons in 2006 to 388 thousand tons in 2007. Emissions from purchased energy were reduced from 873 thousand tons to 866 thousand tons in the same period.

Along with reductions, Novartis is funding its own carbon-offset reforestation project in Latin American (785 hectares, each with 600,000 saplings) and an African plantation (350 hectares) to grow a plant used to produce a biofuel and electric power. An interesting dimension in selecting these particular carbon offsets is that they "can foster long-term economic growth for local populations."[21]

Overseeing this process are managers and energy advisors appointed in the Novartis operating divisions and country business units. In all, there are 501 Novartis Associates who commit half of their time or more working for HSE. In 2006, a revised Data Management System was introduced to facilitate the collection of data in the 208 sites across the world.[22]

The environmental effort has led to a burgeoning of initiatives in the country units. The Corporate Energy Excellence Awards are expected to provide $40 million in net savings over five years, starting in 2007. That figure is equivalent to 3 percent of projected worldwide energy consumption costs at Novartis in the same period. Alternative energy projects include a process for converting sugarcane-based residue to steam in India and woodchip heating in Germany. A major program, initiated in Germany, is underway to recycle a waste product from the generic production of "bulk antibiotics and filtration of culture broths" as a source of biogas used for heat and steam. The reduction in greenhouse gas emissions from these projects has been 7,000 tons. Other alternative energy projects are now in process in India and Austria. In short, Novartis is extending its historic HSE efforts and demonstrating the importance of local initiatives.

Human Rights

Convincing each manager of the necessity for a human rights concern continues to be a major undertaking. In accepting the UNGC principles through the Corporate Citizenship Policy and Guidelines (as outlined above), Novartis internalized the implementation of these principles in the management structures and processes. As Leisinger notes, "Once the guidelines are defined, they have to be implemented through normal corporate-management processes, from individual target setting to performance appraisals to compliance management to auditing to reporting. Only if corporate-responsibility metrics are part and parcel of normal business can they be successful. If the bonuses of managers depend on achieving targets in this area, it becomes a different ball game. But if it is simply the icing on the cake, everybody will talk about it at Rotary lunches or on Sunday mornings in church and then forget about it."[23]

As a means of enhancing its commitment to the UNGC and ethical business conduct, Novartis established a Corporate Integrity and Compliance Department in 2007, which reports directly to the head of Corporate Affairs on the Executive Committee. As with environmental impacts, targets are set for key performance indicators and verified through managerial reviews with internal and external audits. The department includes 205 full-time and part-time compliance officers in ninety-eight country organizations working to implant the Integrity and Compliance Program. This program is an attempt to extend the traditional process based on standards, awareness training, monitoring and auditing, including the idea of leadership skills training and decision making. A significant effort is devoted to inculcating the ideas of corporate integrity into the performance assessments. The Head of Integrity and Compliance described the purpose as follows: "Managers make decisions every day, sometimes based on unclear facts. They are under pressure, and they may find that local culture or competitors' standards are different from or even in direct conflict with Novartis values. We must continue to develop managers' skills to deal with difficult dilemmas."[24] The Business Practices Office, created in 2005 to investigate complaints of misconduct, works closely with the Corporate Integrity and Compliance Department. These efforts reflect the attempt at Novartis to embed principles of the UNGC as a standard of ethics throughout its organization.

Novartis continues to take its own pulse in terms of corporate culture. The results of a survey of forty thousand associates in the pharmaceutical division suggest that the ideals of the UNGC are taking root. Five areas of particular strength included "clarity of strategic direction, performance focus, confidence in senior leadership and effective immediate managers, training and career development opportunities, and the Corporate Citizenship Program."[25] A survey of the four hundred senior managers indicated that they believe the values and behaviors of the company are clear and that Novartis operates with integrity in its external dealings.[26]

The Novartis Foundation for Sustainable Development continues to serve as the key access-to-medicine outreach of the firm. In the drive to eliminate leprosy, Novartis extended the free donation of its multidrug therapy to the World Health Organization. This has led to the cure of about four and a half million patients and the promise of the global elimination of this disease. The Foundation has also applied the idea of social marketing in its Comprehensive Leprosy Care Project. In the case of malaria, the Foundation continues its work initiated in 1990. In 2007 alone, 66 million treatment courses of the Novartis drug Coartem were delivered to more than thirty countries across Africa. Given the effectiveness of Coartem, it has become the entry point for governmental healthcare efforts.

The two outreach projects highlighted in the first part of this chapter continue to make important contributions. Promising early results from the Novartis Institute for Tropical Diseases in Singapore, as reported in the 2007 Annual Report, were that at least two new compounds should be ready for clinical testing by the end of 2008.[27] The Glivec International Patient Assistance Program administrated by the Max Foundation (with the assistance of Axios International) has now risen to 900 qualified physicians treating over 27,000 patients in more than 80 countries. National healthcare systems and other donors are now funding part of the cost of providing Glivec.[28]

As a means of emphasizing human rights and making them a conscious part of enterprise network-wide managerial actions, Novartis has undertaken two programs: (1) the measurement and implementation of a living wage policy, and (2) driving the U.N. Global Compact principles down the supply chain.

The Network-Wide Living Wage Initiative

Novartis supported the idea of a living wage well before joining the UNGC. In 2005 a formal survey and policy were initiated, making Novartis one of the first international companies to pursue a living wage commitment. The implementation of the network-wide requirement as an essential dimension of fair working conditions was chosen as a framework to involve management at all levels in a human rights issue. The process engendered substantial discussion between the headquarters center of the enterprise network and local business unit management.

Defining the concept of a living wage goes back to the Universal Declaration of Human Rights (Article 25) and Pope Leo XIII's 1891 encyclical *Rerum Novarum*. Article 25 states, "Everyone has the right to a standard of living adequate for the health and well-being of himself and of his family, including food, clothing, housing and medical care and necessary social services."[29] To quote one study, "Pope Leo wrote that duties of an employer include 'not to look upon (employees) as bondsmen, but to respect in every man his dignity' and to enable him 'to earn an honorable livelihood' defined as 'necessary for the satisfaction of his needs.' Among such 'needs,' he added, 'A father should provide food and all necessities for those he has begotten' and the family's children should be provided 'with all that is needed to enable them to keep themselves decently from want and misery, amid the uncertainties of this mortal life.'"[30]

The decision to pay a living wage involves a complex balance between a nation's low-wage economic advantage and the worker's human right. In addition, for the purpose of measurement, decisions about what items to include and at what levels varies from county to country depending upon economic differences in countries and in consumption patterns.

Specific definition and measurement of a "living wage" was a major challenge. The first approach to measurement was organized under the Human Resources department. As Vasella has observed, "When you say you will do something and you communicate it, you ought to measure it."[31] Basic measuring methodology was determined in connection with the Business for Social Responsibility (BSR) as a "market basket" valuation; the costs of items a typical family would need (by certain defined criteria) in that environment are measured.[32]

The process was that "HR would propose a minimum living wage for each country, based on the agreed-upon methodology of calculation. Local management in each country would be consulted about the calculation and given an opportunity to propose an alternative living wage level based on local conditions. Ultimately, the vast majority of countries accepted the initial calculation as its living wage standard. In a few countries, Novartis affiliates proposed a living wage higher than the initial calculation based on their own market basket research."[33]

Some countries, such as India, Canada, and the United States, commissioned their own studies, finding substantial differences among cities and regions. Others pointed to conflicts with collective bargaining agreements. In the end, of the sixty countries included in the exercise, fifteen proposed higher living wages, one proposed lower, and six argued for regional differences.

This living wage determination demonstrates how UNGC principles can be moved to the grassroots, in a process where local management participates in measurement and its input is critical to the effort. Novartis and BSR summarized their experience as follows: "Rollout of the living wage project required greater investments than expected. The consultation process was also more time-consuming than expected—though at the same time it provided valuable feedback from local organizations. Often, local management embraced the living wage initiative as a clear reaffirmation by Novartis of its commitment to company values."[34]

In 2005, of the total Novartis workforce of 90,000 people, only ninety-three employees were found to be earning less than the living wage. Novartis continued to refine its measurements and applications. In 2006, another twenty-one associates were identified whose salaries needed to be adjusted. In 2007 there were eleven, and in 2008, just three.[35] The effort put into this program to support so few people underscores the individuality of human rights: justice requires that no one be ignored.

Human Rights and Third Parties

Novartis is operationally sensitive to the performance of third parties (suppliers and subcontractors). In the pharmaceutical industry, supplier components are technically complex and can be the source of enormous risk. Pharmaceutical manufacturers work closely with their suppliers. As their corporate social responsibility was extended to the supply chain (following the pattern in the apparel industry toward the end of the last century),[36] Novartis was already deeply involved with the human rights practices of its suppliers. As reported in the initial interviews, Eigenmann commented on the problems in supplier selection: "How do we assess those who share our values; how is giving preference different from imposing specific standards; how does one balance how far to press one's values on third parties and what legal liabilities are created; how does responsibility differ for subcontractors using Novartis technology, for suppliers where Novartis takes most of their output, or where national legal environments are weak?"

Novartis issued a Third Party Code of Conduct supported by a set of internal application guidelines for third-party management in 2003. In 2007, Novartis joined other major pharmaceutical companies in formulating a framework for third-party management—The Pharmaceutical Supply Chain Initiative.[37] These include requirements in ethics, labor, health and safety, the environment and, interestingly, management systems. The requirements to manage the code components follow the idea of the "reflexive" approach to regulation described in chapter 3.

The code requires that suppliers "shall pay workers according to applicable wage laws, including minimum wages, overtime hours, and mandatory benefits." It also states, "Suppliers shall respect the rights of workers, as set forth in local laws, to associate freely, join or not join labor unions, seek representation, and join workers councils. Workers shall be able to communicate openly with management regarding working conditions without threat of reprisal, intimidation, or harassment."[38]

In applying these standards, the Head of Corporate Affairs notes:

> As Novartis operates all over the world, we are faced with differences in the legal, social, and cultural environments. This means that many of our suppliers apply standards that are different from ours. While some of these differences are not material, there are limits to what a company competing with integrity can accept: Novartis expects our third parties to adhere to all national and other applicable laws and regulations governing protection of the environment, occupation health and safety, and labor and employment practices wherever we do business. Beyond that, we work with our business partners toward achieving the goals of Corporate Citizenship on a long-term and sustainable basis.[39]

Following the structure created to ensure the implementation of Global Compact principles, specific responsibilities have been assigned for third-party management. The Division heads have the responsibility for guideline implementation within their divisions and business units. Third-party officers, generally from the purchasing function, are assigned operating responsibility. Finally, third-party managers work directly with local purchasers. Contracts include a specific reference to The Third Party Corporate Code of Conduct. A detailed management process is followed, with guidelines for auditing and remediation follow-up.

Novartis evaluates its relationships with its suppliers via a corporate citizenship questionnaire, based on the level of business impact, and gives preference to those that meet all aspects of third-party social responsibility. Suppliers who are found to have human rights issues are given one week's notice to demonstrate unconditional compliance to human rights requirements (such as no bonded or forced labor). In case of insufficient evidence of full compliance, the business relationship will be terminated.

Compliance checks and external audits are based on a classification system according to the degree of risk. Classification factors include the nature of the product provided (infrastructure or logistics are low risk, while products using Novartis materials, processes, and techniques are higher risk); geographic location; the judgment of third-party managers; or past auditing experience.

Audits are generally undertaken by specialized firms, such as Intertek,[40] in accordance with a standardized procedure. Between 2004 and March 2008, 243 suppliers were audited, corresponding to 20 percent of all high-risk suppliers.

As anticipated in the 2002 study, external monitoring continues to be a challenge. Leisinger articulates the problem:

> The traditional management approach uses auditing firms like PricewaterhouseCoopers or KPMG to verify what is being done. After Enron and Arthur Andersen, there is a credibility gap. But suppose that Novartis were to approach Amnesty International and say, "We have nothing to hide. Why don't you audit our human rights record?" They would probably say, "No, we don't have the capacity." If Novartis then offered to pay for it, they would be likely to respond, "We can't accept money from industry, as this could jeopardize our credibility." So those who have the best know-how and experience on human rights matters can't be part of compliance.[41]

For Novartis the emphasis on third-party human rights practices is a work in progress. Issues include the following: Which are the relevant criteria to segment high-risk from low-risk suppliers? How do we set priorities for conducting on-site audits? When should we use external auditors? How do we encourage improvement programs beyond corporate compliance, recognizing that monitoring and audits do not themselves create workable standards of business conduct? And what is the best way to interact with NGOs in this process? Novartis is working on external dialogue with research institutes and academia to refine its process and internally to assist group companies in implementing supply-chain management through the local business units.

Human Rights from the Bottom Up

The creativity and diversity of local initiatives demonstrate how human rights have taken root in the business units. These outreach efforts signal the internalization of the Global Compact principles at the local level. The variety of approaches reflects the ingenuity of bottom-up development.[42] A brief summary of local and foreign Novartis outreach programs demonstrates this diversity. The year in parentheses indicates the time of project initiation.[43]

Local Outreach

- Helping poor communities in Mexico
  Novartis Mexico has established a comprehensive corporate citizenship program uniting the efforts of Novartis associates, physicians, NGOs, and local authorities to provide material (blankets, meals, clothing, baby items), medicines, and free medical check-ups in poor communities (2004).
- Proximology: caring about caregivers
  Novartis France has created a Health and Proximology Department and a Company Foundation to assist caregiving relatives of aging patients. The Proximology approach is to improve the care provided and, at the same time, support the caregiver through scientific study and the development of innovative approaches (2001).
- The Compass Consultation in Australia
  The Compass Project undertaken by Novartis Australia is a broad, nationwide consultation to better understand the implications of an aging population in the Australian society. This process led to a Novartis pilot effort, the "Neighborhood Contract Program," to address the problem of social isolation among the aging (2005).
- Diversity and Disabilities in Brazil
  This project arose from a Brazilian law requiring companies with more than 1,000 employees to have people with disabilities comprise at least 5 percent of their work force. Novartis Brazil embraced this requirement with gusto. Within a campaign of "Valuing Differences" they recruit "great people" and then find positions for them within the firm. They found they have "enhanced our corporate culture through diversity" (2005).[44]
- Public Health Awareness
  Novartis Greece has joined with the National Research Institute to sponsor an annual symposium on public health issues, including

public lectures and a one-day symposium for medical experts and political officials (2003).

- Supporting Tiny Hearts
  Novartis Finland donates five cents of every package of Diovan sold in
  Finland to buy equipment for the Heart Unit at the Children's Hospital
  at the Helsinki University Central Hospital (2005).
- Novartis Comunidad
  Novartis Argentina in conjunction with a Catholic and a Jewish NGO
  is providing free counseling, medical advice, and medicines to the
  poorest members of Argentine society (2005).
- The Mammography Bus
  In Japan, where breast cancer is growing at alarming rates, outreach has
  been focused on mammography. Novartis provides the bus and screens
  applicants for mammograms performed by an NGO, The Breast Cancer Research Group (2006).

Foreign Outreach

- Malaria in Ethiopia
  Fighting malaria in Ethiopia is an extension of the 2001 agreement
  between Novartis and the World Health Organization to provide the
  antimalarial drug Coartem at cost to governments of malaria-stricken
  countries. Novartis Italy has joined with the Italian Ministry of Health
  to provide free diagnosis, health education, and Coartem for rural
  communities in northern Ethiopia (2005).
- One Euro in Solidarity
  In Novartis Spain, associates are asked to donate one euro from their
  monthly pay to support health care for poor communities in Western
  Africa (2005).

This 2008 update demonstrates the persistence necessary on the part of
many people to embed the idea of human rights in an organization. As
with other characteristics, such as innovation, trust, or openness, these
dimensions of corporate culture can be elusive. There are many immea-
surable variables and surprises, particularly in dealing with human rights
in a multinational setting. The term "human rights" and the cohesiveness

of human rights ideas tied to numerous aspects of corporate involvement constitute new ground for business managers. Yet attention to human rights reflects the soul of an organization. Although difficult to measure, its presence or absence is clear.

For Novartis, beginning with the commitment of senior managers, the combination of organization structures—guidelines, policies, assignment of responsibilities—seems to be working. Within these structures, Novartis has continued its implementation of the UNGC.

The principles of the UNGC are the easy part. Making them work within the firm and, beyond that, in the complicated pharmaceutical supply chain is, indeed, a challenging task. A network-wide focus such as the payment of a living wage to each employee draws the attention of everyone in the organization to this right, reminding each person of the need for action and the connection to broader, more subtle and less measurable, rights.

In a multinational enterprise there is a natural tension between enterprise-wide network standards and the uniqueness of local settings (an underlying theme of previous chapters). The Novartis experience reported here is an attempt to understand how one organization is addressing this tension.

APPENDIX: 2002 INTERVIEWEES

URS BAERLOCHER
Head, Legal and General Affairs
Novartis International AG

TERRY BARNETT
President and Chief Executive Officer
Novartis Corporation (United States)

MARTIN CH. BATZER
Head, Pharma Affairs
Novartis Pharma AG

JEFF BENJAMIN
Vice President and Deputy General Counsel
Novartis Corporation (United States)

KASPAR EIGENMANN, PH.D.
Head, Corporate Health, Safety, and Environment
Novartis International AG

DAVID EPSTEIN
President, Novartis Oncology
Novartis Pharma AG
(telephone interview)

JOHANNES M. FREY
Head Corporate Affairs
Novartis International AG

PAUL L. HERRLING, PH.D.
Head, Global Research
Professor for Drug Discovery Science
University of Basel
Novartis Pharma AG

JULIE M. KANE
Vice President
Novartis Corporation (United States)

KLAUS LEISINGER, PH.D.
Executive Director
Novartis Foundation for Sustainable Development

MARIA LOURDES LASQUITE
Stakeholder Relations Manager, P.R.
Novartis International AG

ERWIN SCHILLINGER
Head, International Coordination
Novartis International AG

KARIN SCHMITT
Head, Foundation Affairs
Novartis Foundation for Sustainable Development

ANDREAS SEITER, M.D.
Head, Stakeholder Relations
Stakeholder Relations/Editing Office
Novartis International AG

GLORIA STONE
Director, Global Public Relations
Novartis Oncology
Novartis Pharma AG
(telephone interview)

PETER TOBLER
Compliance Officer
International Coordination
Novartis International AG

DANIEL VASELLA, M.D.
Chief Executive Officer and Chairman
Novartis International AG

NORMAN C. WALKER
Head, Human Resources
Novartis International AG

DIETER H. WISSLER
Head, Corporate Communication
Novartis International AG

PART V

MANAGING THE FIRM
AS A COMMUNITY

This part of the volume completes the argument outlined in the preface by focusing on the relationship between the enterprise and the individual. It is a generalization of the implementation of human rights strategy as described in the case study of Novartis. It addresses the fundamental question of leadership: How does the enterprise serve its role in society while simultaneously serving the needs of its internal stakeholders who have committed their efforts to the firm? This question embraces much of the literature on organizational behavior. Two dimensions will be addressed here: (1) the nature of the person whose needs are to be fulfilled, and (2) how the enterprise serves the needs of this person within the social rules it has set for itself—in this case, meeting the human rights standards of the United Nations Global Compact.

In this final part, the focus is shifted to the local business unit as the starting point—the unit that manages the firm's operations (including the implementation of a human rights standard) in the local community. This is a bottom-up grassroots concern as distinct from the top-down determination of uniform enterprise network standards. Bottom-up analysis (grassroots analysis in economics, or the principle of subsidiarity in Catholic social thought) must begin with the idea of human flourishing. A person is an end unto himself or herself and should never be treated as a means to some other end.

Chapter 9 approaches this issue by drawing a distinction between an "individual" and a "person" from the perspectives of psychology, religion, and economics. In this discussion, psychological and religious considerations add to the more traditional moral, philosophical basis of business ethics. Building on this foundation, the "person" is then positioned in the enterprise.

This part also examines the balance between human flourishing and rules of the organization (in this case, the rules of the enterprise network as defined by the uniform standards established in Parts III and IV). In chapter 10 this balance is interpreted in a proceduralist and a communitarian context.

Given the multiplicity of local situations, as outlined in chapter 4, the exceptions to the rule cannot be treated in the same general empirical way as global trends. Thus, Part V shifts to a more conceptual treatment. We return to several threads that have run throughout the previous chapters and have emerged as key questions in the implementation of values-based management principles: the relationship between universality, on the one hand, and diversity and consequent relativism on the other; the relationship between the individual holder of inherent rights and the group holder of claims on that individual in the form of obligations or responsibilities; and the ultimate question of whether, or to what extent, I am my brother's keeper, and how I am to balance the various demands and needs of my various brothers.

The Individual in the Organization

Two dimensions of the individual in the organization are considered in this chapter: (1) the distinction between the individual and the person, and (2) the relationship between the person and the organization.

I. THE INDIVIDUAL AND THE PERSON

Casual observation demonstrates the differences in human motivation. Some of us strive to be the rugged individual. Others concentrate on nurturing relationships with those around us.

Psychological theory makes this distinction in terms of the individual drive for "more," as opposed to our social embeddedness. This same distinction can be seen in religious traditions as they have developed over the centuries. Economists struggle with this distinction, as reflected in chapter 3. Adam Smith's concept of the invisible hand regulating the economy is based on the individual's striving for more, while his theory of moral sentiments emphasizes society's role in shaping individual morality.[1]

In Psychology

The Drive for More

Several psychological traditions recognize that humans exhibit what Alfred Adler called "the striving for superiority":

> It runs parallel to physical growth and is an intrinsic necessity of life itself. It lies at the root of all solutions of life's problems and is manifested in the way in which we meet these problems. All of our functions follow its direction. They strive for conquest, security, increase.... The impetus from minus to plus never ends. The urge from below to above never ceases. Whatever premises all our philosophers and psychologists dream of—self-preservation, pleasure principle, equalization—all these are but vague representations, attempts to express the great upward drive.[2]

This is a difficult notion to define precisely; as Adler notes, many have tried. In some ways, the Buddha captured it best in his discussion of the desire that is the root of all suffering. An enormous amount of ink has been spent through the centuries defining and redefining the nuances and subtleties of the term "desire," but most Buddhists would agree that the Buddha was describing some sort of attachment to things for the sake of the individual. That is, the individual experiences himself as the center of the universe, the primary reality, and relates with objects, people, ideas, emotions, or other phenomena in terms of their relevance to the enlargement or preservation of that sense of self.

Freudian psychoanalytic theory seems to identify this drive with the pleasure principle, and many writers have equated it with the id. However, this drive seems to underlie the functioning of all three components of the traditional psychoanalytic model. The id is the seat of the drive for pleasure, but the ego and superego function largely to preserve the self against the pressures of the internal and external worlds.[3] Later modifications of psychoanalytic theory have recast this essential drive in other forms. For example, neo-Freudians[4] typically refer to the individual's intense desire to deny or somehow overcome death and limitation, while object relations theorists emphasize the individual's need to develop an autonomous sense of self.[5] Adler himself interpreted this drive as an urge to overcome the deep sense of weakness and inadequacy that we experience as young, dependent children.[6] He argued that this overcoming can take different forms, depending on other personality factors, social influences, and circumstances.

Humanistic psychologists, especially Carl Rogers[7] and Abraham Maslow,[8] have described a drive for self-actualization, which they viewed as analogous to the natural growth of living organisms. Thus, humans are organically oriented toward growth and development, psychologically as well as physically. One can discern echoes of Adler in this humanist view, although the humanists regard self-actualization as a positive goal, whereas Adler is more sensitive to its moral ambiguity.

Behaviorist theory and research may be the source of the strongest psychological arguments for the power of the "drive for more." An early behaviorist theory of learning, called associationism, was based on the observation that animals (including humans) tend to associate two events occurring close together. Ivan Pavlov trained dogs to salivate at the sound of a bell by repeatedly ringing the bell at feeding time.[9] However, learning by association is much less powerful than operant conditioning,[10] which rewards or punishes the animal for producing the targeted behaviors. Operant conditioning has emerged as one of the most powerful methods of influencing someone's behavior, even without that person's conscious knowledge that she is being conditioned.[11] In the terminology of this volume, we could say that the urge to gain pleasure and avoid pain is an expression of the desire for more.

The philosopher Thomas Hobbes, in his classic work *Leviathan*, seems to have focused on this drive in its rawest form in his anthropology. He argued that this is the root of all our behavior, however much we may construct rationalizations. However it is conceived, most of us would agree that this drive for more is a defining characteristic of human behavior. It is an important reason for the failure of socialism or of any system which assumes that individuals are able or willing to act solely for the good of the group and against their own interests at all times. Ignoring basic features of human nature is a sure path to failure in social planning.

On the other hand, if the drive for more is our core motivation, that is, if Hobbes is right, then why does society not repeatedly degenerate into a Hobbesian war of all against all? The notion of a social contract, based on the recognition of mutual self-interest, is not an adequate response, since there will always be situations in which one's own Hobbesian self-interest would be best served by cheating on the social contract. Further, how do we explain altruism and self-sacrifice in terms of self-interest?

Selfish gene theory, to use the term coined by Richard Dawkins,[12] argues that the individual organism's sacrifice for the survival of other members of its species, and especially close genetic relatives, is the result of natural selection. Although the self-sacrificing individual organism may die, if its death promotes the survival of others who carry very similar genetic material, then that genetic material, including the tendency to altruistic self-sacrifice, will tend to be passed on. But this argument seems thin, especially when we consider that humans are known to sacrifice themselves for others who are not genetically related, sometimes not even members of the same racial or ethnic group.

One could argue that such self-sacrifice is selfish in the sense that it supports a self-image desirable to the person in question. For example, a soldier who throws himself on a grenade in order to save his companions (such an incident in Vietnam was reported by the news media in the mid-1960s) arguably acted to support his self-image as a good soldier and comrade. But the notion that a psychologically healthy person would destroy himself for the sole purpose of preserving an aspect of his self-image also seems implausible. The argument that self-sacrifice serves some selfish purpose, whether genetic or psychological, gets stretched even thinner when applied to the various winners of the Carnegie Hero Fund's Carnegie Medal. A candidate for the medal "must be a civilian who voluntarily risks his or her life to an extraordinary degree while saving or attempting to save the life of another person. The rescuer must have no full measure of responsibility for the safety of the victim."[13] From its beginning in 1904 through 2008, the Fund awarded 9,243 medals; a significant portion of recipients died while saving the lives of others. Medal recipients in 2008 included several people who rushed into raging fires to save others, including total strangers; people who drowned or died of suffocation while trying to save others; and a man who leapt in front of a train to save a teenager who was walking on the tracks.[14]

Social Embeddedness

According to Ira Progoff, "Adler, Jung, and Rank . . . based their work on a social conception of the psyche in contrast to Freud's insistence, derived from his connection with 18th Century romanticism, on the fundamental conflict between the individual and civilization."[15] Of these three, Adler was the most articulate spokesman for the importance of social embeddedness in any understanding of human nature. Most Western psychologists have followed Freud in emphasizing individual, intrapsychic processes and assuming that the individual can be evaluated as an independent unit. Adler argued that "[b]efore the individual life of man there was the community. In the history of human culture, there is not a single form of life which was not conducted as social. Never has man appeared otherwise than in society."[16]

Adler's ideas and the social aspects of the theories of Carl Jung and Otto Rank have been largely overlooked in American psychology. However, several findings in psychological and anthropological research support the inherently social nature of human beings. Konrad Lorenz, for example, noted that across cultures, adult humans are predisposed to respond to infant facial features with caretaking emotions and behavior.[17] Sarah Sternglanz, James Gray, and Melvin Murakami[18] have used more modern psychological techniques to verify and extend Lorenz's original observation across a wide variety of adults reporting different socioeconomic backgrounds and different degrees of experience with children.

On the other hand, human infants are "genetically pre-programmed to immediately seek out, register and exuberantly respond to" an emotional relationship with the caregiver.[19] Newborns demonstrate a preference for shapes that resemble human faces,[20] exhibit a preference for human voices, and in a variety of other ways are "endowed with complex emotions for a vital intersubjectivity, emotions that estimate and activate affectionate and alert engagements with caregiving persons."[21]

Taken together, such findings suggest that adults and infants are neurologically predisposed to intense emotional relationships at a level more primal than that of personal choice. Of course, appropriate infant-caregiver relationships sometimes fail to develop for a variety of reasons, and in extreme cases infanticide or infant abandonment may be the tragic result. But these are the exceptions, and our mutual horror at them lends further support to the argument that we are biologically predisposed to participate in certain fundamental relationships that are necessary for our physical survival.

Neurology influences social relationships, but social relationships also influence neurology. As one researcher states, "It is now accepted that a baby's emotional environment will influence the neurobiology that is the basis of mind."[22] Indeed, to quote another study, "The emotional and communicative precocity of human newborns indicates that the emotional responses to caregivers must play a crucial role in the regulation of early brain development."[23]

Infants experience an astonishing rate of neurological development. During the first few years of life, each of the billions of neurons in the human brain forms connections to an average fifteen thousand other neurons. By the age of three, an estimated one thousand trillion neural synapses have developed. But this is only half the story; synaptic pruning begins in early childhood, accelerates in late childhood, and, by late adolescence has discarded half of the neural connections. Both the growth and the death of synaptic connections are guided by the individual's experiences. Emotional, relational experiences seem particularly crucial to the healthy development of brain circuits that are important to emotional regulation, impulse control, language, symbolic thinking, stress tolerance, and the capacity to emotionally or cognitively appreciate another person's point of view.[24]

The crucial role of early relationships in healthy neurological development is demonstrated by the effects of abuse and neglect. "Impoverished environments appear to have the opposite effect of rich and varied surroundings. They suppress brain development."[25] The orbitofrontal cortex, amygdala, and temporal lobes are all negatively affected by deleterious experiences in early childhood; these structures are vital in the mature brain's functioning in the areas of memory, emotion, motivation, interpersonal relationships, and impulse control. Further, endocrine responses to stress in early childhood can profoundly alter the brain's functioning in the areas of memory, anxiety, depression, information processing, and problem solving. Unhealthy development may include improper synaptic connections, excessive synaptic sensitivity, or even atrophy of brain structures which are underutilized.[26]

Neurology and the social matrix are so closely intertwined that, as Robert Wright[27] has stated, "The evolution of human beings has consisted largely of adaptation to one another." As another researcher put it, "Human beings are equipped at birth with abilities prepared for sympathetic and cooperative mental life in a society that creates cultural meanings, seeks to be governed by them, and transmits them to the young."[28] In fact, there is evidence that the neocortex, the most uniquely human part of the brain, co-evolved with language and social complexity. Both R. J. M. Dunbar and A. Whiten[29] argue that the development of larger, more complex social groups encouraged the development of a larger, more complex neocortex, which in turn encouraged further development of larger, more complex social groups, and so on. As Carl Zimmer put it, "Hominid evolution may have become a feedback loop of ever-increasing social intelligence, producing our ever-expanding brains."[30]

Evidence from both ontogeny and philogeny supports the social embeddedness of human beings. But this social embeddedness is not an abstract thing; we are always embedded in a particular social context composed of particular social and cultural meanings and mores. As William Sullivan notes, "A social context, moreover, is always and necessarily a moral order."[31]

In Philosophy and Religious Traditions

It is increasingly apparent that the notion of a human being as independent of social context is inaccurate and misleading. Any attempt to address motivation and moral choice must recognize the multiple links between the individual and the social networks in which she participates. A good person is often defined as "virtuous" or "moral." Although the two concepts are distinct,[32] they both are directed to characteristic patterns of thought and behavior in which social embeddedness dominates the "drive for more."

Aristotle defined virtue in terms of individual excellence, where excellence is measured by its *telos* or purpose.[33] For Aristotle, virtue is closely associated with social embeddedness. It is "an exemplary way of getting along with other people, a way of manifesting in one's own thoughts, feelings, and actions the ideals and aims of the entire community."[34] Aristotelian virtues include both social virtues of congeniality and those that can be categorized as moral.[35]

The philosopher Jacques Maritain distinguishes between "individuality" and "personality" in discussing the common good. "In each of us, individuality, being that which excludes from oneself all that other men are, could be described as the narrowness of the ego, forever threatened and forever eager *to grasp for itself*."[36] "Personality," Maritain holds, "is a much deeper mystery, and to probe the depths of its meaning is considerably more difficult."[37] "Unlike the concept of the individuality of corporeal things, the concept of personality is related not to matter but to the deepest and highest dimensions of being."[38] Having made this distinction between individuality and personality, however, Maritain stresses "that they are not two separate things. There is not in me one reality, called my individual, and another reality called my person. One and the same reality is, in a certain sense an individual, and, in another sense, a person. Our whole being is an individual by reason of that in us which derives from matter, and a person by reason of that in us which derives from spirit."[39] For purposes of our current discussion, we will adopt Maritain's distinction between the individual (motivated by the drive for more) and the person shaped by and opening to things beyond the self, without assuming Maritain's distinction between matter and spirit.

Religious traditions stress the web of relationships within which individuals function. In the Christian tradition, beginning with the teachings of Christ and formalized in doctrine, faith is expressed through our interactions with one another. "What good is it, my brothers, if a man claims to have faith but has no deeds? Can such faith save him? Suppose a brother or sister is without clothes and daily food. If one of you says to him, 'Go, I wish you well; keep warm and well fed,' but does nothing about his physical needs, what good is it? In the same way, faith by itself, if it is not accompanied by action, is dead. But someone will say, 'You have faith; I have deeds.' Show me your faith without deeds, and I will show you my faith by what I do" (James 2:14–18, *NIV*). For Augustine, for example, "human nature . . . was always created social."[40] Thomas Aquinas, for another, recognized that people are essentially social and cannot be good by themselves.

Buddhist recognition of the essentially social nature of moral and religious activity is exemplified in the three middle elements of the Eightfold Path (Right Speech, Right Action, and Right Livelihood) and in the Sangha as the third of the Three Jewels. While each of the eight elements making up the Eightfold Path may be seen as having a social dimension, the middle three are explicitly social. It is not possible to achieve the release from suffering that is the Buddhist goal without interacting properly with others. Indeed, Theravada Buddhists argue, "*Sila* (virtue, moral conduct) is the cornerstone upon which the entire Noble Eightfold Path is built."[41] Nor is it possible to achieve release from suffering without the assistance and support of the well-intentioned community. The Sangha (literally, association, assembly, or community) refers in the narrow sense to the community of Buddhists, especially ordained monks and nuns. In its broader sense, Sangha refers to all those who are trying to live a good and moral life and striving for wisdom.[42]

The Hindu concept of *dharma*, often translated as morality or righteousness, is central to both individual conduct and the well-ordered society and links the two. Bansi Pandit explains:

> *Dharma* (morality or righteousness) is the cornerstone of a just and equitable state. *Dharma* preserves the individuals and the society. The oft-quoted axiom is: "Hunger, sleep, fear, and sex are common to all animals, human and sub-human. It is the additional attribute of *dharma* that differentiates man from the beast." Thus, the political philosophy (*danda-nîti*) of the state must be grounded in *dharma*. In ancient literature, the righteous king (state) is believed to be *Dharma* itself, created by God for the protection of all beings (Manu 7.3 and 7.14).
>
> In personal life *dharma* is expressed as virtues and duties. In the political life *dharma* is expressed as the just and equitable laws which restrain evil and promote virtuous life. In the Hindu polity, politicians are required to inspire virtue and loyalty to the laws of the state by their own examples. In Hindu legal literature the word *dharma* conveys the same meaning as the words *ethical, reasonable,* and *equitable* in Western legal literature.[43]

In the Confucian view, morality consists primarily in the cultivation and conduct of proper social relationships. This emphasis on proper social relationships has often been misunderstood in the West as an emphasis on etiquette for its own sake. However, the core Confucian concepts of *ren, li,* and *yi* are much deeper, linking individual morality with social order. *Ren* includes notions of benevolence, kindness, kindheartedness, humanity, and virtue.[44] It can also be understood as a commitment to moral improvement.[45] *Ren* is expressed in and governed or shaped by *li,* the proper ordering of social relationships. In its narrowest sense, *li* refers to correct conduct of rituals, but in its broader sense it refers to the ordering of social life and conduct in harmony with *ren. Yi,* a refinement to Confucian thought introduced by Mencius (as stated in Chan), emphasizes the importance of duty and righteousness in sustaining *li.*[46]

The deep interconnections between virtue ethics and religion, as these examples indicate, are not accidental.[47] It is difficult to form a basis for defining what constitutes virtue without appealing to some transcendent moral authority. Christians, Jews, and Muslims ascribe that authority to a personal God. While many non-Western religions are not monotheistic (and in some cases not theistic at all), they nonetheless make some claim to transcendental authority for their moral positions. Even Aristotle appealed to the nature of the Unmoved Mover.

In the Market

At first glance, Adam Smith's market participant in his *The Wealth of Nations* appears to be an utterly self-interested individual:

> He generally, indeed, neither intends to promote the public interest, nor knows how much he is promoting it. By preferring the support of domestic to that of foreign industry, he intends only his own security; and by directing that industry in such a manner as its produce may be of the greatest value, he intends only his own gain, and he is in this, as in many other cases, led by an invisible hand to promote an end which was no part of his intention.[48]

Smith's market participant, however, did not operate in a moral vacuum. He was formed and informed by his moral sentiments, the topic of which was the other great preoccupation of Smith's intellectual life. While Smith would have agreed that "market relationships are in no way social,"[49] he would also have pointed out that the people who engage in market relationships are very social beings indeed. They have been profoundly influenced by the moral contexts in which they live; their views, goals, and the limits of the options that they allow themselves to consider have been shaped by those same contexts. In his *Theory of Moral Sentiments*, Smith provides a rich analysis of sociality, based on the premise that benevolence and a capacity for fellow-feeling are properties of human nature.[50] And he explicitly noted the role that some moral sentiments, such as honesty and trustworthiness, play in business transactions. However, these two works remained separate, and their topics were never integrated within an overarching theory of human activity.

While Adam Smith does not appear to have fully explained how the moral and market aspects of his human being are integrated into one person, another economist and philosopher, writing at about the same time as Smith, included the fully socially embedded person in the market transaction itself. Like Smith, Antonio Genovesi wrote from a moral perspective.[51] Genovesi agreed with Smith's concept of the market in that the pursuit of wealth generates public benefits, but he did not make the distinction between market transactions and other personal relationships in his civil society. His idea of all-embracing moral behavior comes as no surprise from an eighteenth-century Catholic priest. What is surprising is the good fit between Genovesi's notions of a mutually beneficial reciprocity and all personal interrelationships within and beyond the market—even though he developed those ideas through an assessment of the marketplace, rather than the other way around (the direction one would anticipate from one grounded in the theology of the natural law).

Smith's notion of the invisible hand in *The Wealth of Nations* reflects the emphasis on the individual and on individual freedom that was characteristic of his time, and it endures today. His concern for moral sensibilities, however, is all but forgotten.

In the Business Enterprise

In the institutionalized markets of today, the interactions within the firm are as essential to its performance as are the firm's interaction with the marketplace. The strategic positioning of the firm must be matched by relationships within the organization, and the social values of the market must be matched by the personal morality of the people in the firm. The positioning of the firm within its environment and of the person within the firm raises the question of which set of interests and needs, the institution's or those of persons, should take priority. As noted in previous chapters, there is a tension between the rules of the institution and the interests and needs of the persons who comprise it.

II. THE PERSON AND THE ORGANIZATION

The tension between the goals of the institution and those of the person in the organization can be expressed in many ways. In terms of institutional management, the strategic positioning of the firm in its environment can be at odds with the specific interests of those working within the firm. For the multinational firm, the uniform standards of the enterprise network may find different applications to fit the unique circumstances of the local community and culture in the settings of the individual business unit. The values underlying the rules of the organization can be distinct from the morality of the individual. In such cases we can speak of the *good* of the virtuous individual set against the *right* of the rules.

The notion of the good presents a vision of the virtuous and moral person, who exhibits a definitive set of personal characteristics (the virtues) formed through the individual's interaction with others. Values-based moral management at its core depends on the capability of individual managers to have and act on a vision of the good and thus to put their sense of social embeddedness ahead of their "drive for more." Excess careerism, vicious corporate cultures, and numerous corporate scandals are the result of perverse priorities involving these two basic human motivations—a failure on the part of the individual to pursue the good.

Definitions of the good by virtue theorists provide a kind of moral clarity, but it is achieved at a price. There is considerable variation among individual visions of the good, even among highly moral people, and it is difficult to draw together the efforts of people with disparate interests and motivations and direct these efforts toward common goals. But this is precisely the nature of the business enterprise. With rare exceptions, large business organizations are not composed exclusively of people who agree on all aspects of a moral code and all issues regarding its implementation. In the case of multinational corporations, members of the business enterprise are likely to hold quite different religious and cultural beliefs regarding the nature of the good. How is *ren* to be expressed in *li* if the members of the group disagree on the nature and elements of *ren*? How is personal *dharma* to be translated into *danda-nîti*?

———————

A concentration on the individual, albeit one who is recognized as a *person* formed through interaction, does not in itself provide a structure or process through which group efforts can readily be directed toward common goals, such as the Principles of the United Nations Global Compact. In a business enterprise, the relationships among the internal stakeholders are organized in some manner through sets of rules or procedures directed at creating correct behavior (that which is "right"). A good manager is one who can harmonize the personal good and the institutional right. Chapter 10 considers two approaches to achieve this balance: the procedural model of contracts and the communitarian emphasis on relationships.

CHAPTER TEN

The Person and the Enterprise

Management Models

Two approaches to dealing with the tension between the person and the organization are the proceduralist and the communitarian models. Both are of interest to the multinational manager who is faced with cross-cultural issues on a network-wide basis and must discern appropriate actions within local communities.

I. PROCEDURALIST MODELS

Proceduralist approaches can be grouped roughly into three categories: deontological (e.g., the moral philosophies of Immanuel Kant, John Rawls, and Lawrence Kohlberg); utilitarian (e.g., John Stuart Mill and some readings of Adam Smith); and contractarian. The basis of the claim for moral authority is different in each case. The deontological approach relies on abstract analysis, based on principles of fairness which are asserted to be universal; the utilitarian approach relies on maximization of net benefit; and the contractarian approach relies on the importance of honoring contracts in order to establish and maintain social order. The essential argument is the same for all three: The broad social good is best achieved by structuring the interaction among a group's members rather than by attempting to improve the character of each member. In the terminology of this volume, the common good is best achieved by an emphasis on the right rather than on the good.

Whatever their philosophical basis, proceduralist models focus on rules and their application. These explicit and implicit rules guide the interaction among individuals, between individuals and the communities of which they are members, and among the communities. At all of these levels, the concentration on procedure as the determinant of correct action leads in application to a focus on contracts, first among individuals, and then extending to contracts among organizations, among countries, and among global systems. Thus, at the level of implementation, all proceduralist models become contractarian in the sense that they rely on contracts among participants for their viability. (It is noteworthy that Rawls, perhaps the preeminent contemporary liberal rights theorist, melds both deontological and contractarian elements in his theory.) Rule definitions can be approached on a macro basis, with a view toward the rules and constraints imposed by the systems, or at the micro level of interaction among individuals.

On a macro basis, the discussion in chapter 3 of the basic market model and its extensions to long-term enterprise sustainability was based on contractarian models. Both the shareholder and stakeholder models are contractarian. In this market model, contracts are not devoid of values beyond those reflected in law and regulation. Certain social values are implicit in the contractual relationship itself. For example, trust among the individual contracting parties is a necessary foundation for the pyramid that becomes the market.

Philosopher Robert Audi makes the following comparison:

> Utilitarians maintain that to maximize the good we must not only cooperate with others but also respect their rights, even when we have no ongoing relationship with them. Instrumentalists tend to

hold a similar view concerning desire satisfaction: Concentrate exclusively on your own and you will tend to get little of it. Kantians see us as properly aiming at coexistence in a kingdom of ends, and they insist, as do virtue theorists, on honesty with others and, within certain limits, beneficence toward them.[1]

Richard De George proposes that a fair negotiation is one in which each participant must be satisfied with the fairness of the process itself, distinct from the outcomes. "All interested parties must be allowed to have a say."[2] In addition, "agreements in general are fair if both parties enter into them freely, both sides benefit from the arrangement, and both sides believe the terms fair."[3] De George thus extends the moral requirement from the individual to the process itself. Mattias Storme and James Gordley emphasize the legal tradition that contracts be negotiated in good faith.[4]

The contractarian emphasis can also be found in organizational theories that have been developed to counter traditional shareholder models. For example, the difference between the stakeholder and shareholder models lies in the priority given to shareholders, not in the underlying contractarian base. In stakeholder theory, the manager becomes the arbiter among the interests, needs, and rights of the stakeholder, each possessing an implicit or explicit contract with the firm.

The contractarian model serves well the individual drive for more. Each of us can pursue our drive for self-expansion in creative ways through explicit and implicit contracts with other individuals or institutions. The interacting complex of these contracts then forms the market, which translates intense personal preferences into the material well-being of society.

This model is less than sanguine about the positive dimensions of social embeddedness and the personal concern for others, and therefore it focuses on the procedures by which the individual participant is directed toward the correct or *right* behavior. Aside from Hobbesian constructions, these models generally do not envision the person as completely devoid of virtues or morality or as totally motivated by the drive for more. The focus, however, is on the procedures for interaction rather than the personal qualities of the actors, and the latter are generally left largely unexplored.

Such procedural emphases can lose track of the person, and hence the importance of virtue as self-fulfillment; personal faith as a guide to morality; and the individual's influence on the procedures and vice versa.

Their basic fallacy is in mistaking the means (correct procedure) for the end (the common good). Elements of both the *good* and the *right* are needed. What is missing is a sense of community, a notion that links the importance of the individual to procedures within which the person can contribute to the common good. The communitarian model attempts to make this connection.

II. THE COMMUNITARIAN MODEL

There is a natural extension from the distinction between the individual and the person to the role of the person in a community as expressed in philosophy, religion, and psychology. Aristotle's definition of virtue, as noted earlier, was in the context of community. For Jacques Maritain, the person requires membership in a society for both his or her dignity and the fulfillment of needs.[5] As an extension of what he terms "the social side of our nature" to an involvement in community, Audi notes: "It is not unnatural to go further and to maintain that human good itself is realizable only in community."[6] He ties the added dimension of community to notions of the common good in communitarian terms: "In addition to an individual's good being in part socially constituted, communitarianism reflects an emphasis on 'the common good.' Aquinas described law itself as 'ordained toward the common good,' and communitarians have criticized the political theory of Rawls and others as insufficiently providing for it."[7]

From a psychological perspective, there is a natural flow from a person's social embeddedness to participation in a community. The Hebrew Bible and the New Testament also emphasize this community context, as do Augustine, Aquinas, and the Roman Catholic tradition generally. A similar transition exists in the Buddhist, Hindu, Confucian, and Islamic traditions.

The challenge of managing the business enterprise as a community is based on the tensions between the good of society and that of its members. The addition of a communal purpose to personal morality introduces the possibility of conflict between personal and communal goals. Helen Alford and Michael Naughton opt for community goals: "The notion of the common good entails the primacy of the whole (the community) over the parts (the community's individual members). . . . In one sense, individual persons are ends in themselves, and their development is an inherent good, not to be sacrificed to anything else. Yet, insofar as the individual person's development and fulfillment follows from participation in the common good—in fact, *is* a participated good—the community may call upon the individual to make outright sacrifices for its preservation."[8] In contrast, as we have argued elsewhere, "if . . . the individual is inextricably intertwined with the social group in which she participates, then it follows that her personal fulfillment, her individual good, is also intertwined with the common good. But, 'intertwined with' does not mean 'subsumed under'; there are always tensions between the person and her social matrix. It is a mistake to attempt to resolve these tensions in favor of either pole."[9]

These tensions, then, imply the necessity of procedures for resolving them. Thus, communities must define their communal good in parallel with the good of the individual members and establish procedures through which both sets of goods can be nurtured and balanced—a major task. The communitarians address this task. The communitarian model as proposed by Amitai Etzioni includes elements of the *good* of individual morality and the *right* of correct procedure. It envisions a minimal set of core values in a pluralistic society. with an emphasis on procedural structures that link and influence but rarely coerce individual actors and their moral choices.

Etzioni's Communitarianism

Etzioni frames communitarian ideals in terms of a "good society," which he describes as "a society that fosters a limited set of core values and relies largely on the moral voice rather than upon state coercion."[10] There are two instruments of his good society: the communal moral voice and the reality of overlapping communities.

Sources of the Communal Moral Voice

Etzioni ties his concept of a moral voice to social embeddedness. "One main instrument of the good society, the mainstay of 'culture,' is the moral voice which urges people to behave in pro-social ways. While there is a tendency to stress the importance of the inner voice, communitarians recognize the basic fact that without continual external reinforcement, the conscience tends to deteriorate."[11]

This moral voice is what distinguishes the communitarian ideal from the notion of civil society.[12] While most proponents of civil society avoid any ranking of voluntary organizations according to their substantive values, communitarians stress a core of values: "The concept of the good society differs from that of the civil one in that while the former also strongly favors voluntary associations—a rich and strong social fabric, and civility of discourse—it formulates and seeks to uphold some particular social conceptions of the good. The good society is, as I have already suggested, centered around a core of substantive particularistic values."[13]

Etzioni would accept personal religious beliefs as part of a personal "inner voice." However, he is suspicious of religious influence in defining the common social morality or the common good. He has a deep distrust of coercion by the state and a keen awareness of the possibility that religious groups might impose their values through the state. This is the basis for his emphasis on voluntary organizations of civil society as a counterbalance to the state. "All that I argue here is that good societies promote particularistic, substantive formation of the good; that these are limited sets of core values that are promoted largely by the moral voice and not by state coercion."[14] Thus, while the state may be the only institution in our society with the right of coercion, Etzioni is in a continuous search for offsetting influences.

The appropriate role of religion in determining state policy for liberal democracies (as distinct from theocracies, such as in ancient Judaism or modern Islam) is a hotly debated topic in the philosophy of law, generally in the framework of the separation of church and state. Richard Neuhaus, for example, supports the religious voice:

> As with individual citizens, so also with the associations that citizens form to advance their opinions. Religious institutions may understand themselves to be brought into being by God, but for the purposes of this democratic polity they are free associations of citizens. As such, they are guaranteed the same access to the public square as are the citizens who compose them. It matters not at all that their purpose is to advance religion, any more than it matters that other associations would advance the interests of business or labor or radical feminism or animal rights or whatever.... What opinions these associations seek to advance in order to influence

our common life is entirely and without remainder the business of citizens who freely adhere to such associations.[15]

In contrast, Daniel Conkle objects to some aspects of religious input. While he accepts that there is a public role for religion, he does not accept a role for religious fundamentalism, which he defines as "a type of religion that regards its sacred texts (or other religious authority) as a source of truth that is absolute, plain, and unchangeable."[16] For Conkle, a fundamentalist approach interdicts the appropriate "deliberative, dialogic decision-making process, a process that at least permits the possibility that argument or discourse will lead to a change of mind."[17]

Audi adds an interesting dimension to this discussion of the role that faith and religion do, can, and should play in our interaction with others. He supports a religious voice in liberal democracy but adds that faith-based thought should be similar to philosophical reasoning, in that God wants us to be clear thinkers as well as faithful people. Regarding the relationship between religion and secular arguments, Audi asserts that God would support (even desire) a correctly reasoned secular argument:

> Indeed, on the assumption that God is omniscient and omnibenevolent—all knowing and all good—any cogent argument, including an utterly non-religious one, for a moral principle is in effect a good argument for God's knowing that conclusion, and hence for urging or requiring conformity to it. How could God, conceived as omniscient and omnibenevolent, not require or at least wish our conformity to a true moral principle? . . . I should think, moreover, that in some cases good secular arguments for moral principles may be better reasons to believe those principles divinely enjoined than theological arguments for the principles, based on scripture or tradition; for the latter arguments seem more subject than the former to extraneous cultural influences, more vulnerable to misinterpretation of texts or their sheer corruption across time and translation, and more liable to bias stemming from political or other non-religious aims. This turns one traditional view of the relation between ethics and religion on its head; it may be better to try to understand God through ethics than ethics through theology.[18]

In his encyclical letter *Fides et Ratio*, Pope John Paul II carefully assesses this same relationship and concludes that reason and revelation should come to identical conclusions,[19] although revelation will trump reason in cases of disagreement.

Faith and religion play an important role in the way we think, in the way we interact with others, and in the way communities are organized and governed, including the broadest systems of national and international governance. Thus, faith, religious tradition, and institutionalized religion have a role—both beneficial and potentially problematic—in the social definition of the business enterprise and in its management.

Overlapping Communities

Communities are the structures through which social interactions take place. They are a central part of our moral formation. Each of us is a member of multiple communities, some defined by common values, others by work, still others by geography. Laurie Richardson describes the interaction among communities in terms of "nesting boxes": "Communities are the most important sustaining source of moral voices other than the inner self. . . . Communities are best viewed as nesting boxes. Less encompassing communities (families, neighborhoods) are nestled within more encompassing ones (villages and towns), which in turn are situated within still more encompassing national and cross-national communities. Nongeographic communities criss-cross the others."[20] Thus, the community and nests of communities provide the means by which the person is linked to the larger society, as distinct from the web of contractual relationships that comprise the market.

The communal linkage, as Etzioni observes, is not without difficulties:

> The challenge to the communitarian paradigm is to point to ways in which the bonds of a more encompassing community can be maintained without suppressing the member communities. In many ways, the sociological formation required is similar to what is needed in the relations between an individual and a single community: autonomy that is bounded rather than unfettered. And just as individual rights must be balanced with a commitment to a shared

core of values, so the commitment to one's community (or communities) must be balanced with commitments to the more encompassing society.[21]

In addressing the problem, Etzioni stresses the importance of what he calls "thick shared frameworks" of layered loyalties, which nurture a split loyalty between a person's immediate community and the more encompassing community.[22] He makes an important point relative to the individual freedom within the community: "Most people in contemporary free societies are able to choose, to a significant extent, the communities to which they are psychologically committed, and can often draw on one to limit the persuasive power of another."[23] On the part of the community, the frameworks need to recognize people as members of multiple, overlapping, and interlaced communities.[24]

Richardson treats nongeographic communities as different from the others, a distinction of importance for the business enterprise. "Nongeographic communities, which are made up of people who do not live near one another, may not have foundations as stable and deep-rooted as residential communities, but they fulfill many of the social and moral functions of traditional communities. Work-based and professional communities are among the most common of these."[25] (Here, Richardson is referring to a community of personal relationships as distinct from the Internet communities discussed in chapter 2.)

Communitarian thought clearly has much to contribute to managing the business enterprise as a community, although surprisingly little of the work that is generally classified as business ethics begins with the communitarian tradition.

The Multinational Firm as a Community

A view of the business enterprise as a community involves a different approach from our traditional organizational guidelines. It implies the management of relationships rather than contracts. It involves careful attention to the good of the person, his or her personal virtue, flourishing, and morality. Individual rights are defined and assured by the community, while individual responsibilities are determined with respect to communal goals. The enabling structures within which these personal relationships are nurtured must benefit the community as well as the individual.

People associated with the business enterprise are already members of multiple communities. Each person in a business enterprise or business unit of a multinational corporation belongs to numerous communities, such as family, voluntary organizations, religious institutions, or governmental units—each with its, perhaps subtle, differences in core values. As noted above, membership in overlapping communities provides protection for the minorities in each community from coercion by the majority. In terms of the business enterprise, this protection would be conferred by membership in the sometimes overlapping institutions that represent the various stakeholder groups.[26]

As communities overlap and nest within one another, societies are formed[27] with institutions that reflect the particular values of that society.[28] This creates a unique challenge for the multinational enterprise, as an organization that spans multiple societies.

Of the many crosscurrents in this communitarian view of the firm, two warrant specific comments: (1) the overall determination of network-wide standards versus the implementation of those standards, and (2) the question of how to deal with the persistent cultural differences in the settings of the individual business units.

Network Standards verses Business Unit Implementation

In our discussion of strategically positioning the firm within its environment, the emphasis was on universal principles translated into uniform standards for the enterprise network. The concept of human rights served this purpose well. The Universal Declaration of Human Rights specifies principles of human rights that are supported in Catholic social thought and liberal rights theory. The first step was to codify a set of principles for the business enterprise, as expressed in the United Nations Global Compact. These can then become the uniform standards for the business enterprise, as in the case of Novartis.

But action occurs at the grassroots—the business unit. As argued above, the locus of social embeddedness for the person is in her or his relationships. The communitarian model holds the most promise for effective moral (fair and just) implementation at the local level. It has historic roots in philosophy and in Catholic social thought, with its concern for overarching principles and local exceptions.

The "common good" is a phrase used frequently in communitarian literature. The common good is defined as the goal of all communities, but at the same time it refers to the fulfillment of each individual person within these communities—the macro and the micro view, respectively. This raises the problem of what Paolo Carozza terms "the polarity of pluralism and the common good."[29]

Maritain describes the common good in terms of both "the end of the social whole" and "the *person* as a social unit."[30] The common good "is the good *human* life of the multitude, of a multitude of persons; it is their communion in good living"[31] and "the good of a people and a city."[32] Maritain also ties this macro version of the common good to each of the persons participating in society: "But the end to which it tends is to procure the common good of the multitude in such a way that the concrete person gains the greatest possible measure, compatible with the good of the whole, of real independence from the servitudes of nature. The economic guarantees of labor and capital, political rights, the moral virtues and the culture of the mind, all contribute to the realization of this independence."[33] Thus, Maritain ascribes the same common good to all of society and to each member who comprises that society.

The philosophical macro/micro distinction is also evident in Catholic thought. In *Pacem in Terris*, John XXIII referred to "the universal common good; the good, that is, of the whole human family," and John Paul II continued this theme in terms of the unity of the human family.[34] He stressed the principle of solidarity, which calls each of us to respond to one another as persons, that is, to make a real commitment to the good of our neighbor. As Elshtain states,

> John Paul's name for this alternative aspiration is solidarity, not "a feeling of vague compassion or shallow distress at the misfortunes of so many people" but, instead, a determination to "commit oneself to the common good; that is to say, to the good of all and of each individual because we are really responsible for all." Through solidarity we *see* "the 'other' . . . not just as some kind of instrument . . . but as our 'neighbor,' a 'helper' (cf. Gen. 2:18–20), to be made a sharer on a par with ourselves in the banquet of life. . . ." The structures that

make possible this idea of solidarity are the many associations of civil society "below" the level of the state.[35]

In defining the common good as a set of broad human principles, the communitarian notion of nested communities is useful. The common good can be defined institutionally, beginning with the goals of those organizations in our government and civil society that have the broadest reach, and then specified for all of those communities nested within the broader community, with narrower and narrower reaches until we arrive at the smallest local, grassroots, formal or informal community. Thus, beginning as an international good, the common good is nested in smaller and smaller communities of interaction. Conversely, actions implementing the common good go in the other direction, from the smallest community to the broadest reach. In Catholic social thought, this is expressed as the principle of subsidiarity.

Beginning at the grassroots, subsidiarity is based on the idea that those closest to the problem are best positioned to deal with it. Subsidiarity focuses on the smallest definable group and then expands as broader, more inclusive communities intervene temporarily to address issues that cannot be solved at the more basic level. In line with the principle of subsidiarity, we start at the bottom and support those with whom we have a linkage, but not in a way that damages those with whom we have no linkage. Subsidiarity is based on the idea of participation. Each person finds fulfillment in participation with other persons.

Subsidiarity has both a negative and a positive dimension. Negatively, the principle restricts intervention on the part of a broader, higher, more inclusive community in the affairs of a smaller, lower, less inclusive community. And, when intervention becomes necessary, it should be temporary. This dimension generally refers to the overextension of powers on the part of the state, an intervention that restricts the freedom of the subordinate group and the participation of its members. Carozza describes the positive dimension as follows: "The 'higher' grouping exists not just for their own sake but to assist the smaller, more limited association in realizing their task, just as the community of the friendship of family is oriented toward providing the individual with the conditions enabling him to realize freely his own dignity. . . . In short, subsidiarity takes the freedom necessary to human dignity and extends it to a regard for freedom at all levels of social organization."[36] In this sense, achieving subsidiarity is a procedural principle, ensuring the participation of each person.

These conceptual guidelines should enhance managerial thinking about implementing a human rights strategy in the enterprise community; about dealing with universal principles and cultural relativism, narrowly defined; and about balancing the right and the good in managing across cultures.

Cross-Cultural Concerns

Cultural differences have deep roots in society and religion. Even though cultural differences are eroding, many persist, especially those perceived as coming from a divine mandate. Part of the remarkable adaptability of multinational firms has been their ability to cross cultural lines, based on many years of operating in multicultural environments with multinational management teams. Again, the idea of nested communities provides guidance. Each person in a firm, steeped in his or her own cultural cluster, becomes part of the business unit community and, further, the enterprise network community. The longer the exposure, the more the person becomes part of the firm's unique corporate culture.

The persistence of cultural beliefs and values is illuminated by the psychological notion of narrative consciousness. The application of these concerns is reflected in the culture of the organization. The mapping of individual relationships in social capital research distinguishes between those who cling to their group (and thus are less likely to change) and those who build bridges to other groups. Finally, a guide to cross-cultural interaction is social embeddedness from a theological perspective.

Narrative Consciousness

In psychology, the notion of narrative consciousness illuminates some of the ways in which our social relationships affect our values and attitudes.[37] An extended analysis of how our consciousness is formed alerts us to the depth of cultural bias and the difficulty of cross-cultural dialogue. Certainly, a significant portion of this transmission occurs nonverbally, in the disapproving glance, the affectionate gesture, the parental emotions which even infants seem exceptionally adept at detecting.[38] However, much of our socialization is too complex to be communicated nonverbally.

The link between verbal communication and socialization is dramatically demonstrated in autism. Two of the three core features of autism are "qualitative impairment in social interaction" and "qualitative impairments in communication."[39] Regarding the former, people with autism seem to lack a "theory of mind," the capacity to imagine another person's point of view or internal experience. This capacity emerges in most humans by five years of age and is so basic to our interpersonal experience that most of us have trouble articulating it, let alone imagining what life would be like without it. One unusually eloquent adult with autism, Temple Grandin, has said that other people are so baffling to her that she feels like "an anthropologist on Mars."[40] Regarding impairments in communication, Lorna Wing reports that perhaps 20 to 25 percent of persons with autism are completely nonverbal, although some of them can reproduce animal or mechanical noises quite accurately. Even the most linguistically skilled individuals often have difficulty with the pragmatics of speech, that is, the social use of language as opposed to its informational use. They are often very literal; Wing gives the example of a young man who exhausted himself riding subway trains until midnight because his card stated "valid for travel until midnight," and he thought it was an order.[41]

The impairments of autism suggest that language and neurology are interrelated in much the same ways as social relatedness and neurology, and that in fact there is some deep, as yet unidentified connection among the three of them. Studies of infant and child language acquisition support this association. As infants, "[o]ur brains are programmed to recognize human speech, to discriminate subtle differences between individual speech sounds, to put words and meaning together, and to pick up the grammatical rules for ordering words into sentences."[42] By the age of one year, children are able to distinguish and respond to fearful vocalizations in the absence of facial cues.[43] However, they are beginning to lose the ability to distinguish subtle differences in speech sounds that are not used in the language they hear every day.[44] This is a very preliminary example of the ways in which language development and neurological development influence each other, which is the subject of a rapidly developing field in neurocognition.[45] The complex interplay among language, neurology, and cognition in philogeny and ontogeny is traced by Gary Cziko,[46] and, as previously noted, R. J. M. Dunbar explicitly ties together the evolution of language, social complexity, and the neocortex.

So, socialization and language are intertwined, as we would expect, given the ways in which language and neurological development are intertwined. But how is language used to communicate cultural meanings? Jerome Bruner has proposed two modes of cognition, the first being paradigmatical or logical-scientific and the second being narrative. The former is more familiar to academics and corporate executives. This is the mode of propositional logic and argument, of mathematics and science, and of bullet points and memos. This is the sort of linguistic communication seen in linguistically skilled individuals with autism. The latter has more to do with the communication of cultural values and social patterns. This is the sort of linguistic communication which is seriously impaired in most persons suffering from autism.[47]

The difference between abilities in these two cognitive modes in persons with autism hints that narrative may be the more important mode for the transmission of socially relevant information, and, in fact, this is the argument made by narrative psychologists. Dan McAdams suggests that "children with autism do not understand people as intentional agents or do so only to a limited degree. Their lack of understanding applies to the self as well, suggesting that at the heart of severe autism may reside a disturbing dysfunction in 'I-ness' and a corresponding inability to formulate and convey sensible narratives of the self."[48]

Drawing on a large body of evidence in developmental, cognitive, and personality psychology, McAdams emphasizes the central role of narrative in the construction of self-understanding throughout life, beginning with "the 1-year-old's emergent understanding of intentionality, the development of the agential 'I' and the objective 'me' in the 2nd year of life, the maturation of a theory of mind in years 3 and 4, and the early conversations children enjoy with their parents, siblings, and friends as they co-construct the remembered past."[49] It is worth noting that autobiographical memory, which "helps to locate and define the self within an ongoing life story,"[50] seems to emerge late in the second year of life.[51] This co-construction, along with an enormous amount of mutual storytelling throughout childhood, educates the individual in "the norms, rules, and traditions that prevail in a given society, according to a society's implicit understandings of what counts as a tellable story, a tellable life."[52] George Rosenwald has pointed out that "[w]hen people tell life stories, they do so in accordance with the models of intelligibility specific to the culture."[53]

Or, in McAdams's words: "Life stories mirror the culture wherein the story is made and told. Stories live in culture."[54]

Narrative self-understanding continues to develop in adolescence and young adulthood as the individual uses newly acquired cognitive tools to begin constructing a life story, which knits together diverse elements of self-experience in a more or less coherent way, providing a sense of meaning and purpose. This process continues throughout adult life, particularly in the face of life stages or events that call for redefinition of the self, such as reaching midlife or divorce. These life stories are "psychological texts that are jointly crafted by the individual himself or herself and the culture within which the individual's life has meaning. Our autobiographical stories reflect who we are, and they also reflect the world in which we live."[55]

McAdams notes that narrative ideas have been applied in various areas within psychology, including developmental psychology, cognitive psychology, clinical and counseling psychology, and industrial-organizational psychology. While narrative may not have become the new root metaphor for psychology, as Theodore Sarbin[56] has suggested, many psychologists do seem "newly sensitized to the power of societal myths and cultural narratives in shaping human behavior in social contexts."[57] It is not necessary to take the position of George Howard,[58] who argues that stories are the dominant mode of human cognition and sociocultural interaction and that the paradigmatical mode is actually a subset of the narrative mode. For our purposes, it is sufficient to note that issues of personal and cultural meaning, identity, value, and morality are generally and most powerfully conveyed in narrative and that storytelling "is a fundamental human activity we all do."[59] The individual absorbs the narrative motifs (both structural and content-specific) from his culture, uses them to tell himself the story of his life, and influences the cultural trove of stories by telling his own story to others. The role of paradigmatical thought in this context is to serve as a sort of literary criticism, elucidating but never exhaustively cataloging the meanings and insights buried in the complex weave of individual and cultural narratives.

In discussing concepts of narrative and story in this context, it is important to be clear that we are not referring to the self-contained, highly structured, generally immutable pieces of contemporary literature. Our model is the sort of folk narratives that compose oral traditions. These narratives are interwoven, loosely structured, and very fluid. They change from telling to telling, both influencing the life experience of listeners and being influenced by the life experience of the storytellers. In this context, the emphasis is on the process of storytelling rather than on the finished product, and the stories and narratives are rarely if ever finished.

This more folklore-oriented view of narrative is consistent with the current understanding of the workings of memory. Recent research and theory suggest that memory is reconstructive. Snapshots of personal experiences are not stored, let alone videotapes. Rather, experiences are woven into an associational web, linked to many other elements of past experience. (There are some indications that this weaving is an important part of the brain's activity during sleep and dreaming.) When an event is remembered, it is actually reconstructed according to the person's understanding of its meaning, extrapolating from associations and editing the details (and sometimes larger elements as well) to fit. Memory is not fixed; the passage of time and repeated acts of remembering can alter memory of an event drastically. Therefore, it could be said that remembering is really storytelling. This applies to individual memory, but also to group and organizational memory.

Various researchers have noted several recurring motifs in personal and cultural narratives; for example, agency versus communion and redemption versus contamination.[60] We propose another: The stories humans tell as individuals and as cultures are often concerned with the complementarity and contradictions between our "drive for more" and our social embeddedness. We also note a crucial characteristic of the values carried in individual and cultural narratives: They often remain implicit in the narrative, and in some ways are more powerful for not being explicitly articulated and therefore subject to critical examination.

Pluralistic Corporate Cultures
"Corporate culture" is meant to capture the various dimensions of the ethos of a particular business firm. A recent term in the literature of organizational behavior, it is generally defined in communitarian terms. It is, for example, a "pattern of shared basic assumptions that the group learned as it solved its problems of external adaptation and internal integration, that has worked well enough to be considered valid and, therefore, to be taught to new members as the correct way to perceive, think and feel in relation to those problems."[61] Some aspects of a given corporate culture are

explicit, but others are communicated implicitly through stories and by example, and are often the more powerful for being the less visible.

Definitions are often tied to values. As one author has put it, "a cultural tradition emerges around values," where "a value is an enduring belief that a specific mode of conduct or end-state of existence is personally or socially preferable to an opposite or converse mode of conduct or end-state of existence."[62] Linda Trevino notes, "Culture also can provide the collective norms that guide behavior. . . . Collective norms about what is and what is not appropriate behavior are shared and are used to guide behavior. . . . These help individuals judge both what is right and who is responsible in a particular situation."[63]

A preferred culture would provide a balance between individual flourishing and community goals—the same balance sought by internal governance procedures. Organizational behavioralists have studied the congruence between individual characteristics and corporate cultures, and the hypothesis that satisfaction results from a harmonious relationship between the individual and the corporate culture has generally been supported. Following a careful empirical study, Charles O'Reilly, Jennifer Chatman, and David Caldwell conclude, "These results demonstrate that the fit between an individual's preference for a particular culture and the culture of the organization the person joins is related to commitment, satisfaction, and turnover."[64]

Concern about corporate culture is of a different dimension from concern about uniform moral standards and their governance. It must be initiated individually, a requirement well beyond corporate procedures. It can be envisioned in terms of the freedom of managerial decision making within hard and soft constraints. Hard constraints, as we have discussed, are those imposed on the enterprise by the external forces of product and financial markets, national regulatory regimes, global governance networks, and the expectations of society. The soft constraints are corporate policies and procedures, such as those intended to implement Principles 3 through 10 of the Global Compact. Within these guidelines, multinational managers need to be attentive to the good of the local people who are part of their particular business unit and to the common good of the communities of which these people are members. The behavior of good managers reflects a genuine, socially embedded concern for their colleagues.

Two examples taken from the Novartis case make this point. The first has to do with implementing Principles 1 and 2 of the Global Compact—those of unspecified human rights. The second example focuses on the critical issue of understanding cultural differences among the members of the enterprise community.

The case of pregnancy testing outlined in the Novartis experience (chapter 8) captures the tension between enterprise standards and local practices. The practice of undisclosed pregnancy testing of job applicants in the subcontracted plant in a free trade zone was common not only across the free trade zone, but across the respective country. Management of the subcontracted plant was clearly aware of human rights concerns and did not see this practice as a violation of a woman's human rights. In this case, senior Novartis management overruled the local practice.

The second example draws upon multinational management structures. The people within the firm come from different and often only partially articulated value sets based on their personal narrative consciousness and the culture in which they were nurtured. These values are then influenced by the business culture of their own country and, finally, by the culture of the individual multinational. Two distinct business cultures are the relational social market notions of continental Europe and the individualism of Anglo-American capitalism. In the Novartis experience, this distinction was underscored by the different attitudes toward the United Nations Global Compact among Swiss managers and their American counterparts (see, again, chapter 8).

Social Capital

"Social capital" is a technical way of analyzing social embeddedness and corporate culture in a business enterprise. The idea of social capital is that interpersonal relationships make a difference. It is "the advantage created by a person's location in a structure of relationships."[65] The use of this concept is an attempt to understand why some people flourish in an organization more than others, in that their interests are better served than those of others. In analyzing this difference, social capital must be distinguished from human capital. "The human capital explanation of the inequality is that the people who do better are more able individuals; they are more intelligent, more attractive, more articulate, more skilled. Social capital is the contextual complement to human capital in explaining advantage. Social capital explains how people do better because they are somehow better connected with other people."[66] There is a communal dimension to social capital. "At an intuitive level, social capital represents the resources that arise from relationships and that can accrue to either the individual or the collective. These assets can help individuals reach their own goals or assist members of the collective in working toward the common good."[67] Thus, social capital can provide value to the person as well as both intra-organizational and interorganizational benefits.

A key component of social capital is organizational trust. Organizational trust is "the cumulative willingness of members of a group to be vulnerable to the actions of that group, even if they do not know all the other members of the group and even if the actions of other members cannot be monitored or controlled."[68] Trust depends on both individual traits and organization structures; "the level of organizational trust within a community depends directly on the strength of the networks among its members, the degree of shared collectivist norms such as reciprocity and helpfulness, and the abilities of its members and the group itself."[69]

Social capital is based on the ideas of bonding and bridging.[70] One who bonds is following her natural tendency to seek out relationships with others like herself. Bonding is a powerful lens for viewing the firm as a community, since bonding is the most comfortable and therefore most common form of relationship.

A bridger is one who explores links to people unlike herself. These kinds of linkages are more difficult than those of bonding. Bridgers need to find a sense of comfort before they can reach out. Bridgers are of particular interest to students of multinational management. They are the ones most likely to reach across cultural gaps within the firm. A bridger would also be the one to reach beyond the boundaries of her own firm. When institutional boundaries become more porous as a function of globalization, the personal cross-institutional involvement can be expected to increase and effective bridging to become more important. In the multinational firm, the institutions being bridged can be quite different in terms of both their institutional and their social cultures. Chapter 4 stressed the difference between corporate cultures and those of NGOs, and the institutional risks of exposure on both sides.

This same bridging risk holds for a personal bridger. No institution or community is uniform in the personal attitudes (such as those of conservatives and liberals, on multiple dimensions) of its decision makers. As a person reaches out to someone in an institution identified with a different public position, such as a corporation or an NGO, he can incur a risk to his reputation within the firm. In the Novartis case, Kaspar Eigenmann described an example of a bridging relationship (see chapter 8) when a small group of participants from Ciba-Geigy and two scientific institutes initiated a series of informal discussion meetings, without telling their colleagues since they expected disapproval. This example underscores the exposure of cross-cultural dialogue. The corporate lesson here is that when senior management sets a policy with involvement across institutional boundaries, as in the case of management dialogue and collaboration with an NGO, those same senior managers must strive to support the individual bridgers.

Understanding the Culture of Another

Many different cultures are represented in the multinational community (the enterprise network) itself consisting of communities (business units). A moral corporate culture must be based on true understanding and acceptance of another person's cultural heritage. Such a movement beyond tolerance to appreciation requires a movement beyond intellectual understanding to empathy.

The theologian John Dunne offers a way toward this empathic understanding and acceptance, through his notion of "passing over." Starting with one's own most central concerns, one explores another person's life and beliefs in terms of how these concerns are addressed: "You find yourself able to pass over from the standpoint of your life to those of others, entering into a sympathetic understanding of them, finding resonances between their lives and your own, and coming back once again, enriched, to your own standpoint."[71] It is important to remember that this passing over is not the acceptance of another's belief system; it is passing over to her life experience, the story of her life, her narrative with all its embedded values, in an attempt to appreciate how certain central questions are addressed.

Much of Dunne's work rests on a belief in core human commonalities, among which is the centrality of death.[72] The great religions, each in unique ways, offer "insight into the common experiences of mankind"[73] and opportunities to experience an ineffable "peace that is spoken of in all the religions."[74] Dunne's "passing over" is not a form of spiritual tourism. It rests on the deep-seated awareness that the key issues in our own lives are unresolved, and the hope that another person's life or culture will offer us new insights into our own. Dunne understands that empathy is rooted in uncertainty; in order to truly appreciate another person's life experience, I must not be satisfied that my own perspective is the final word. Throughout his writings, Dunne argues for the assurance of faith rather than the certainty of dogma. This distinction may suggest both an avenue for transcultural cooperation within the multinational enterprise and a means of recognizing and encouraging the role of faith and virtue in the lives of individuals (and therefore of groups) without falling into the moral certitude that characterizes fundamentalism of all stripes.

Empathic understanding poses a deep communitarian challenge to our notions of management. Still, for a multinational enterprise, this kind of local appreciation must exist if local stakeholders are to flourish within the procedures of the enterprise network and if responsibilities such as those espoused in the first two principles of the United Nations Global Compact are to be implemented at the grassroots.

The rapid growth of the global business environment has demonstrated that we cannot predict the cultural clashes and ethical dilemmas that lie ahead.[75] The principled flexibility offered by a communitarian approach to business ethics may help us develop an ethic for the multinational enterprise that will promote both the flourishing of individual stakeholders and local communities, and the furtherance of the goals expressed in the Compact principles.

Pluralism and Relativism: One Last Time

The concern over uniform network standards and the uniqueness of local business-unit implementation, as well as the importance of cross-cultural understanding and dialogue, return us to the discussions of universalism versus relativism in chapters 5 and 6. For the network, corporate management struggles with this distinction in identifying global standards as the basis for strategically positioning the enterprise for long-term sustainability. From the grassroots, local management also faces this distinction in implementing those rules at the level of the local business unit.

Thomas Donaldson and Thomas Dunfee provide a careful, insightful structure within which the tensions between uniform global standards and unique community norms can be analyzed. They extend the notion of a social contract reflecting global social preferences as the basis of legitimacy for the multinational firm (see chapter 3) to the uniqueness of "micro" social contracts in local communities. Their approach is thus different from the narrow contractarian basis of the proceduralist models.

They define a dual base for ethical norms. One is a set of global hypernorms, which are valid across all cultures and communities. The other is a set of micronorms, which are valid within specific communities. The hypernorms, then, determine the moral free space within which each community can establish its own norms. This hierarchy and distinction are built upon what Donaldson and Dunfee term "integrated social contract theory" (ICST). ICST is an "attempt to find a middle course between ethical universality and cultural particularity."[76]

In Donaldson and Dunfee's conceptual structure, local communities generate their own ethical norms. To be "authentic," these norms must be "supported by the attitudes of a clear majority of the community as well as reflected in community behavior."[77] "Authentic ethical norms represent the consensus of the individuals who constitute a given organization or group on the propriety of particular behaviors. . . . An authentic ethical norm exists within a group or community whenever a substantial majority of membership holds the attitude that a particular behavior is right (wrong) and a substantial majority act consistently with that attitude."[78] These ethical norms are generated for their members through "extant" or "micro" social contracts.

Local community norms must, however, be within the boundaries of global hypernorms. These hypernorms reflect cross-cultural truths such as human rights.[79] Hypernorms define the moral free space within which local communities define their own norms. Authentic local norms must be within the requirements of the hypernorms if they are to be "legitimate."

Hypernorms transcend communities, creating obligations for all communities. "No matter how large, however, any community is capable only of generating authentic ethical norms, not hypernorms."[80] Hypernorms are based on macrosocial contracts that reflect hypothetical agreement among rational members of a community. Thus, while hypernorms transcend communities, authentic norms must be grounded in specific communities.

Hypernorms can be grouped into three distinct categories: procedural, structural, and substantive. Procedural norms are based on the rights of voice and of exit: the right to speak and to be heard, to participate fully in the life and decision making of the community; and the right to leave that commmunity either physically or by severing relationships. They are norms essential to the consent necessary for authentic microsocial contracts.[81] Structural hypernorms provide the foundation for political and social organizations. These principles "establish and support essential background institutions of society."[82] Donaldson and Dunfee describe structural hypernorms, such as the right to private property, to fair treatment under the law, or the condemnation of bribery, in terms of an "efficiency" hypernorm.[83] Substantive hypernorms specify fundamental conceptions of the good. These hypernorms represent the "convergence of human experience and intellectual thought."[84] They cover a broad range, from the promise-keeping of the contractarians to respect for human dignity as the foundation for human rights.

Structural hypernorms are based on macrosocial contracts at the level of the overall economic system, and procedural hypernorms are found within the macrosocial contract.[85] In contrast, substantive hypernorms are not part of the social contract. They exist outside these contracts.

Donaldson and Dunfee expend great efforts to clarify the foundation for their microsocial community norms and their hypernorms, and they tie the determinations of measured authentic, legitimate, local norms, as well as theoretical hypernorms, to individual management decisions. However, in both cases, they resist the temptation to define a preferred set of norms. For microsocial contracts, the emphasis is on how to make ICST useful in day-to-day decisions.[86] They cite eleven examples of authentic, legitimate norms among "millions of examples of norms like these."[87] Competing norm sets, arising from the uniqueness among communities, are a major concern. They consider various types of tensions: (1) within communities, which could arise from an individual's membership in multiple communities, or from the tension between individual and community goals; (2) the horizontal tension when two communities have competing microsocial norms, as could be the case for business units located in different cultural settings; and (3) tensions from vertical relationships when one community is subordinated to another larger or broader community, similar to the concept of nested communities.[88]

Stressing flexibility, Donaldson and Dunfee pose six rules of thumb to guide managers in resolving these tensions:

- Transactions solely within a single community, which do not have significant adverse effects on other humans or communities, should be governed by the host community's norms;
- Existing community norms indicating a preference for resolving conflicts of norms should be utilized, so long as they do not have significant adverse effects on other individuals or communities;
- The more extensive or more global the community that is the source of the norm, the greater the priority that should be given to the norm;
- Norms essential to the maintenance of the economic environment in which the transaction occurs should have priority over norms potentially damaging to that environment;
- Where multiple conflicting norms are involved, patterns of consistency among alternative norms provide a basis for prioritization;
- Well-defined norms should ordinarily have priority over more general, less precise norms.[89]

These provide insightful, but still general, guidance to the implementation of the United Nations Global Compact.

Donaldson and Dunfee are careful not to endorse any set of general principles as a specific basis for substantial hypernorms, in spite of the many calls for this list since their early published work on ICST. They regard the statement of a preferred set of hypernorms as a form of absolutism.[90] Instead, they note, "Most communities must, as a matter of moral necessity, find and articulate their own [substantial] hypernorms, using the concepts and linguistic terms that are right for them."[91]

They look primarily to uniformity among cultures as the source of commonality: "Rather, ethics is inevitably expressed in ways that are 'thick' with culture, tradition, and institutional significance. Thus limited, the claim for the existence for hypernorms becomes the claim for a significant area of overlap among local cultures. . . . Because hypernorms are by definition capable of gaining an overlapping consensus of reasonable religious, philosophical, and moral doctrines, then *if* they exist, we should hope to discover a real world convergence of religious, philosophical, and cultural beliefs."[92]

They explain their approach further:

While granting that a convergence of ethical views is likely, we do not take a position about whether hypernorms have a purely rational basis as Kant argues, or a partially empirical and historical basis as Hegel argues . . . instead, we propose to use the existence of the convergence of religious, cultural, and philosophical beliefs around certain core principles as an important *clue* to the identification of hypernorms. We proceed in this manner because, again, even if hypernorms are certified solely through the light of reason, we should expect to encounter patterns of the acceptance of hypernorms among people around the world. Hence, patterns of religious, cultural, and philosophical beliefs can serve as a clue, even if not as complete validation, for the identification of hypernorms.[93]

In short, Donaldson and Dunfee attempt to provide enterprise management with guidelines for specific decisions by emphasizing extant authentic, legitimate, community microsocial contracts as the primary sources of ethical norms and by looking to the commonality among community norms as the basis for generalization, informed by a thin set of reasoned hypernorms.[94] In their model we see perhaps the most promising current communitarian business model, and one which allows for the sort of crossing over and mutual self-discovery that is crucial to the successful management of the multinational business enterprise.

This chapter has argued that personal flourishing depends on our ability to embrace our need for social fulfillment over our inherent drive for more. This personal characteristic is also central to the achievement of worthy communal goals and to the contribution of a community to the common good. Faith, and organized religion to the extent it expresses and supports faith, support this ordering of personal characteristics. Therefore, we advocate the inclusion in the conversation of faith, religious traditions, and organized religious institutions as supporting both individual growth—through dominance of the sense of social embeddedness over the drive for more—and individual interaction—through nested, overlapping communities that seek the common good (with the exception, perhaps, of extreme fundamentalism).[95] The challenge for business management is to foster the sense of social embeddedness for the individual benefit of those associated with the enterprise, and to establish procedures that are compelling but not always compulsory in channeling personal energies toward appropriate goals without over-encouraging the personal drive for more.

This sense of balance between the individual and the community is captured in the responsibility of multinational management to ensure a set of uniform ethical norms across the local communities spanned by the organization, while, at the same time, ensuring the unique rights of people in each local business unit, extended where possible to their multiple communities. Principles of the United Nations Global Compact provide a guide to both the uniform requirements and the call for a response to diverse local needs beyond those uniform principles.

Creation of a corporate culture where local diversity is recognized and respected is a true challenge. Nothing short of a cultural "crossing over" will fully ensure this sensitivity yet maintain the balance with uniform enterprise ethical norms. Support of personal religious belief can be an asset in creating this kind of corporate culture. This means understanding and respecting the faith commitments that form the core of the various communities and cultures comprising the business enterprise community, particularly the diverse communities spanned by a multinational firm.

This chapter completes our sequence of steps addressing the values concerns of management, based on principles as distinct from rules. That sequence has been to strategically position the enterprise to ensure long-term sustainability in its rapidly changing economic, political, social, and cultural environment; to select a human rights standard as defined in the United Nations Global Compact; and to recognize the importance of a community culture in applying that standard within the organization.

This volume has addressed three questions: How has society changed its views on what it wants from the business enterprise and why? How does business, particularly the multinational enterprise, strategically position itself to meet these new demands? How, then, does the enterprise implement this strategy?

The underlying argument is straightforward:

- As a result of the technical revolution and availability of information, society is changing its views on what it wants from the artificial person (the corporation) that it has created.
- As national governments lose policy freedom and adaptable multinational enterprises gain power, the guide to corporate behavior must turn to principles as distinct from regulation.
- In order to ensure long-term corporate viability and prepare itself for the future, enterprise management must anticipate shifting social preferences now, in order to adopt a strategy and implement it.
- The most effective standard is a human rights stance, beginning with the Universal Declaration of Human Rights, which is framed for the business enterprise in the Principles of the United Nations Global Compact.
- To implement this strategy, the enterprise must adapt the United Nations Global Compact Principles in accordance with its own unique circumstances, and ensure that they are deeply implanted within the enterprise and its corporate culture in order to affect decisions at the level of the local business units.

This argument has drawn us into a thicket of issues at the levels of both theory and application. At the level of theory, the issues involve:

- Universalism and relativism
- Principles and rules
- Social values and individual morality
- Community and contract

At the level of application they involve:

- Enterprise-wide standards and local uniqueness
- Internal principles and external regulatory bodies as guides for the behavior of the business enterprise
- Sustainability and normative ethics as bases for managerial decision making
- The nature and character of the business enterprise as a nexus of contracts and as a nest of communities

The astute reader will have noticed that the boundary between these two levels has been porous throughout this volume. The experiences of firms and managers grappling with the issues have been the primary means of testing and refining our understanding of those issues. To paraphrase the Epistle of James, "Show me your theory without application, and I'll show you my theory alive in—and enlivened by—its application."

Many of the issues in application come into tight focus in relation to the multicultural character of the multinational enterprise. Because of this character, the tensions between hypernorms, expressed as network-wide standards, and local values can be acute. The same can be true for potential tensions between local business units or among individual members of the management team.

These are not simple challenges, and they do not have simple solutions. However, finding even the beginning of an answer often depends on how one frames the question. For example, the issues summarized above are given in pairs, as is customary, but the pairs are connected by "and" instead of "versus." This was done intentionally. "Universalism versus relativism" implies that the two are mutually exclusive and that there are no other choices. Neither of these implications is necessarily true. It may be that there are certain universal themes of human life that do not exist in some abstract realm but are only and always experienced in the living of individual human lives. If this is true, then the universal is always expressed through the individual (or relative) and is only known through reflection on that expression. By understanding the expressions better, we may come to a better (but never complete) understanding of these deeper themes.

And such reflection is best accomplished in dialogue with others. Whether it is through mutual storytelling, confidences between friends, or psychotherapy, interaction with someone whose viewpoint is different from our own provides us with greater insight into both ourselves and the human situation in general. This process of sharing perspectives, rooted in mutual openness and respect, begins with the assumption that neither of us has a claim on universal truth or ultimate principles and that both of us face similar challenges and core experiences in our lives.

Dunne's notion of crossing over is a particularly rich form of such dialogue, but all of us are capable of the sort of open interchange with others that is described above. Such dialogue across religious and cultural boundaries is essential to successfully carrying out the ideas discussed in this book. Openness to dialogue and openness to individuals and communities steeped in another culture or subculture are central to true respect for human rights in any political, economic, or social setting, especially for the multinational firm. Dialogue has been at the center of the Universal Declaration and the broad reach of its applications across the world. Within the firm, participation and dialogue are the keys to respecting the dignity of the persons in the enterprise community while achieving its goals.

ONE.   Global Integration: Its Driving Force and Pervasive Impact

1. For a history of the evolution of this technology, see Kurzweil, pp. 261–80.

2. Ibid., pp. 20, 27.

3. Ibid., p. 25.

4. Ibid., p. 4.

5. See *Computer Science: Reflections on the Field, Reflections from the Field.*

6. A high rate of change can be observed in other areas, such as biotech-nology, where researchers are beginning to understand the full role of RNA in a cell's operating system. The impact of these findings has been compared to the 1932 discovery of the neutron in physics. See "Biology's Big Bang."

7. Feinstein.

8. DiMaggio et al., p. 307.

9. T. L. Friedman 2005, p. 53.

10. Ibid., p. 56.

11. Ibid., pp. 61–63.

12. Ibid., p. 66.

13. Ibid., p. 80.

14. Ibid., p. 159.

15. "Internet World Stats: Usage and Population Statistics."

16. DiMaggio et al., p. 308.

17. "Web Server Survey."

18. This section is an update and extension of material from an article that appeared in the *Vanderbilt Journal of Transnational Law.* See Tavis, March 2002.

19. The term "multinational enterprise" is preferred to the more commonly used "multinational corporation" or the United Nation's "transnational enter-prise" even though all three terms refer to the same set of institutions. Since each business unit of a global firm is incorporated in the host country, making it a legal citizen of that county and subject to its laws, the word "enterprise" is in-tended to embrace a range of countries, cultures, and legal regimes. Multinational

is intended to indicate that most global companies are still anchored in a single country, although a growing number are becoming truly transnational in governance and management. Since "corporations" or "enterprises," "multinational" or "transnational," generally refer to business enterprises, the more general term "firm" includes financial institutions and service enterprises. At times, these terms will be used interchangeably, particularly when quoting other authors. In the discussions that follow the focus will be on the management of these institutions.

20. The flow in 2001 was $2.8 trillion, up from $2 trillion in 2000. See Longworth.

21. See Hummels, Ishii, and Yi. Vertical specialization includes three dimensions: "(1) A good must be produced in multiple sequential stages, (2) Two or more countries must specialize in some, but not all, stages and, (3) At least one stage must cross an international border more than once." For the purpose of measurement, economists would classify the first two conditions as outsourcing, while vertical specialization would include the third. See Yi, p. 56.

22. Krugman.

23. Keohane and Nye, Jr., p. 15.

24. Technological change is a key component of growth. "Cross-country studies suggest that technological change accounts for a large portion of differences in growth rates." *Human Development Report 2001*, p. 29.

25. Annan 2000.

26. These numbers are a purchasing power parity basis in constant 2005 prices.

27. Rodrik, p. 20.

28. Ibid.

29. "The Gini coefficient is the mean difference of income in the population. A Gini coefficient of one (1) would indicate the maximum possible degree of inequality, where one household had all of the income. A Gini of zero (0) would indicate that there is no inequality, that incomes were equally distributed. The World Gini coefficient was 65.9 in 1993, an increase on 62.5 in 1988 (intercountry comparisons based on purchasing power parity). The implied increase of about 0.7 Gini points per year is very high." Milanovic, p. 11.

30. Väyrynen, p. 235.

31. Leisinger 2008, p. 200.

32. Ibid., pp. 221–22. See also *The World Health Report 2005*, p. xiv.

33. *World Development Report 2006*, p. 2.

34. *The Millennium Development Goals Report 2007*, p. 4.

35. Comparative costs of living are based on purchasing power parity comparisons, not exchange rates. Thus, $1 is reasonably comparable country to

country. A dollar a day reflects desperate poverty. In August 2008 a World Bank Policy Research Working Paper analyzed the Purchasing Power Parity methodology and bias. It determined that the 2005 measurements were superior to the previously reported 1993 data and concluded that a more appropriate poverty line was $1.25 per day. It stated: "Extreme poverty—as judged by what 'poverty' means in the world's poorest countries—is found to be more extensive than previously estimated." The authors calculated that a full one-quarter of the population in the developing world (1.4 billion people) live in the destitution of $1.25 a day or less. They continued, "Yet the data also provide robust evidence of continually declining poverty incidence and depth since the early 1980s." In 1980 there were 1.9 billion poor people, representing half the developing-country population. See Chen and Ravallion, p. 1.

36. Leisinger 2008, p. 200.

37. *World Development Report 2000/2001*, p. 45.

38. Freedom House 1999, p. 1.

39. Ibid., p. 3.

40. Huntington 1991. For a general explanation of the third wave, see Freedom House 1999, pp. 34–46.

41. Huntington 1991, p. 17.

42. Ibid., pp. 18–21.

43. Michael Novak claims that "the natural logic of capitalism leads to democracy," but specific empirical linkages are elusive. See Novak, p. 362.

44. Black, pp. 517–18.

45. Ibid., pp. 518–19.

46. See, generally, Muravchik, which outlines the various tactics and organizations used to promote democracy.

47. Diamond 2008, p. 79.

48. Heydemann, p. 174.

49. Ajami, p. 142.

50. See Tavis 1997, pp. 133–40.

51. Ajami, p. 142.

52. Soroush, p. 45.

53. Diamond 2008, p. 74.

54. Lewis, p. 55.

55. Ibid., p. 57.

56. Ibid., p. 63.

57. Ibid., p. 54.

58. Ibid., p. 55.

59. Abu-Nimer, p. 256.

60. Soroush, p. 154.

61. Diamond 2008, p. 277.

62. Ibid. Diamond 2008 summarizes these surveys, pp. 34–36 and 277. "In 2005 Freedom House reported a five-year 'positive regional trajectory'—a phase that subsided with the political turmoil in Iraq and the unnerving election of Islamic Fundamentalists in the region" (p. 266).

63. In an efficient financial market, all participants have access to the same information. For democracies, the advantage of an increasing amount of readily available information, which should enhance political participation, may be offset by information overload and the related hectic pace of a life where citizens do not have time for the thought and reflection necessary for full participation (DiMaggio et al., p. 320). Note that the amount of new information electronically and in print nearly doubled between 1999 and 2002 (Levy, p. 6). Levy concludes "that living in an accelerating, information-saturated culture is taking its toll on us—on our bodies and psyches as well as our ability to govern ourselves with the wisdom and compassion of which we are capable (more, faster, better)" (p. 24). Unfortunately, in politics we do not have a profession analogous to that of the financial analyst, where the overwhelming amount of data related to governance can be assessed with objectivity.

64. Sen 1999, p. 58. Note that Sen's emphasis on freedom supports Lewis's concern that faith, not freedom, would be the necessary foundation of Islamic democratization (Lewis, p. 63).

65. Huntington 1991, pp. 115–16.

66. Freedom House 2006.

67. "When Freedom Stumbles," p. 63 (in a summary of the 2006 Freedom House report).

68. The Economist Intelligence Unit looks at sixty indicators in five broad categories to measure the texture of democracy. Classifications of the 165 independent states and two territories evaluated in 2006 by the Unit include "Full democracy (28), Flawed democracies (54), Hybrid regimes (30), Authoritarian (55)." See Kekic.

69. Diamond 2008, p. 64.

70. "Internet World Stats: Usage and Population Statistics."

71. DiMaggio et al., p. 312.

72. *Human Development Report 2001*, p. 40.

73. For a careful review of sociological studies of Internet use as of 2001, see DiMaggio et al.

74. Nordstrom and Ridderstrale, pp. 115–16.

75. DiMaggio et al., p. 319.

76. Kluth, p. 19.

77. Grossman, p. 44.

78. Poniewozik, pp. 63–64.

79. Grossman, p. 46.

80. Stein, p. 76.

81. See http://braintalk.blogs.com/brigadoon/2005/01/about_brigadoon.html.

82. Toyota has launched a virtual Scion car as a means of reaching Second Life users. Toyota opened a virtual office and sells and market-tests digital replicas of products. See Jana and McConnen, p. 17.

83. M. Hill.

84. See Glade. This is a narrower sense than the full anthropological definition that Harrison and Huntington describe as referring to the "entire way of life of a society: its values, practices, symbols, institutions, and human relationships." In their work *Culture Matters*, Harrison and Huntington also restrict their definition. "Hence we define culture in purely subjective terms as the values, attitudes, beliefs, orientations, and underlying assumptions prevalent among people in a society. See Harrison and Huntington, p. xv.

85. For numerous careful studies of cultures changing with modernization, see *Grassroots Development: Journal of the Inter-American Foundation*, http://www.iaf.gov.

86. French Minister of Culture Renaud Donnedieu de Vabres, as quoted in Riding.

87. *World Investment Report 2000*, p. xv.

88. Ibid.

89. Ohmae; Guéhenno.

90. "Indeed, in all the domains surveyed, it is evident that in key respects, many states, but most especially SIACS [states in advanced capitalistic societies] have become more active, although the form and modalities of this activism differ from those of previous eras." See Held et al., p. 436.

91. Slaughter, p. 200.

92. Väyrynen, p. 234.

93. Ibid., p. 243.

94. The loss of policy freedom exacerbates the problem for national regulation of an international institution. The control of the state is limited to the local operation of a multinational enterprise—the local business unit. The local unit can readily bypass governmental controls through its extensive connections with the multinational enterprise network. In strategic alliances, for example, the fluid horizontal relationships among competing firms change the nature of competition, making the antitrust dimension of regulation even more complex.

95. A 1997 estimate of the cost for developing countries to implement just four of the WTO agreements—customs, valuation, sanitary and phytosanitary measures, and intellectual property rights—was $140 million. See Rodrik, p. 5. In addition to these flows, resources must be held in reserve to support open-market policies. In Peru, for example, the foreign hard-currency reserves held

by the Central Bank are equal to about 1 percent of its annual gross domestic product. Ibid., p. 6.

96. Of course, in a world free of internal and external conflict, military budgets for most countries would be vast sources of funds for social programs. Diverting just 10 percent of sub-Saharan Africa's military spending in 1999 would have raised $700 million. See *Human Development Report 2001*, p. 6.

97. By governance, we mean the processes and institutions, both formal and informal, that guide and restrain the collective activities of a group. Government is the subset that acts with authority and creates formal obligations. Governance need not necessarily be conducted exclusively by governments and the international organizations to which they delegate authority. Private firms, associations of firms, nongovernmental organizations (NGOs), and associations of NGOs can form quasi-governing structures (Keohane and Nye, Jr., p. 12).

98. J. Johnson, p. 94.

99. Kline 1988, p. 27.

100. Held et al., p. 53.

101. Slaughter, pp. 204–14.

102. Ibid., pp. 214–18.

103. The code of conduct movement is substantial. For a collection of individual ethics statements—including credos, value statements, and codes of ethics or conduct—see Murphy 1995. For a comparison of the Johnson & Johnson aspirational statement and the Caterpillar Code of Conduct, see Tavis 1997, pp. 388–93.

104. Murphy 1998, p. 732.

105. Ibid., p. xiv.

106. For a summary of global codes, see Williams 2000, pp. 305–90. This volume includes copies of twenty-seven international codes.

107. Cavanagh, pp. 169, 172.

108. Ibid., p. 179.

109. Schilling, p. 234.

110. Ibid.

111. See Interfaith Center on Corporate Responsibility (ICCR), Press Release.

112. A smaller network, the initial Global Alliance for Workers and Communities, was an unusual combination of corporations such as Gap and Nike, a multilateral institution (The World Bank), universities such as St. John's and Penn State, cooperating organizations (Atma Jaya University Research Institute of Indonesia, the Center for Economic Studies and Applications in Vietnam, the Chalalongkom University Social Research Institute in Thailand), and others to survey workers and study working conditions in the apparel industry. For the successor organization to this initial effort, see http://www.theglobalalliance.org.

113. Fair Labor Association website, http://www.fairlabor.org.

114. Haufler, pp. 121, 129.

115. Ibid., p. 129.

116. Salter, p. 112.

117. Evans and Lindsay, p. 488.

118. Haufler, p. 127.

119. Ibid.

120. Ibid., p. 128.

121. Keohane and Nye, Jr., quoted in Tavis, March 2002, p. 492 n. 10.

122. Väyrynen, pp. 234–35.

TWO.   Responding to the Future

1. From Yeats's poem "The Second Coming."

2. This theory, developed by Richard Foster, is summarized by Beinhocker, p. 254.

3. Kurzweil, p. 106.

4. Bullis, pp. 26–30.

5. Kurzweil, pp. 35–106.

6. Joy, p. 8.

7. These data on nanotechnology are drawn from "Small Wonders: A Survey of Nanotechnology," p. 5.

8. See "NanoTech: Are Non-Materials Over-Hyped? Part 2."

9. See "Orion's Belter: The World's First Practical Quantum Computer is Unveiled," p. 81.

10. Ibid. The Orion computer was demonstrated in February 2007. Described as a 16-qubit processor, it must sit in a bath of liquid helium cooled to just a fraction of a degree above absolute zero (minus 273 degrees Centrigrade) to work.

11. See Pontin 2007a (April 8).

12. Kurzweil, p. 105.

13. For example, "a 26-year-old quadriplegic was hooked up to a computer via an implant smaller than an aspirin that sits on top of his brains and reads electrical currents. Using that technology, he learned how to move a cursor around a screen, play simple games, control a robotic arm." See Taylor.

14. Mankin.

15. Language translation, of course, is complex. Although translation was one of the earliest challenges to be addressed by computers, it has proven to be one of the most difficult. A word or phrase in one language may map onto multiple words or phrases in another, specific phrases have their own meanings, and punctuation is problematic. The process has moved from one based

on rules of grammar to the statistical analysis of previously translated texts selected as parallel texts. A recent approach is to "divine the statistical probabilities of words and phrases in one language ending up as particular words or phrases in another" (see Ratliff, p. 211). Still another approach relies on translating five-to-eight-word chunks from a dictionary that includes all of the possible conjugations and variations of each word. The Spanish-to-English dictionary, for example, is about twenty times the size of the standard Merriam-Webster (ibid., p. 212).

16. Kurzweil, p. 143.

17. Lohr, pp. 1, 8, 9.

18. Pontin 2007b (January 28).

19. Companies such as Intentional Software are working on an approach whereby their programmers collaborate closely with people working within an organization, who know what the programs should do, with the production of actual target codes automated. See ibid.

20. "Reinventing the Internet," p. 32.

21. Ibid.

22. Ibid.

23. See http://www.research.ibm.com/autonomic/overview. Last accessed March 28, 2009.

24. The extension from computer games to computer video games to virtualization can place us in whole different worlds. "Later in the 21st Century, as neural implant technologies become ubiquitous, we will be able to create and interact with virtual environments without having to enter a virtual reality booth. Your neural implants will provide the simulated sensory inputs of the virtual environment—and your virtual body—directly in your brain" (Kurzweil, p. 144).

25. See Dixon.

26. Joy.

27. "Splitting the Digital Difference," p. 3.

28. Valles-Bedregal.

29. Einhorn, Smith, and Edwards.

30. This is the Ndiyo Program. See "Splitting the Digital Difference," p. 4.

31. See "Splitting the Digital Difference." An example from India as reported in 2005 highlights the importance of access to PCs. The village of Embalan contains a "knowledge" center with five computers and a wireless connection to the Internet. Users come from the surrounding twenty-five villages. Students are the most frequent users. Through this center, the status of women has been enhanced. Local and global information is now readily available. Thus the center serves a social as well as a knowledge function. The great majority of the local Indian villagers, many of whom are illiterate, get their information from televi-

sion and loudspeakers atop the knowledge center, or from the center's newsletter. See "Behind the Digital Divide," p. 22.

32. "Gartner Says Emerging Markets Hold the Key to Future Telecoms."

33. "Economics Focus: Calling Across the Divide," p. 74.

34. "Gartner Says Emerging Markets Hold the Key to Future Telecoms."

35. "The Real Digital Divide," p. 11.

36. Ibid.

37. The World Bank, *Global Economic Prospects 2008.*

38. T. L. Friedman 2008, p. 31.

39. Lucas, pp. 17–18.

40. Baker and Green.

41. For example, in local Indian elections (Oberman), 2008 Malaysian national elections (Lucas, p. 18), and the aftermath of the 2009 Iranian elections.

42. Diamond 2008, p. 294.

43. See Markoff.

44. Mandel. Nanotechnology is particularly problematic, as a complex technology with a diversity of potential applications.

45. Feder. Following the Berkeley lead, regulatory attempts are being undertaken in other locations such as Cambridge, Massachusetts.

46. Caruso, p. 3.

47. A late 2006 patent application was for rights to a "minimal bacterial genome"—a synthetic bacterium consisting of 381 genes necessary to keep an organism alive. See "Artificial Life: Patent Pending," p. 92.

48. "Rio Declaration on Environment and Development," Article 15.

49. Termed the "precautionary approach," this is Principle 7 in the code, as discussed in chapter 7 of this volume. The application of the principle in a specific corporation is discussed in chapter 8.

50. As a percentage of global gross domestic capital formation, FDI inflows have increased from 2 percent in 1979 to an impressive 14 percent in 1999. In terms of production, the gross product of international production has grown from one-twentieth in 1982 to one-tenth of the GDP in 1999. Investment, acquisition, and production data are taken from *World Investment Report 2000*, pp. xv–xix. This report provides valuable information on these activities.

51. *Human Development Report 2007/2008*, p. 293.

52. *World Investment Report 2000*, pp. xv–xix.

53. Capaldo, Dobbs, and Suonio, pp. 8–9.

54. "Briefing: Emerging-Market Multinationals," pp. 62–64.

55. See Ghislanzoni, Penttinen, and Turnbull. Booze and Company stress the same need to be organizationally close to developing country action. They suggest a gateway approach. See Prahalad and Bhattacharyya.

56. Manyika, Roberts, and Sprague, p. 69.

57. Tavis 1997, p. 54–55.

58. Brunet.

59. For a discussion of joint ventures in Korea and Mexico and the relationships among the partners and with the governments, see Kim, p. 173; Jameson and Rivera, p. 204.

60. Kline 1991, p. 26.

61. Manyika, Roberts, and Sprague, p. 65.

62. "Tired of Globalisation."

63. The WTO is not a perfect agreement, as demonstrated in the difficulties of the Doha Round. Its rule-based system has been called fragile. The number of cases brought since its creation—three hundred cases involving the 150 members—is "staggering." The biggest offenders (also by far the largest trading partners) have been the United States and Europe. Whereas the most fundamental principle of the WTO is the most favored-nation principle, only nine of the 150 members follow it. See "The WTO: A 'Fragile' Body under Attack by Protectionist Policies in the U.S. and EU."

64. Following a long history of U.S. agricultural protectionism, the U.S. made a proposal in October 2005 to reduce the highest tariffs in agricultural goods—90 percent—and to reduce farm subsidies that were the most trade-distorting by 60 percent. See "World Trade Talks in the Rough," p. 77.

Europe has made progress in reducing agricultural subsidies. While only 2 percent of the European workforce are farmers, subsidies have been substantial, with 40 percent of the EU budget going to farming under the common agriculture policy. The EU support for agriculture has its roots in the concern for food security and rural poverty in the 1940s and 1950s, but today 80 percent of the support goes to the richest 20 percent of the farmers. Subsidies have been reduced. European farmers as of 2005 were paid about a third above world prices, down from 80 percent in the 1980s. Probably of greater importance is that the subsidy is now a direct single payment rather than in the form of higher prices for agricultural output, resulting in less trade distortion. See "Charlemagne: The Farmer's Friend," p. 58.

65. "In the Twilight of Doha." See also Castle and Landler; Einhorn and Srivastava.

66. "In the Twilight of Doha."

67. See Khanna.

68. "The WTO: A Fragile Body under Attack by Protectionist Policies in the U.S. and EU," p. 5.

69. See Jensen and Weston.

70. Gates.

71. See Baughn and Buchanan

72. Delacroix with Bornon.

73. Renaud Donnedieu de Vabres, the French Minister of Culture, quoted in Riding.

74. Woodward, p. 68.

75. Hamdi, p. 84. *Sharia* is the Islamic law of Sunni tradition. Also see Robin Wright, p. 64, who argues that resistance to political change is not necessarily a function of Islamic faith.

76. R. S. Appleby, p. 43.

77. Ibid., p. 44.

78. J. Johnson, p. 110.

79. Ibid., pp. 110–11.

80. R. S. Appleby, p. 44.

81. Wallensteen.

82. Ramadan, in an interview as quoted in Buruma.

83. Shachtman, Mackall, and Stevick.

THREE.   Assessing the Appropriate Role of the Enterprise

1. Every facet of the argument presented in this chapter has benefited from open debate in MBA and Executive MBA classes at the University of Notre Dame.

2. For a discussion of the nexus of contracts theory in finance as developed by Coase as well as Jensen and Meckling, see Tavis 2002, p. 529. See also M. Friedman 1970.

3. The managerial area of discretion is determined by external factors. For earlier discussions of this concept, see Tavis 1997, pp. 96, 105–7.

4. For an earlier statement of this distinction in terms of a "productivity/ social separation" principle, see Tavis 1982.

5. Hill and Jones.

6. Fort 2007, p. 136; Tavis 1997, p. 114.

7. Fort 2007, p. 15.

8. Ibid.

9. Berle and Means, p. 336.

10. Fort 2007, p. 138.

11. York, p. 2.

12. Wagner and Kaplan, p. 29.

13. York, p. 3.

14. The majority of this paragraph is taken from Tavis 1997, p. 116. Further, "The collaborative nature of the German economy is clearly evident in the governing structure of corporations. German industrial democracy is based on co-responsibility. As described by [Michael Albert, in his 1993 work, *Capitalism Against Capitalism*, p. 110]: 'In Germany, all parties are invited to participate

in company decision-making: Shareholders, employees, executives, and trade unions alike cooperate in a variety of ways to achieve a unique form of joint management.' There are two boards in all German firms of over 2,000 employees: a supervisory board and a board of directors. The supervisory board is the senior body with the assignment to oversee the activities of the board of directors. Representation on the supervisory boards is divided equally between owners and employees, although the chair is always a shareholder representative. The board of directors is a management board. Worker rights are also legislated in the form of works councils. It is mandated that management interact with the council in a broad range of decisions" (Tavis 1997, pp. 116–17). For an extension of the tension between Anglo-American and social market economies, see pp. 108–24.

15. Fort 2007, p. 134.

16. Ibid.

17. Ibid, p. 157.

18. Legitimacy can be seen as the third step in a sequence of transparency and accountability on the part of the firm, leading to a judgment of legitimacy on the part of society. For a discussion of this necessary sequence, see Tavis, March 2002, pp. 511–13. Sethi and Sama make this distinction between what they describe as "ethical business conduct as defined by legal norms" and conduct that involves "conform[ing] to and abid[ing] by the prevailing societal norms, traditions, and culture of the relevant environment" (p. 88).

19. Hasnas, p. 29.

20. Alford 2006.

21. See Campbell, pp. 7, 64.

22. Ibid., p. 123.

23. Edel, p. 1271. This notion of "values" has evolved over time. "In the last hundred years a *general theory of value* attempted to unify all normative fields from ethics and aesthetics to social and religious philosophy. Even when the general theory receded, its language and the way it formulated methodological issues remained standard for most of twentieth-century moral philosophy. Its influence dissipated only when use of the term 'value' becomes so commonplace as to lose all determinate significance" (p. 1269).

24. O'Rourke IV provides an analysis of the relationship between identity and reputation.

25. Hatch and Schultz, p. 19.

26. Fombrun, p. 277.

27. For procedures, see Fombrun, p. 91, and Merchi, p. 52. The value of these brands can be very large. As measured by *Business Week*'s international survey for 2005, the value of the Coca-Cola brand (the leader) was $68 billion, fol-

lowed by Microsoft at $60 billion and IBM at $53 billion. See "Top 100 Global Brands Scorecard."

28. For a careful study of reputational capital, see Roberts and Dowling. They define reputational capital as embracing both external and internal factors as outlined above. "Because reputation is valued in its own right, customers value associations and transactions with high-reputation firms. Because reputation also serves as a signal of the underlying quality of a firm's products and services, consumers may pay a premium for the offerings of high-reputation firms, at least in markets characterized by high levels of uncertainty" (p. 1079). They also note the role of reputation in leading potential consumers to accept advertising claims more favorably and in supporting new product introductions. With respect to the internal impact, they comment, "A firm with a good reputation may also possess a cost advantage because, *ceteris paribus*, employees prefer to work for high-reputation firms, and should therefore work harder, or for lower remuneration" (p. 1079). Their research, based on data from the annual *Fortune* report of "America's Most Admired Firms," "consistently suggests that superior-performing firms [based on financial performance] have a greater chance of sustaining superior performance over time if they also possess relatively good reputations." See also Fombrun, p. 6.

29. The *Fortune* list of "America's Most Admired Companies" is based on sample surveys of executives and outside directors of Fortune 1000 and Global 500 companies. The ten attributes of representation include "social responsibility to the community and the environment," along with the quality of corporate culture ("ability to attract and retain talented people, quality of management, and innovativeness"), "quality of products or services," and a series of financial performance measures. The surveys are conducted by the Hay Group. See *Fortune* "Most Admired Companies: FAQs," http://www.haygroup.com/ww/Expertise/index.asp?id=900.

30. Margolis and Walsh, p. 277. These general findings have been confirmed by another research review by Orlitzky et al. Reviewers have not been kind to these studies, finding numerous methodological concerns with many of them. Nevertheless, the uniformity in these conclusions based on different methodologies suggests a positive relationship. At least, there is little evidence suggesting that corporate social performance destroys value (Margolis and Walsh, p. 278).

31. Kielstra et al., p. 7.

32. A sampling of these organizations includes: CERES Principles, the Dow Jones Sustainability Index, FTSE4Good Index, International Organization for Standardization ISO14001 and ISO 26000, KLD Indices, and Social Accountability International SA8000. Specifically for the banking industry, the International Monetary Fund has issued the "Equator Principles" as a financial

industry benchmark for world banks providing funds to emerging market development projects.

33. Geczy, Stambaugh, and Levin, p. 2, quoting from "The Social Investment Forum."

34. See "Socially Responsible Investing."

35. The financial markets watch corporate social performance. See Geczy, Stambaugh, and Levin. In addition, skeptics continue to analyze social claims with care. See Loughran, McDonald, and Yun.

36. Eurosif, *European SRI Study 2008*. The total European SRI market is segmented into "core" and "broad" investors. Core investors follow screening strategies representing $710 billion. Broad investors (representing the other $3 trillion) are those who explicitly include SRI in their traditional financial analysis.

37. Figure 3.1 represents stakeholders in the first concentric ring. In this figure there is no distinction between external and internal stakeholders. The second concentric ring lists the institutions that represent the interests of these stakeholder groups. The power of each representing institution is changing with globalization. As noted earlier, shareholder and creditor power is increasing along with globalization and the information flowing to market participants. This holds, but to a lesser extent, for customers. Other institutions such as labor unions have proven to be less adaptable and are losing the power to represent their members. The third and fourth concentric rings represent governmental bodies as overarching stakeholders. Local governments can be crassly arbitrary and ineffective and, as noted, national regulators are losing their policy freedom. The final ring represents the global governance networks as outlined in chapter 1.

38. Tavis 2006.

39. The Ethical Trading Initiative is a London-based consortium of trade unions, NGOs, and major retailers and suppliers to United Kingdom markets established in 1998 to develop and implement fair labor practices throughout the supply chain.

40. In 2005, after two years of negotiations, Ethical Trade Initiative and FLA joined with four other activist groups and eight companies (including Nike, Patagonia, and Gap) to launch the Joint Initiative on Corporate Accountability and Workers' Rights, aimed at developing "a single set of labor standards and a common factory-inspection system . . . to replace today's overlapping hodgepodge of approaches with something that's easier and cheaper to use—and that might gain traction with more companies." Their initial pilot project was a thirty-month trial in several Turkish factories that supplied the companies involved (see Bernstein). The Turkey project was completed and a final report issued in December 2007. That report can be found at http://www.jo-in.org/english/resimler/080623_JO-IN_Final_Report.pdf.

41. For an analysis of the decision to produce and donate MECTIZAN, see Case 3 in Tavis 1997, pp. 244–75.

42. Costa 2006.

43. Costa 2008.

44. See http://www.accesstohivcare.org.

45. See http://www.pmtectdonations.org.

46. Concerned with the extensive criticism of drug prices, pharmaceutical companies have initiated discount policies for the estimated 45 million people in the United States who do not have health insurance, such as the Pfizer Helpful Answers (http://www.pfizerhelpfulanswers.com) or the Merck program (http://www.merchuninsured.com). Discounts in these kinds of programs range from 15 to 40 percent. Recipients of these programs do not need to meet age or income requirements.

47. As part of the Global Alliances to Eliminate Leprosy, Novartis donates at cost a multidrug therapy for treating a type of malaria, as described in chapter 8.

48. Focusing on healthcare delivery, Pfizer has launched the "Pfizer Global Health Fellows Program." Fellows are Pfizer personnel selected to work with NGOs on health needs (particularly for HIV/AIDS patients) in Africa, Asia, Eastern Europe, and Latin America on three-to-six-month assignments, while Pfizer continues salaries and pays expenses (http://www.pfizer.org).

49. Executives of Novartis (a Swiss pharmaceutical with a long history of interacting with NGOs, particularly in environmental issues) report that the window of open discussion with NGOs is far more effective before the issue becomes politicized. The period between the emergence of an issue and its politicalization can last up to six years. See chapter 8.

50. Management can easily be trapped in a no-win situation, caught in what *Business Week* labels the "culture wars." "While the experts debate the imponderables, CEOs are being caught by surprise in the cultural crossfire." See Greene and France, p. 91.

51. Wal-Mart also has developed a computer system second only to the Pentagon's. See "Special Report on Wal-Mart," pp. 9, 67–69.

52. Wal-Mart has attempted to bypass local planning committees and appeal directly to voters, although with mixed results. The company also faces "invisible picket lines" in the form of boycotts and obstruction for its anti-union stance (see "Special Report on Wal-Mart," p. 68). Prior to the 2005 annual meeting, institutional investors expressed a concern that the company's reputation over workplace issues was beginning to affect its share values (see "Wal-Mart Urged by Investors to Improve Its Reputation," p. 6).

53. See Barbaro and Gills.

54. Barbaro.

55. For a discussion of The Body Shop commitment, see "Our Values" at http://www.thebodyshop.com/bodyshop/values/index.jsp.

56. For a most informative analysis of the Energy Conversion Devices history and insight into the motives and determination of the founder, see Howard 2006.

57. See Whirlpool website: http://www.whirlpool.com/custserv/habitat.jsp.

58. Romig.

59. For a discussion of the contractual theories of the firm, see Tavis 2002. The idea of implicit contracts draws, in part, from social contract theory.

60. As reported earlier, see Coase as well as Jensen and Meckling.

61. Velasquez, pp. 122-24.

62. R. Anderson 2004 and 2005.

63. Interface, Inc. (August 31, 2004 press release).

64. R. Anderson 2004 and 2005.

65. Annas, p. 330.

66. Etzioni 2001.

67. Paine, p. 55.

68. Ibid., p. 140.

69. Chami, Cosimano, and Fullenkamp, p. 1718. In the same issue of *The Journal of Banking and Finance,* an article by Hausmann uses the term "reputational capital" to indicate the value of trustworthiness; see Hausmann.

70. Leisinger 2007a, p. 338 n. 10.

71. See Carroll, p. 275. The Committee for Economic Development is a nonprofit, nonpartisan public policy organization composed of senior corporate executives and university leaders formed in 1942.

72. Bowen, as quoted in Carroll, p. 282.

73. Epstein, as quoted in Carroll, p. 288.

74. Alford, Sena, and Shcherbinina, p. 10.

75. Crook.

76. The Crook four-way classification of CSR is analytically useful: good management (raise profits and advance the well-being of society at the same time); borrowed virtue (increase social welfare at the cost of profits); pernicious CSR (raise profits but reduce social welfare); delusional CSR (reduce profits and welfare). His distinction between good management and borrowed virtue roughly fits the boundary between ensuring sustainability and pursuing moral corporate behavior, as presented earlier, where his "good management" would be ensuring long-term enterprise sustainability.

Crook condemns managerial attempts to meet extra-legal social demands at the cost of profits. He discusses concern for sweatshop labor, classifying concerned corporate action as pernicious CSR where "emphasis is laid on responsible behavior toward workers and communities in developing countries" (p. 9).

Here, he creates a false dichotomy between investment flowing to developing countries and the issue of sweatshop labor. He misses the goal of remediation embedded in the apparel codes.

At one point, however, he does concede the possibility of paying attention to society: "In a way, this is to concede an important point to the advocates of CSR. Capitalism does function on top of, and in one way or another, is molded by prevailing popular opinion" (p. 10). Beyond that, Crook would reject a normative departure from the market model.

77. Franklin, p. 8.

78. For a summary of environmental issues, see Hunt, pp. 289–302.

79. Esty and Winston.

80. Enderle and Tavis.

81. See Earth System Research Laboratory Global Monitoring Division, NOAA Research, National Oceanic and Atmospheric Administration, http://www.esrl.noaa.gov/gmd/ccgg/trends/co2_data_mlo.html (accessed March 2009).

82. For a summary of data on greenhouse gas emissions and alternative energy sources, see *The McKinsey Quarterly*, no. 1, 2007. For an extended treatment, see Bressand et al. Another useful summary is "A Special Report on Business and Climate Change," pp. 1–30. A third comprehensive useful source is the *Human Development Report 2007/2008*. Finally, see "Intergovernmental Panel on Climate Change, Fourth Assessment Report, Climate Change 2007."

83. As an example, see Murray, who concludes: "Global warming is a natural and cyclic solar phenomenon with CO_2 being, at best, a piggyback amplifier," p. 4.

84. Bonini, Mendonca, and Oppenheim.

85. In preparation for the meeting, the Intergovernmental Panel on Climate Change issued its Fourth Assessment Report, which contained its strongest statement on the potentially devastating effects of global warming.

86. "Some Like It Cool," p. 10.

87. Brazil as of 2008 was the fourth largest global producer of greenhouse gases, most of which come from the massive deforestation in the Amazon—areas the size of New Jersey or larger are razed each year. As in the United States, the Brazilian effort to reduce such emissions is beginning at the level of the individual state. The state of Amazonas, the largest in Brazil, has announced a climate-change law with compensation for "environmental services." For more information, see Rohter. India is experiencing a major loss of the Himalayan ice pack. For more information, see Sengupta.

88. For an insightful review of Chinese environmental efforts, see T. L. Friedman 2008.

89. Burtraw, Palmer, and Kahn.

90. Broder.

91. T. L. Friedman 2008, p. 393.

92. *The Economist*, June 2, 2007, contained a special report on business and climate change. See "The Final Cut: Business Can Do It, with Governments' Help," pp. 28–30 in that section.

93. Harvey.

94. See http://www.chicagoclimatex.com.

95. Specific-use carbon-offset pricing mechanisms are emerging. Individual airplane travelers can now purchase carbon offsets that go toward planting trees or supporting renewable energy sources. See Tennesen. Or, see Native Energy (http://www.nativeenergy.com), the Conservation Fund (http://www .conservationfund.org/gezero), or Atmosfair (http://www.atmosfair.de).

96. As reported in 2007, 40 percent of CO_2 emissions are from energy production. In the United States 50 percent of this energy is produced from coal; in India it is 70 percent; in China, a whopping 80 percent comes from coal-fired plants. See "Dirty King Coal: Scrubbing Carbon from Coal-Fired Power Stations Is Possible but Pricey," p. 22.

97. Ibid., p. 24.

98. "Sunlit Uplands: Wind and Solar Power Are Flourishing, Thanks to Subsidies," p. 16.

99. See "The Final Cut: Business Can Do It, with Governments' Help," p. 30. For a graph of the global cost curve for various greenhouse gas abatement measures, see Bozon and Nyquist, pp. 38–39.

100. Mufson.

101. Fitzgerald; Pacala and Socolow.

102. Revkin.

103. Porter and Van Der Linde, pp. 128–29.

104. An example is the Scandinavian paper industry. With forward-looking regulation, Scandinavian companies developed a new market for chlorine-free paper and, based on innovative improvements in the production process, have become the producers of new pulping and bleaching equipment. See Porter and Van Der Linde, pp. 128–30. A broad example in the chemical industry is the expansion of Canada's Responsible Case Program, evolving into the Intergovernmental Forum on Chemical Safety, a global governance network as mentioned in chapter 1.

105. Hart, pp. 71–73.

106. For the results of this 2006 survey of 4,238 executive respondents from 116 countries, see "The McKinsey Global Survey of Business Executives: Business and Society." Also see Bonini, Mendonca, and Oppenheim.

107. "The McKinsey Global Survey of Business Executives: Business and Society 2006," p. 34.

108. Kielstra et al., p. 5.

109. Ibid., p. 14.

110. Ibid., p. 6

111. Ibid.

112. Ibid., p. 7.

113. Ibid., p. 8.

114. Finkelstein, Hambrick, and Cannella, Jr., report on a series of studies that rate U.S. industries by their managerial discretion. Industries such as computer programming, perfumes and cosmetics, and motion picture production were rated as having high discretion. Industries such as natural gas transmission, electric services, and water supply were rated as low discretion (pp. 29–30). Comparing studies over time, the authors see an expansion of managerial discretion: "It is also possible that macro-environmental factors have brought about a general expansion of managerial discretion in recent years. . . . Beyond the obvious trend of deregulation in many countries, more options simply exist on the organizational landscape. Companies can select unique combinations of businesses in which to be active; they can be fully active in a business or partly active through joint ventures or other alliances; they can select among myriad geographic locales for producing their products and still others for selling them; they can use full-time permanent employees or contingent temporary workers. In short, societal and economic trends, as well as organizational innovations, have expanded the choices for senior executives, perhaps well beyond what existed when Lieberson and O'Connor (1972) conducted their study that pointed to limited managerial effects" (p. 31).

115. The generous healthcare and pension benefits, job security, long vacations, and short workweeks of "Old Europe" will decrease. Although the process will be impeded by European workers, as demonstrated by the dramatic French and Dutch rejection of the Constitution for Europe in 2005 and the Irish veto in 2008, continuing global economic integration will drive down production costs. The technological edge maintained so long by German firms will become increasingly difficult to support. Although this trend is clearly forcing European firms to be more attentive to the productivity and efficiency dimensions of the basic market model, at the level of the firm other facets of the social market economy will persist: the representation of workers on the advisory boards will continue to be reflected in productivity; corporate/community retraining efforts will continue to provide worker flexibility; ownership structures will dampen the pressure for short-term performance beyond solvency; managerial involvement with NGOs will continue to provide a link to social expectations. For a detailed analysis of these forms of corporate governance, see Fort and Schipani; Monks and Minow; Tavis 2002.

116. A comment on the measurement of wealth is in order. The wealth measure needs to capture the full benefits minus costs of enterprise sustainability

commitments. In financial theory, wealth is based on cash flows projected for the life of the project, or to perpetuity in the case of dividends. Thus, the cash emphasis is long term. With the application of discount rates, however, the present value of distant cash flows can be low. In high-risk situations the present value of cash flows is reduced to the point where the cash returns from long-term strategic positioning become irrelevant (i.e., $100 to be received in ten years at a discount rate of 20 percent is worth just $16 today). Thus, when an alert management team is strategically positioning the enterprise today for long-term sustainability, a net present value measure may discount the downstream cash flows inappropriately.

As a financial measure of value, the price of a firm's stock should theoretically reflect the present value of the cash that will accrue to that share to perpetuity. As a practical measure, share price varies substantially and seldom captures the full impact of potential cash flows. The charge that the stock market is short-sighted appears to be correct. This is a widespread (almost unanimous) observation of executives. Academic empirical studies of this phenomenon encounter methodological and measurement problems (Abarbanell and Bernard). Experimental tests of professional traders suggest this is the case (Haigh and List).

Compared to this precise but flawed present-value measure, other metrics that capture the long-term results of today's strategic positioning are imprecise. Strategic positioning involves very long planning horizons. This fits the time frame of cash flow projections but not their present value. A metric that gives greater weight to longer-term strategies is necessary. Measures such as "the strategic management scorecard" have been proposed. Enderle and Tavis use the "balanced scorecard" as developed by Kaplan and Norton as a way of capturing the three-phase managerial process of strategic positioning, resource commitments, and assessment. In this process, the scorecard can assure that "the long term is firmly entrenched in all planning efforts" (Enderle and Tavis, p. 1141). In terms of an accurate, single measure of corporate wealth, however, there are still limitations. Jensen argues that the balanced scorecard contains the same flaw as pluri-objective stakeholder theory, with no way to keep score (see Jensen). To date, beyond Donaldson's rolling dividend theory, the risk-adjusted discount-rate problem persists (see Donaldson).

117. For a review of this history, see Tavis 1997.

118. "The Mensch of Malden Mills: CEO Aaron Feuerstein Puts Employees First."

119. See "Body Shop—Capitalism and Cocoa Butter," pp. 66–67.

120. Undaunted, Ovshinsky, an Abron investor group, and a longtime counselor, George Howard, began to produce the hydrogen storage and fuel cell technologies.

121. *Value Lines*, "Interface, Inc." Interface financial performance has consistently improved over the past decade with a dip in 2002 and 2003 reflecting the softening of the economy. Return on total capital reached 11 percent in 2007 and a robust return in equity of 19.5 percent. The demand for modular carpet is holding in the office market and expanding in nonoffice applications.

FOUR.   **Partnering with Nongovernmental Organizations**

1. The analysis and cases in the chapter are based on the conference "Peace Through Commerce: Partnership as the New Paradigm," held at the University of Notre Dame, Notre Dame, Indiana, November 12–13, 2006. Conference proceedings have been published in *Peace Through Commerce: Responsible Corporate Citizenship and the Ideals of the UN Global Compact*, edited by Oliver F. Williams, C.S.C. Much of the analysis in this chapter is drawn from chapter 20 in this volume, "Multinational Enterprises Interacting with Nongovernmental Organizations," by Lee A. Tavis.

2. M. Anderson.

3. For a concrete example of these policies and their local impact, see Tavis 1997, pp. 169–204, "Case 1, The Dolefil Operation in the Philippine Islands."

4. See Lowry 2008.

5. See Abdelnour et al.

6. Litow.

7. Newton and Bee.

8. Greenhut with Corcoran.

9. Eugenio.

10. Tavis 1997, pp. 60–93.

11. Leisinger 2004, p. 54.

12. Civil society is composed of all nongovernmental formal and informal organizations. In addition to the institutions generally recognized as nongovernmental organizations, civil society includes academic and public policy institutions, faith-based groups, and labor representatives, as well as individual companies and business associations. Business (companies and their associations) is generally separated as a distinct for-profit category from this milieu. In this volume, we use the term NGO broadly to include all of those institutions of civil society (except business) that interact with business and independent agents.

13. Reilly.

14. Commission on Global Governance, p. 254.

15. Fisher.

16. Keohane and Nye, Jr.

17. Anheier, Glasius, and Kaldor.

18. For a careful review of NGO accountability, see Ebrahim, p. 194; and Mayer.

19. Chisholm, p. 141.

20. Ebrahim, pp. 194–95.

21. Ibid., p. 198.

22. Mayer, p. 4.

23. Ibid., p. 10.

24. Malhotra.

25. Bishop, pp. 4, 5.

26. Ibid., p. 5.

27. An interesting early example of a social entrepreneurial bank is the ShoreBank of South Chicago. It describes its role as follows: "ShoreBank International Ltd. (SBI) delivers a broad range of financial services to financial institutions and their funders globally, dedicated to expanding access to capital for small businesses, entrepreneurs, and households. Within our core sectors of small business finance, microfinance, and housing finance SBI develops innovative solutions to catalyze the financing of entrepreneurial and housing investments around the world by working with interested finance institutions and by introducing independent platforms." For more information, see http://www.sasbk.com.

Another interesting example is the Business Planning Model Competition at the University of Notre Dame. The Sustainable Social Venture Competition combines entrepreneurship with a social mission or purpose, serving a "double or triple bottom line" by incorporating financial, social, and/or environmental sustainability. This competition puts a distinctively Notre Dame spin on entrepreneurship, pairing it with our history of social mission. Past winners include a unique housing solution for working families in underdeveloped countries, a company that mixes tourism in Cambodia with volunteerism, and a reseller of used books who supports literacy programs and provides environmental benefits. For additional information about Social Entrepreneurship or the Sustainable Venture Competition, contact Melissa Paulsen by e-mail at mpaulse1@nd.edu.

28. "INGO Accountability Charter."

29. Ebrahim, pp. 204–8.

30. Den Hond and De Bakker.

31. Ebrahim, pp. 204–8.

32. Den Hond and De Bakker.

33. Fort and Westermann-Behaylo.

34. Brak and Echard, p. 9.

35. Cavanagh et al.

36. T. L. Friedman, 2007.

37. Lederach, pp. 98–99.

38. M. Anderson, p. 131.

39. Lederach, p. 103.

40. For an example of business serving as a convenor in the Southern Philippines, see again Case 1 in Tavis 1997, pp. 169–204.

41. Scherrer.

42. Holloway.

43. Leisinger 2007b, p. 128.

44. Leisinger as quoted in Kumra, pp. 80–81.

45. Weber and Barrett.

46. Malan.

47. Guáqueta, p. 393.

48. Leisinger 2003, p. 125.

49. See Lowry 2006.

50. World Economic Forum, p. 40.

51. See O'Neill.

52. Scherrer, p. 277.

53. Guáqueta, p. 397.

54. Leisinger 2009b, p. 23.

55. Leisinger 2007a, p. 333.

FIVE.   **The Nature of Human Rights**

1. Haakonssen, p. 885.

2. Weinreb, p. 278.

3. Haakonssen, p. 886; Weinreb, p. 278.

4. Rubenstein.

5. Velasquez and Brady, pp. 88–89.

6. Ibid., p. 88.

7. Weinreb, pp. 278–79.

8. Campbell, p. 59.

9. Hollenbach 1994a, quoting Locke, p. 131.

10. M. Perry 1998, p. 130.

11. Rawls 1971, p. 302.

12. This is the same as assigning preemptive weights in a goal programming objective function.

13. Campbell, p. 66.

14. Hollenbach 1994a, p. 131.

15. See Fortin, pp. 37–38; also quoted by Hollenbach 1994a, p. 127.

16. Steinfels, p. 19.

17. Ibid.

18. Ibid., p. 21.

19. Hollenbach 1994a, p. 127.

20. Monsignor Franco Biffi has identified this period of human rights history—the papacies of Leo XIII through Pius XII—as the "Phase of Discernment." From notes by S. Cornish in the authors' possession, on unpublished writings of Biffi.

21. Adequately summarizing this rich tradition in a few pages is impossible. Nevertheless, a brief review is a necessary step in understanding the uniqueness of human rights teachings as part of the Catholic social tradition. This summary closely follows that of Hollenbach 1979.

22. Quote from *Rerum Novarum,* in Hollenbach 1979, p. 47.

23. Cornish, p. 2.

24. Pius XII, 1951 Christmas address, in Hollenbach 1979, p. 58.

25. Pius XII, 1952 Christmas address, in ibid.

26. Hollenbach 1979, p. 41.

27. Cornish, p. 2.

28. Glendon 2001, p. 132.

29. René Cassin, *La Pensée et l'Action* (Boulogne-sur-Seine: F. Lalou, 1972), p. 152, as reported in Glendon 2001, p. 132.

30. Cornish, p. 2.

31. Christiansen et al., as quoted in Hollenbach 1979, p. 98.

32. Hollenbach 1979, p. 75.

33. Elshtain, p. 156.

34. Hollenbach 1994b, p. 328.

35. Elshtain, p. 160, with quotations from Cahill. Michael Perry would add that "rights-talk is also a way of talking about duties and obligations from the side of the beneficiary of the duty." M. Perry 1990, p. 186.

36. These extremes and intermediate points on the spectrum are articulated by Donaldson and Dunfee, p. 23.

37. Rawls was careful not to say in his *Theory of Justice* that he was making universal claims. Hollenbach 1994a, however, argues that the approach of both Kant and Rawls was universalistic, p. 134.

38. Campbell, p. 63.

39. Elshtain, p. 154.

40. M. Perry 1998, p. 68.

41. Ibid., p. 65.

42. Ibid.

43. Ibid., p. 67.

44. Pope John Paul II, *Veritatis Splendor,* as quoted in M. Perry 1998, p. 57.

45. Brems, p. 9.

46. Sen 1997, p. 33.

47. Ibid., p. 39.

48. Brems, p. 9.

49. Statement delivered on Saturday, 18 October 1997, to the Communications Conference at the Aspen Institute, Colorado, United Nations Press Release SG/SM/6366, 20 October 1997. Quoted by Brems, p. 10.

50. M. Perry 1998, p. 75. See Marty, who proposes an approach to cultural dialogue and acceptance in terms of "hospitality."

51. MacIntyre 1988, p. 354.

52. MacIntyre 1981, p. 67, as quoted in Hollenbach 1994a, p. 129.

53. Terms taken from Hollenbach 1994a, p. 143.

54. M. Perry 1998, pp. 82, 86.

55. Velasquez and Brady, pp. 88–89, referring to Aquinas, *Summa Theologiae*, I-II, q. 94, a. 4.

56. Aquinas, *Summa Theologiae*, I-II, q. 94, a. 4, quoted by Velasquez and Brady, p. 103 n. 29. Velasquez and Brady comment: "Aquinas remarks, for example, that norms that pertain to temperance—i.e., to the regulation of the desires and pleasures of sense—are not universally binding 'because the practice of temperance varies according to different times . . . and according to different human laws and customs.' Aquinas, *Summa Theologiae*, II-II, q. 170, a. 1, obj. 3. In a passage that was almost universally ignored, *Summa Theologiae*, II-II, q. 57, a. 2, Aquinas argues, also, that 'man's nature is changeable, wherefore that which is natural to man may sometimes fail.' Consequently, in *Summa Theologiae* [I-II], q. 94 a. 4 and a. 5, Aquinas notes that the derivative precepts of natural law can change" (p. 104 n. 30).

SIX.   The Universal Declaration of Human Rights

1. For an interesting discussion of this period in the history of the United Nations, with rich analyses of the people and the debates, including the impressive role of Eleanor Roosevelt, see Glendon 2001.

2. Ibid., p. 6.

3. See U.N. Charter Preamble § Article 55 (c). Cf. Article 1 (3), as quoted in Brems, p. 20.

4. Glendon 2001, p. 32.

5. Ibid., p. 31.

6. Ibid., p. 186.

7. Glendon 1998, p. 24.

8. Glendon 2001, p. 153.

9. Ibid., p. 154.

10. Ibid., p. 169.

11. Ibid., p. 162.

12. Honduras and Yemen had no representatives present.

13. Glendon 2001, p. 170.

14. See Agi; this classification is drawn from René Cassin. Or see Glendon 2001, p. 172.

15. Glendon 2001, p. 180.

16. Ibid., p. 182.

17. Ibid., p. 184.

18. Ibid., p. 186.

19. For an analysis of this requirement in the global apparel industry, see Tavis 2006.

20. Glendon 2001, p. 190.

21. Brems, pp. 20–21.

22. American Anthropological Association, "Statement on Human Rights," *American Anthropologist* 49, no. 4 (1947): 539–43, reprinted in Morton E. Winston, ed., *The Philosophy of Human Rights* (1989), pp. 116–20, as quoted in Brems, p. 24.

23. Glendon 2001, p. 225.

24. Glendon 2001 describes Pen-chun Chang as a Renaissance man, ibid., p. 33.

25. Ibid., p. 225.

26. *The International System of Human Rights*, Université d'été des droits de l'homme Genéve, Switzerland, http://www.aidh.org/uni/Formation/02Les Pactes_a.htm (accessed April 2, 2009).

27. *United Nations Treaty Collection: Multilateral Treaties Deposited with the Secretary General: Status of Treaties*, http://treaties.un.org/Pages/Participation Status.aspx (accessed April 3, 2009). Note that Russia has signed and ratified both covenants. The United States has signed but not ratified the Covenant on Economic, Social and Cultural Rights. The U.S. has ratified the Covenant on Civil and Political Rights with a declaration that it is not self-executing, which many view as nullifying the ratification. See, for example, Human Rights Committee, General Comment 24 (52), General comment on issues relating to reservations made upon ratification or accession to the Covenant or the Optional Protocols thereto, or in relation to declarations under article 41 of the Covenant, U.N. Doc. CCPR/C/21/Rev.1/Add.6 (1994); Concluding Observations of the Human Rights Comm.: United States of America, U.N. Doc. no. CCPR/C/USA/CO/3/Rev.1, para. 10 (2006), available at http://tb.ohchr.org/default.aspx?country=us.

28. Brems, p. 22.

29. Ibid., p. 11.

30. Among these groups in the United States are the Jesuit Center of Concern and Catholic Relief Services, the latter more focused on action than influencing policy.

31. See, for example, Malkin.

32. Brems, p. 27.

33. Brems's analysis is of a different kind from that of Sen 1997, described in chapter 5. Sen analyzes the religious belief systems of Asian cultures, whereas Brems looks only at documents.

34. Ibid., p. 292.

35. Ibid., p. 291.

36. Ibid., p. 293.

37. Ibid., p. 290.

38. John P. Humphrey, "The Revolution in the International Law of Human Rights," *Human Rights* 4 (1975): 207–8, as quoted in Hollenbach 1979, p. 30.

SEVEN.   The United Nations Global Compact

1. Annan 1999.

2. Annan 2002.

3. See chapter 10 for a discussion of hypernorms as defined by Donaldson and Dunfee.

4. This section follows the arguments made by the author in Tavis 2004.

5. Shue, p. 55.

6. Ibid., p. 61.

7. Ibid., p. 63.

8. Tavis 2006, p. 344.

9. Ibid.

10. United Nations Global Compact, Appendix IX, p. 237.

11. Ibid., p. 241.

12. For a discussion of the distinction between prevention and precaution, see the interview with Kaspar Eigenmann, Head, Corporate Health, Safety, and Environment, Novartis International AG, in chapter 8 of this volume.

13. United Nations Global Compact, Appendix IX, p. 242.

14. Ibid., p. 244. These requirements are in concert with the environmental opportunities and responsibility discussed in chapter 3.

15. United Nations Global Compact, http://www.unglobalcompact.org/anti-corruption.

16. Ibid.

17. As of June 2009, 923 companies had been removed from the list of participants for failure to communicate progress. United Nations Global Compact, http://www.unglobalcompact.org.

18. Kline 1985, pp. 21–22, 59–70.

19. Sethi 2000, p. 120.

20. For a partial list of projects between U.N. agencies and the private sector, see Sethi 2003, p. 13.

21. Sethi 2003, p. 116.

22. Cassel and O'Brien, p. 84.

23. Ibid., p. 87.

24. Ruggie.

25. Leisinger 2009a, p. 181. See this essay for an insightful analysis of the Ruggie report from a business perspective within an overall view of rights and responsibilities for human rights.

26. Ruggie, para. 24, p. 9.

27. Ibid, para. 69, p. 20.

28. For the text of the first letter, addressed to Kofi Annan, July 20, 2000, and of the second letter dated only five days later, July 25, 2000, see Sethi 2003, pp. 126–32.

29. Ibid., p. 127.

30. Ibid.

31. Ibid., p. 116.

32. Panel on Corporate Accountability held at the United Nations, February 15, 2001, under the headline "Global Compact with Corporations: "Civil Society Responds," as reported in Sethi 2003, p. 118.

33. http://www.unglobalcompact.org/ParticipantsAndStakeholders/index .html.

34. Tesner and Kell, p. 53.

35. A more specific response is the Citizens Compact, formed by more than seventy NGO and environmental groups. "It lays out a foundation for cooperation between the U.N. and nonbusiness, nongovernmental groups to work toward building better relationship between the U.N. and business, emphasizing the need for monitoring and enforcing a legal framework for corporate behavior." Bruno and Karliner, as quoted by Sethi 2003, p. 119.

36. Examples of successful monitoring exist in the apparel industry. As noted in chapters 2 and 3, the Fair Labor Association along with a number of monitoring organizations is currently conducting extensive global monitoring in the apparel industry at a modest cost per plant visit. The International Center on Corporate Advocacy conducts more in-depth investigations of apparel plants at a much higher cost. In both cases, the monitoring and verification is limited to a specific component of corporate operations.

37. For a comparison of financial reporting and the Global Reporting Initiative, see Enderle, pp. 87–99.

38. http://www.globalreporting.org/aboutGRI.

39. http://en.wikipedia.org/wiki/Global_Reporting_Initiative.   Accessed March 3, 2009.

40. http://www.globalreporting.org/Current Priorities/UNGC.

41. Sherwood, p. 14.

42. http://www.unglobalcompact.org.

43. A recent lawsuit (2003) against Nike supports the concern about litigation. An activist, Mac Kasky, sued Nike over its public statements that the workers in its subcontracted plants (Nike owns none of its own production facilities) were being treated fairly. Kasky claimed the statements were "commercial speech" and therefore subject to factual test, and that they were false. Nike argued that the statements were part of Nike's First Amendment rights to free speech. The California Supreme Court held in favor of Mac Kasky. Nike settled out of court by agreeing to pay $1.5 million to the Fair Labor Association. Ironically, the issue of whether Nike claims were correct was never tested in court.

44. Williams 2004, p. 17.

45. See chapter 8.

46. http://www.unglobalcompact.org.

47. For a careful analysis of these networks, see "New Report: Local Networks Gaining Strength and Impact."

48. For examples of local response, see Case 1, "The Dolefil Operation in the Philippine Islands," and Case 5, "Subcontracting Industrial Components in Mexico," in Tavis 1997.

49. Ghislanzoni, Penttinen, and Turnbull, pp. 78–79.

50. Williams 2004, p. 21.

EIGHT.   **Implementing the Global Compact at Novartis**

1. The first part of this chapter is a slight revision of "Novartis and the U.N. Global Compact Initiative" by Lee A. Tavis. The report has been published in the *Vanderbilt Journal of Transnational Law* and is one of three initially published by the United Nations Global Compact Learning Forum.

2. Novartis, *Only One Company, Novartis Operational Review 1996*.

3. Langreth.

4. Harris and Fuhrmans.

5. Vasella.

6. Novartis Policy on Corporate Citizenship, p. 1.

7. Ibid., p. 2.

8. Novartis Foundation for Sustainable Development.

9. Ibid., see "Dare to Dialogue."

10. Novartis Policy on Corporate Citizenship, p. 2.

11. Wynhoven.

12. Novartis Code of Conduct, section 6, "Bribes, Business Entertainment, Gifts."

13. Guideline 3 was revised in January 2008 with emphasis on what can be construed as marketing payments or through intermediaries. It is supported by the Novartis Pharma Promotional Practices Policy and Guidelines of December 2002, and the Novartis Conflict of Interest policy of January 2007.

14. In response to growing awareness of the importance of the cultural, economic, and social dimensions of human rights, an amended version of Guideline 4 was issued in November 2003.

15. Of the more than 2 billion (US$) that Novartis budgets annually for research and development, about one-third is allocated to collaboration with other research centers. This share, in the upper range for pharmaceutical companies, is deemed necessary in order to keep the three hundred scientists at Novartis in close contact with the many drug discovery networks of interest to the firm. The importance of discovery networks is underscored in the history of the Novartis drug Gleevec, summarized in the next section.

16. The official name of the drug is Gleevec in the United States and Glivec in the rest of the world. Before April 2001 it was referred to as STI571, a term still in use.

17. Druker.

18. Rowland.

19. For information on the Novartis implementation of the U.N. Global Compact, see Novartis and the U.N. Global Compact.

20. *Novartis Annual Report 2007: Caring and Curing*, pp. 89–95.

21. Ibid., p. 91.

22. Novartis GRI Report 2006, pp. 14, 29.

23. Kumra, p. 82.

24. *Novartis Annual Report 2007: Caring and Curing*, p. 97.

25. Ibid., p. 81.

26. Ibid.

27. Ibid., p. 75.

28. Ibid., p. 77.

29. Quoted in Brokatzky-Geiger, Sapru, and Streib, p. 1.

30. Ibid.

31. Vasella, as quoted in Kielstra et al., p. 8.

32. This is the same approach used by the University of Notre Dame Anti-Sweatshop Task Force in evaluating apparel suppliers.

33. Brokatzky-Geiger, Sapru, and Streib, p. 6.

34. Ibid., p. 8.

35. Novartis GRI Report 2006, p. 80; Novartis UNGC Communication on Progress 2007, 2008.

36. Inclusion of the supply chain under the corporate social responsibility umbrella has been described as "the next tidal wave in CSR." See Tesler.

37. *Novartis Annual Report 2007: Caring and Curing*, p. 36.

38. Novartis Third Party Code of Conduct, p. 4, available at http://www .corporatecitizenship.novartis.com/business-conduct/business-practice/third -party-management/third-party-code.

39. Novartis, "Chain Reaction: Business Ethics Shouldn't Stop at the Company's Own Gates."

40. Intertek offers a remarkably broad range of analytical and laboratory services across a broad industrial spectrum. In the pharmaceutical industry its labs provide regulatory accreditations as well as auditing and valuation services. See http://www.intertek.com.

41. Kumra, pp. 82–83. Novartis is working with the Danish Institute for Human Rights in its human rights assessment. The DIHR is a broad-based institute of the Danish government. Its Human Rights and Business Project strives to combine the expertise of the human rights research community with the experience of business in order to develop concrete achievable human rights standards for companies, and to help companies live up to those standards in practice through training and advisory services. See http://www.humanrights-business.org. DIHR has developed two reports to assist companies in assessing their local operations:

(1) Country Risk Assessment. "The objective of the CRA report is to determine areas where companies are at risk of human rights violations—both direct and indirect—due to ineffective laws or poor practices in the country of operation. The CRA is based on the Universal Declaration of Human Rights (UNDR) and examines each human right from a corporate perspective."

(2) The Human Rights Compliance Assessment. This has been under development since 1999. It is "a diagnostic tool designed to help companies detect potential human rights violations caused by the effect of their operations on employees, local residents, and all other stakeholders."

These are exhaustive documents worth reading for anyone interested in the human rights nuances of local business operations.

42. These efforts undertaken by Novartis operation units draw on a long company history beginning with the Ciba-Geigy (one of the two companies merged to form Novartis) Foundation in 1979.

43. The detail of these local outreach efforts is available at http://www .corporatecitizenship.novartis.com/citizenship-in-action/case-studies.

44. The Brazilian effort draws on an enterprise-wide diversity program guided by an independent body of experts—the Diversity and Inclusion Advisory Council. See *Novartis Annual Report 2007: Caring and Curing*, p. 82.

NINE.   The Individual in the Organization

1. The following section "In Psychology" is taken from Timothy M. Tavis and Lee A. Tavis, "The Person, the Market, and the Community," in *The Invisible Hand and the Common Good*, ed. Bernard Hodgson (Berlin: Springer-Verlag, 2004), pp. 303–8.

2. Adler 1930, p. 398.

3. See Rieff for an excellent critique.

4. For example, see Becker.

5. See Eagle for a review.

6. Adler 1956.

7. Rogers.

8. Maslow 1973.

9. Pavlov.

10. See Skinner.

11. See, for example, Sasmor.

12. Dawkins.

13. Carnegie Hero Fund Commission, http://www.carnegiehero.org/hero fund.php.

14. See "Carnegie Medals Awarded to 19 for Extraordinary Civilian Heroism," 2008.

15. Progoff, p. 55.

16. Adler 1956, p. 128.

17. Lorenz.

18. Sternglanz, Gray, and Murakami.

19. Balbernie, p. 237.

20. See Johnson and Morton; Easterbrook et al.

21. Trevarthen, p. 97.

22. Balbernie, p. 237.

23. Trevarthen and Aitken, p. 21.

24. See Balbernie; Eliot; Seigel 1999 and 2001; and Schore for detailed discussions of the processes involved.

25. Bownds, p. 158.

26. Balbernie; see also Seigel 2001; Glaser; Karr-Morse and Wiley; Nelson and Bosquet; and B. Perry.

27. Robert Wright, p. 27.

28. Trevarthen, p. 99.
29. Dunbar; Whiten.
30. Zimmer, p. 272.
31. Sullivan, p. 173.
32. Solomon, p. 194.
33. Ibid., p. 158.
34. Ibid., p. 192.
35. Ibid., p. 194.
36. Maritain, p. 27. Emphasis in original.
37. Ibid., p. 28.
38. Ibid., p. 30.
39. Ibid., p. 33.
40. Markus, p. 252.
41. See http://www.accesstoinsight.org.
42. See http://www.buddhamind.info.
43. Pandit, pp. 138–39.
44. Chuanshu.
45. Li.
46. Chan.
47. Groups looking for common threads across religious beliefs have found substantial commonality. For instance, between 1989 and 1994 a group of distinguished Christians, Muslims, and Jews gathered to address their concerns over morality in business. The commonality they found related to our interactions with one another. Four principles occur in the literature of the faiths.

- Justice: "All three faiths agree that God created the world and that justice must characterize the relationship between its inhabitants."
- Mutual Love: "What scripture expresses as love is here rendered as mutual respect or reciprocal regard—love thy neighbor as thyself—that exists between two individuals."
- Stewardship: "The scriptures testify to the beauties and wonders of nature as signs of God's goodness and providence. Man is set over it all with delegated responsibility. . . ."
- Honesty: "It incorporates the concepts of truthfulness and reliability and covers all aspects of relationships in human life—thought, word, and action."

The Interfaith Declaration can be accessed at http://www.banyansociety.org/commmoral/morcodebus/interfaithstatement.html. An extended statement is available in Webley, pp. 96–108.

48. See Adam Smith, *Wealth of Nations*, Bibliomania.com 2000.

49. Bruni and Sugden, p. 2.

50. Ibid., p. 12.

51. For a most informative comparison of the work of Genovesi with Adam Smith, see Bruni and Sugden.

TEN.   **The Person and the Enterprise: Management Models**

1. Audi 2000a, p. 19.

2. De George, p. 34.

3. Ibid., p. 40.

4. Storme; Gordley.

5. Maritain, p. 47.

6. Audi 2000a, p. 19.

7. Ibid., p. 20.

8. Alford and Naughton, p. 59

9. Tavis and Tavis.

10. Etzioni 1988, p. 10.

11. Ibid., p. 4.

12. This section is related to the discussion of social values in chapter 3.

13. Etzioni 1988, p. 7.

14. Ibid., p. 8.

15. Neuhaus, p. 90.

16. Conkle, p. 318. (The authors are reminded of a bumper sticker—"God said it, I believe it, that settles it.")

17. Ibid.

18. Audi 2000b, p. 83.

19. See Pope John Paul II, *Fides et Ratio.*

20. Richardson, p. 46.

21. Etzioni 1996, p. 191.

22. Ibid., pp. 203–5.

23. Ibid., p. 5.

24. Ibid., p. 205.

25. Richardson, p. 47.

26. See Figure 3.1.

27. Richardson, p. 46.

28. Etzioni 1999, p. 5.

29. Carozza 2003, p. 38.

30. Maritain, p. 39.

31. Ibid., p. 41.

32. Ibid., p. 43.

33. Ibid., p. 44. The specific application of Maritain's views on the common good and the person to the issue of principles-based network standards versus the grassroots application within the local business unit is a conceptual step. Most of the discussion of Maritain's distinction has been focused on the role of the state. For an insightful treatment of Maritain's *The Person and the Common Good*, see McInerny.

34. See Carozza 2006, p. 33.

35. Elshtain, p. 156, quoting Pope John Paul II, *Sollicitudo Rei Socialis*.

36. Carozza 2003, p. 52.

37. This section is taken from Tavis and Tavis, pp. 308–13.

38. See Walker-Andrews for a summary of the research in this area, and Kahana-Kalman and Walker-Andrews for more recent discussions.

39. American Psychiatric Association, p. 75.

40. Sacks.

41. Wing, p. 20.

42. Howe and Courage.

43. Mumme, Fernald, and Herrara.

44. Werker and Tees.

45. See, for example Nobre and Plunkett; Hirsh-Pasek, Golinkoff, and Hollich; Booth and Burnam.

46. Cziko.

47. Bruner.

48. McAdams, p. 104.

49. Ibid., p. 116.

50. Ibid., p. 113.

51. See Howe and Courage on the emergence of autobiographical memory.

52. McAdams, p. 112.

53. Rosenwald, p. 265.

54. McAdams, p. 112.

55. Ibid., p. 115.

56. Sarbin.

57. McAdams, p. 102.

58. Howard 1991.

59. Ruiz.

60. On agency and communion see Bakan; Singer. On redemption and contamination see Maruna; McAdams and Bowman.

61. Schein, p. 12.

62. Milton Rokeach, as quoted in O'Reilly, Chatman, and Caldwell, p. 492.

63. Trevino, p. 612.

64. O'Reilly, Chatman, and Caldwell, p. 512.

65. Burt, p. 4.
66. Ibid.
67. Bartkus and Davis, p. 2.
68. Davis and Bartkus, p. 318.
69. Bartkus and Davis, p. 347.
70. Coleman; Putnam 1993; Fukuyama.
71. Dunne 1977.
72. Dunne 1985.
73. Dunne 1978, p. xiii.
74. Dunne 2000, p. 5.
75. Huntington argues that tension among cultural norms will be the source of global conflict in the twenty-first century (Huntington 1996). Although broadly challenged, Huntington's thesis remains a credible argument.
76. Donaldson and Dunfee, p. 8.
77. Ibid., p. 87.
78. Donaldson and Dunfee's definition of community is essentially communitarian: "A community is a self-defined, self-circumscribed group of people who interact in the context of shared tasks, values, or goals and who are capable of establishing norms of ethical behavior for themselves. . . . This open-ended definition is intended to allow for great variety in the way in which people form relationships capable of generating authentic ethical norms. It recognizes that people may develop authentic norms within informal relationships, as, for example, in the context of a 'shadow' or 'informal' organization where information and even decision making flows outside formal organizational channels" (Donaldson and Dunfee, pp. 39 and 98).
79. Ibid. p. 6.
80. Ibid., p. 89.
81. Ibid., p. 51.
82. Ibid., p. 53.
83. Ibid., pp. 117–38.
84. Ibid., p. 53.
85. Ibid.
86. Ibid., p. 175.
87. Ibid., pp. 172–73.
88. This notion ties to the ideas of solidarity and subsidiarity in the Catholic social tradition.
89. Donaldson and Dunfee, pp. 184–90.
90. In the view of Donaldson and Dunfee, "Most of the history of the Western world reveals a preoccupation with the 'universalist' perspective, and a neglect of the 'unique identity' perspective." They cite Etzioni and the communitarians and

their "insistence to take community conceptions of the Good and not merely universal precepts as morally relevant" (p. 80).

91. Ibid., p. 55.

92. Ibid., p. 57. This is Audi's point made earlier, although without the priority given to reason. Throughout their work, Donaldson and Dunfee refer to "convergence of religious, political, and philosophical thought" (e.g., pp. 44, 50, 59). As with other sources of norms, they do not select religion as a unique foundation, other than stressing the commonality among religions and overlapping community values. (See pp. 27, 66, 204, 221, 226.)

93. Donaldson and Dunfee, p. 59.

94. The United Nations Declaration of Human Rights is mentioned twice in passing as an example of hypernorms in Donaldson and Dunfee (pp. 66, 69).

95. This is a normative speculative venture—a leap of faith, if you will—because there is no empirical evidence in Weaver and Agle's thorough review of the literature on the topic to support the assertion that a person's religiosity contributes to ethical behavior in organizations (see Weaver and Agle). Perhaps personal belief and commitment are too nuanced for measurement given the present state of managerial research; perhaps reason and revelation do, indeed, come to the same conclusions.

Abarbanell, Jeffery, and Victor Bernard. 2000. "Is the U.S. Stock Market My-opic?" *Journal of Accounting Research*, vol. 38, no. 2, Autumn, pp. 221–42.

Abdelnour, Samer, Babiker Badri, Oana Branzei, Susan McGrath, and David Wheeler. 2008. "Grassroots Enterprise Development in Post-Conflict Southern Sudan and Darfur: Preliminary Observations." In *Peace through Commerce: Responsible Corporate Citizenship and the Ideals of the United Nations Global Compact*, ed. Oliver F. Williams, C.S.C. Notre Dame, Ind.: University of Notre Dame Press.

Abu-Nimer, Mohammed. 2000–2001. "A Framework for Nonviolence and Peacebuilding in Islam." *Journal of Law & Religion*, vol. 15, nos. 1–2, pp. 217–65.

Adler, Alfred. 1956. *The Individual Psychology of Alfred Adler: A Systematic Presentation of Selections from His Writings*. Ed. Heinz L. Ansbacher and Rowena R. Ansbacher. New York: Basic Books.

———. 1930. "Individual Psychology." In *Psychologies of 1930*, ed. Carl Murchison. Worcester, Mass.: Clark University Press.

Agi, Marc. 1979. *René Cassin: Fantassin des Droits de l'Homme*. Paris: Plon.

Ajami, Fouad. 1997. "The Arab Inheritance." *Foreign Affairs*, vol. 76, issue 5, September–October, pp. 133–48.

Albert, Michael. 1993. *Capitalism Against Capitalism*. London: Whurr Book Publishers.

Alford, Helen, O.P. 2006. Presentation at the Plenary Session on Stakeholder Theory. "The Good Company: Catholic Social Thought and Corporate Social Responsibility in Dialogue," Sixth International Conference on Catholic Social Thought and Management Education, Pontifical University of St. Thomas (Angelicum), Rome, October 5–7.

Alford, Helen, O.P., and Michael J. Naughton. 2001. *Managing as if Faith Mattered: Christian Social Principles in the Modern Organization*. Notre Dame, Ind.: University of Notre Dame Press.

Alford, Helen, O.P., Barbara Sena, and Yuliya Shcherbinina. 2006. "Philosophical Underpinnings and Basic Concepts for a Dialogue between CST and CSR of the 'Good Company.'" Working draft of position paper for "The Good Company: Catholic Social Thought and Corporate Social Responsibility in Dialogue," Sixth International Conference on Catholic Social Thought and Management Education, Pontifical University of St. Thomas (Angelicum), Rome, October 5–7.

American Psychiatric Association. 2000. *Diagnostic and Statistical Manual of Mental Disorders*. 4th ed. Washington, D.C.: American Psychiatric Association.

Anderson, Mary. 2008. "False Promises and Premises? The Challenge of Peace Building for Corporations." In *Peace through Commerce: Responsible Corporate Citizenship and the Ideals of the United Nations Global Compact*, ed. Oliver F. Williams, C.S.C. Notre Dame, Ind.: University of Notre Dame Press.

Anderson, Ray. 2005. "Who We Are." http://www.interfaceinc.com/who/founder.html. Last accessed April 22, 2009.

———. 2004. "Sustainable Success: Interface CEO Ray Anderson on Business and the Environment," Center for Ethics, Emory University, January 28.

Anheier, Helmut, Marlies Glasius, and Mary Kaldor, eds. 2001. *Global Civil Society 2001*. London: The Centre for the Study of Global Governance.

Annan, Kofi. 2002. World Social Forum address, February 4. http://www.revistainterforum.com/english/articles/021102artprin_en1.html. Last accessed April 22, 2009.

———. 2000. *We the Peoples: The Role of the United Nations in the 21st Century*. New York: United Nations.

———. 1999. Office of the U.N. High Commissioner for Human Rights, *Business and Human Rights: A Progress Report*, February, http://www.unhchr.ch/business.htm. Last accessed April 22, 2009.

———. 1997. Address (18 October 1997) to the Communications Conference at the Aspen Institute, Colorado, United Nations Press Release SG/SM/6366, October 20.

Annas, Julia. 1992. "Ethics and Morality." In *Encyclopedia of Ethics*, ed. Lawrence C. Becker, assoc. ed. Charlotte B. Becker, vol. 1, pp. 329–31. New York and London: Garland Publishing.

Appleby, R. Scott. 2002. "Terrorism: America's New Enemy." *World Book Online Americas Edition*, http://www.worldbookonline.com.

"Artificial Life: Patent Pending." 2007. *The Economist*, June 16, p. 92.

Audi, Robert. 2000a. *Religious Commitment and Secular Reason*. Cambridge: Cambridge University Press.

———. 2000b. "The Place of Religious Argument in a Free and Democratic Society." In *Law and Religion: A Critical Anthology*, ed. Stephen M. Feldman. New York: New York University Press.

Bakan, David. 1966. *The Duality of Human Existence: Isolation and Communion in Western Man*. Boston: Beacon Press.

Baker, Stephen, and Heather Green. 2008. "Social Media Will Change Your Business." *Business Week*, Technology section, February 20.

Balbernie, Roger. 2001. "Circuits and Circumstances: The Neurobiological Consequences of Early Relationship Experiences and How They Shape Later Behavior." *Journal of Child Development*, vol. 27, no. 3, pp. 237–55.

Barbaro, Michael. 2008. "Wal-Mart Sets Agenda of Change." *The New York Times*, January 24, p. C3.

Barbaro, Michael, and Justin Gills. 2006. "Wal-Mart at Forefront of Hurricane Relief." *Washington Post*, September 6, p. D1.

Bartkus, Viva Ona, and James Davis, eds. 2008. *Social Capital: Multidisciplinary Perspectives*. Cheltenham, U.K.: Edward Elgar.

Baughn, C. Christopher, and Mark A. Buchanan. 2001. "Cultural Protectionism." *Business Horizons*, vol. 44, issue 6, November–December, pp. 5–15.

Becker, Ernest. 1997. *The Denial of Death*. New York: The Free Press.

"Behind the Digital Divide." 2005. *The Economist Technology Quarterly*, March 12, pp. 22–25.

Beinhocker, Eric D. 2006. *The Origin of Wealth: Evolution, Complexity, and the Radical Remaking of Economics*. Boston: Harvard Business School Press.

Bellah, Robert N. 2002. "Epilogue: Meaning and Modernity: America and the World." In *Meaning and Modernity*, ed. Richard Madsen, William M. Sullivan, Ann Swidler, and Steven M. Tipton. Berkeley: University of California Press.

Berger, Peter L., and Richard John Neuhaus. 1996. *To Empower People: From State To Civil Society*, 2nd ed., ed. Michael Novak. Washington, D.C.: The AEI Press.

Berle, A. A., Jr., and Gardiner C. Means. 1932. *The Modern Corporation and Private Property*. New York: Macmillan.

Bernstein, Aaron. 2005. "A Major Swipe at Sweatshops." *Business Week*, May 23, p. 98.

Biffi, Monsignor Franco. 1988. "Human Rights in the Magisterium of the Popes of the Twentieth Century." In *Human Rights, a Christian Approach*. Manila, The Philippines: International Federation of Catholic Universities Research Coordination Center.

"Biology's Big Bang." 2007. *The Economist*, June 16, p. 13.

Bishop, Matthew. 2006. "The Business of Giving." *The Economist*, February 25, pp. 3–5.

Black, Jan Knippers. 2000. "What Kind of Democracy Does the 'Democratic Entitlement' Entail?" In *Democratic Governance and International Law*, ed. Gregory H. Fox and Brad R. Roth. New York: Cambridge University Press.

"Body Shop—Capitalism and Cocoa Butter." 1998. *The Economist*, vol. 347, issue 8068, May 16, pp. 66–67.

Bonini, Sheila M., Greg Hintz, and Lenny T. Mendonca. 2008. "Addressing Consumer Concerns about Climate Change." *The McKinsey Quarterly*, no. 2, pp. 52–61.

Bonini, Sheila M., Lenny T. Mendonca, and Jeremy M. Oppenheim. 2006. "When Social Issues Become Strategic: Executives Ignore Sociopolitical Debates at their Own Peril." *The McKinsey Quarterly*, no. 2, pp. 20–32.

Booth, James R., and Douglas D. Burnam. 2001. "Development and Disorders of Neurocognitive Systems for Oral Language and Reading." *Learning Disability Quarterly*, vol. 24, no. 3, pp. 205–15.

Bownds, M. Deric. 1999. *The Biology of Mind: Origins and Structures of Mind, Brain, and Consciousness*. Bethesda, Md.: Fitzgerald Science Press.

Bozon, Ivo J. H., and Scott S. Nyquist. 2007. "New Horizons in Global Energy." *The McKinsey Quarterly*, no. 1, pp. 4–5.

Brak, Chabuca, and Pierre Echard. 2005. "Business and NGO Partnerships—for Maximum Impact." *Sustainable Development International*. London: Henley Media Group, pp. 9–12.

Brems, Eva. 2001. *Human Rights: Universality and Diversity*. International Studies in Human Rights, vol. 66. The Hague: Martinus Nijhoff Publishers.

Bressand, Florian, Diana Farrell, Pedro Haas, Fabrice Morin, Scott Nyquist, Jaana Remes, Sebastian Roemer, Matt Rogers, Jaeson Rosenfeld, and Jonathan Woetzel. 2007. "Curbing Global Energy Demand Growth: The Energy Productivity Opportunity." McKinsey Global Institute, May.

"Briefing: Emerging-Market Multinationals." 2008. *The Economist*, January 12, pp. 62–64.

Broder, John M. 2007. "Governors Join in Creating Regional Pact on Climate Change." *The New York Times*, November 15, p. A16.

Brokatzky-Geiger, Juergen, Raj Sapru, and Matthias Streib. 2006. "Implementing a Living Wage Globally—The Novartis Approach." Case study published by the U.N. Global Compact, December, http://www.unglobalcompact.org. Available at http://www.unglobalcompact.org/data/ungc_case_story_resources/doc/E4360C96-351F-4446-8D2D-3B5C7B47D5CB.pdf. Last accessed April 24, 2009.

Browning, Don, ed. 2006. *Universalism vs. Relativism: Making Moral Judgments in a Changing, Pluralistic, and Threatening World*. Lanham, Md.: Rowman & Littlefield Publishers.

Bruner, Jerome. 1986. *Actual Minds, Possible Worlds*. Cambridge, Mass.: Harvard University Press.

Brunet, John E. 2001. "Integrating Technology into the Business Environment." Presentation at the International Association of Jesuit Business Schools, VIII Forum, Manufacturing and Technology in the Global Economy: Issues Confronting Jesuit Business Schools. Detroit/Mercy, Detroit, Mich., June 26.

Bruni, Luigino, and Robert Sugden. 2006. "Fraternity: A Moral Understanding of Market Relationship." Paper presented at "The Good Company: Catholic Social Thought and Corporate Social Responsibility in Dialogue," Sixth International Conference on Catholic Social Thought and Management Education, Pontifical University of St. Thomas (Angelicum), Rome, October 5–7. Available at http://www.stthomas.edu/cathstudies/cst/conferences/thegood company/Finalpapers/Robert%20Sugden%2009.00%20.pdf. Last accessed April 24, 2009.

Bruno, Kenny, and Joshua Karliner. 2000. "Tangled Up in Blue: Corporate Partnerships at the United Nations." Corp Watch, http://www.corpwatch.org. September 1. Last accessed April 22, 2009.

Bullis, Kevin. "Expandable Silicon." *Technology Review*, published by MIT, http://www.technologyreview.com/Nanotech/19901. Last accessed April 22, 2009.

Burt, Ronald S. 2005. *Brokerage and Closure*. Oxford: Oxford University Press.

Burtraw, Dallas, Karen Palmer, and Daniel Kahn. 2005. "CO_2 Allowance in the Regional Greenhouse Gas Initiative and the Effect on Electricity Investors." December 13. http://ideas.repec.org/p/rff/dpaper/dp-05-55.html. Last accessed April 22, 2009.

Buruma, Ian. 2007. "Tariq Ramadan Has an Identity Issue." *The New York Times Magazine*, section 5, col. 1, February 4.

Cahill, Lisa Sowle. 1980. "Toward a Christian Theory of Human Rights." *Journal of Religious Ethics*, vol. 8, Fall, p. 278.

Campbell, Tom. 2006. *Rights: A Critical Introduction*. London and New York: Routledge.

Capaldo, Antonio, Richard Dobbs, and Hannu Suonio. 2008. "Deal Making in 2007: Is the M&A Boom Over?" *The McKinsey Quarterly*, no. 1, pp. 8–12.

Carnegie Hero Fund Commission. http://www.carnegiehero.org/herofund .php. Last updated March 16, 2009. Last accessed April 22, 2009.

"Carnegie Medals Awarded to 19 for Extraordinary Civilian Heroism." 2008. Carnegie Hero Fund Commission, Pittsburgh, December 22.

Carozza, Paolo G. 2006. "The Universal Common Good and the Authority of International Law." *Logos*, Notre Dame Law School Legal Studies Research Paper No. 07-36, vol. 9, no. 1, Winter, pp. 28–55. Available from the Social Science Research Network electronic library, http://ssrn.com/abstract=984746. Last accessed April 24, 2009.

———. 2003. "Subsidiarity as a Structural Principle of International Human Rights Law." *The American Journal of International Law*, vol. 97, no. 1, January, pp. 38–79.

Carroll, Archie B. 1999. "Corporate Social Responsibility: Evolution of a Definitional Construct." *Business and Society*, vol. 38, no. 3, pp. 268–95.

Caruso, Denise. 2007. "Someone (Other Than You) May Own Your Genes." *The New York Times*, section 3, January 28, p. 3.

Cassel, Douglass. 2001. "Human Rights and Business Responsibilities in the Global Marketplace." *Business Ethics Quarterly*, vol. 11, no. 2, April, pp. 261–74.

Cassel, Douglass, and Sean O'Brien. 2008. "Transnational Corporate Accountability and the Rule of Law." In *Peace through Commerce: Responsible Corporate Citizenship and the Ideals of the United Nations Global Compact*, ed. Oliver F. Williams, C.S.C. Notre Dame, Ind.: University of Notre Dame Press.

Castle, Stephen, and Mark Landler. 2008. "After 7 Years, Talks Collapse on World Trade: A Rich-Poor Deadlock." *The New York Times*, section 1, July 30, p. 1.

Cavanagh, Gerald F., S.J. 2000. "Executives' Code of Business Conduct: Prospects for the Caux Principles." In *Global Codes of Conduct: An Idea Whose Time Has Come*, ed. Oliver F. Williams, C.S.C. Notre Dame, Ind.: University of Notre Dame Press.

Cavanagh, Gerald F., S.J., Mary Ann Hazen, Brad Simmons, and David Berdish. 2008. "Ford Motor Company, Human Rights, and Environmental Integrity." In *Peace through Commerce: Responsible Corporate Citizenship and the Ideals of the United Nations Global Compact*, ed. Oliver F. Williams, C.S.C. Notre Dame, Ind.: University of Notre Dame Press.

Chami, Ralph, Thomas Cosimano, and Connel Fullenkamp. 2002. "Managing Ethical Risk: How Investing in Ethics Adds Value." *Journal of Banking and Finance*, vol. 26, no. 9, September, pp. 1697–1718.

Chan, Selina. 2000. "Confucianism—Mortality." *FONI: The International Literary Journal*, vol. 6, Spring, http://www.lehigh.edu/~infoni/essay/confucianism.htm.

"Charlemagne: The Farmer's Friend." 2005. *The Economist*, November 5, p. 58.

Chen, Shaohua, and Martin Ravallion. 2008. "The Developing World Is Poorer Than We Thought, but No Less Successful in the Fight against Poverty." Policy Research Working Paper #4703, The World Bank Development Research Group, Washington, D.C., August. http://www-wds.worldbank.org/external/default/WDSContentServer/WDSP/IB/2008/08/26/000158349_20080826113239/Rendered/PDF/WPS4703.pdf. Last accessed April 24, 2009.

Chisholm, Laura B. 1995. "Accountability of Nonprofit Organizations and Those Who Control Them: The Legal Framework." *Nonprofit Management and Leadership*, vol. 6, issue 2, pp. 141–56.

Christiansen, Drew, Ronald Garet, David Hollenbach, and Charles Powers. 1974. "Moral Claims, Human Rights, and Population Policies." The Yale Task Force on Population Ethics. *Journal of Theological Studies*, vol. 35, pp. 83–13.

Chuanshu, Li, "Confucian Ethics and Universal Ethics." *Lock Haven International Review*, vol. 15, December 2001, http://www.lhup.edu/library/International Review/chuanshu.htm.

Coase, Ronald H. 1937. "The Nature of the Firm." *Economica*, new series, vol. 4, no. 16, November.

Coleman, James S. 1990. *Foundations of Social Theory*. Cambridge, Mass.: Harvard University Press.

Commission on Global Governance. 1996. *Our Global Neighborhood: The Report of the Commission on Global Governance*. Oxford: Oxford University Press.

Computer Science: Reflections on the Field, Reflections from the Field. Publication of the Committee on the Fundamentals of Computer Science: Challenges and Opportunities, Computer Science and Telecommunications Board, National Research Council of the National Academies. Washington, D.C.: National Academies Press, 2004.

Conkle, Daniel O. 2000. "Secular Fundamentalism, Religious Fundamentalism, and the Search for Truth in Contemporary America." In *Law and Religion: A Critical Anthology*, ed. Stephen M. Feldman. New York: New York University Press.

Cornish, Sandie. 1999. "From Rejection to Proclamation: A Brief Overview of the Development of the Catholic Church's Thinking on Human Rights." Proceedings of the Australian Catholic Social Justice Council, Australian Catholic Bishops Conference.

Cortright, Steven, and Michael Naughton. 2002. *Rethinking the Purpose of Business: An Inter-disciplinary Approach within the Catholic Social Tradition*. Notre Dame, Ind.: University of Notre Dame Press.

Costa, Thomas. 2008. "Bristol-Myers Squibb Company: Secure the Future." In *Peace through Commerce: Responsible Corporate Citizenship and the Ideals of the United Nations Global Compact*, ed. Oliver F. Williams, C.S.C. Notre Dame, Ind.: University of Notre Dame Press.

———. 2006. "Corporate Social Responsibility in the Global Village." Berges Lecture Series, Mendoza College of Business, University of Notre Dame, November 14.

Crawford, James. 2000. "Democracy and the Body of International Law." In *Democratic Governance and International Law*, ed. Gregory H. Fox and Brad R. Roth. New York: Cambridge University Press.

Crook, Clive. 2005. "The Good Company: A Survey of Corporate Social Responsibility." *The Economist*, vol. 374, no. 8410, January 22, pp. 3–22.

Cutler, Claire A., Virginia Haufler, and Tony Porter, eds. 1999. *Private Authority and International Affairs*. Albany: State University of New York Press.

Cziko, Gary. 1997. *Without Miracles: Universal Selection Theory and the Second Darwinian Revolution*. Cambridge, Mass.: MIT Press.

Davis, James H., and Viva Ona Bartkus. 2008. "Organizational Trust and Social Capital." In *Social Capital: Multidisciplinary Perspectives*, ed. Viva Ona Bartkus and James H. Davis. Cheltenham, U.K.: Edward Elgar.

Dawkins, Richard. 1976. *The Selfish Gene*. Oxford: Oxford University Press.

De George, Richard T. 1993. *Competing with Integrity in International Business*. New York: Oxford University Press.

Delacroix, Jacques, with Julien Bornon. 2005. "Can Protectionism Ever Be Respectable? A Skeptic's Case for the Cultural Exception, with Special Reference to French Movies." *The Independent Review*, vol. 9, no. 3, Winter, pp. 353–74.

Den Hond, Frank, and Frank G. A. De Bakker. 2007. "Ideologically Motivated Activism: How Activist Groups Influence Corporate Social Change Activities." *Academy of Management Review*, vol. 32, no. 3, pp. 901–24.

Diamond, Larry. 2008. *The Spirit of Democracy: The Struggle to Build Free Societies Throughout the World*. New York,: Time Books, Henry Holt and Co.

———. 1999. *Developing Democracy: Toward Consolidation*. Baltimore: Johns Hopkins University Press.

DiMaggio, Paul, Eszter Hargittai, W. Russell Neuman, and John P. Robinson. 2001. "Social Implications of the Internet." *Annual Review of Sociology*, vol. 27, pp. 307–36.

"Dirty King Coal: Scrubbing Carbon from Coal-Fired Power Stations Is Possible but Pricey." 2007. *The Economist*, vol. 383, issue 8531, June 2–8, pp. 22–24 (in special section "Cleaning Up: A Special Report on Business and Climate Change," between pp. 54–55 of issue).

Dixon, Douglas. 2000. "Our Technological Future: Star Trek or Terminator? A Warning from Bill Joy of Sun Microsystems." April, http://www.manifest-tech.com/society/techfuture.htm. Last accessed April 24, 2009.

Donaldson, Gordon. 1984. *Managing Corporate Wealth: The Operation of a Comprehensive Financial Goals System*. New York: Praeger.

Donaldson, Thomas, and Thomas W. Dunfee. 1999. *Ties that Bind: A Social Contracts Approach To Business Ethics*. Boston: Harvard Business School Press.

Douglass, R. Bruce, and David Hollenbach, eds. 1994. *Catholicism and Liberalism: Contributions to American Public Philosophy*. New York: Cambridge University Press.

Druker, Brian James. 1999. Presentation at the 41st Annual Meeting of the American Society of Hematology, December 3–7, New Orleans.

Dunbar, R. J. M. 1993. "Co-Evolution of Neocortex Size, Group Size, and Language in Humans." *Behavioral and Brain Sciences*, vol. 16, no. 4, pp. 681–735.

Dunne, John S. 2000. *Reading the Gospel*. Notre Dame, Ind.: University of Notre Dame Press.

———. 1985. *The City of the Gods: A Study in Myth and Mortality*. Notre Dame, Ind.: University of Notre Dame Press.

———. 1978. *The Way of All the Earth: Experiments in Truth and Religion*. Notre Dame, Ind.: University of Notre Dame Press.

——. 1977. *A Search for God in Time and Memory*. Notre Dame, Ind.: University of Notre Dame Press.

Eagle, Morris N. 1984. *Recent Developments in Psychoanalysis: A Critical Evaluation*. New York: McGraw-Hill Book Co.

Easterbrook, Megan A., Barbara S. Kisilevsky, Darwin W. Muir, and David P. Laplante. 1999. "Newborns Discriminate Schematic Faces from Scrambled Faces." *Canadian Journal of Experimental Psychology*, vol. 53, no. 3, September, pp. 231–41.

Ebrahim, Alnoor. 2003. "Making Sense of Accountability: Conceptual Perspectives for Northern and Southern Nonprofits." *Nonprofit Management & Leadership*, vol. 14, no. 2, Winter, pp. 191–212.

"Economics Focus: Calling Across the Divide." 2005. *The Economist*, March 12, p. 74.

Edel, Abraham. 1992. "Value, Theory of." *Encyclopedia of Ethics*, ed. Lawrence C. Becker, assoc. ed. Charlotte B. Becker, vol. 2, pp. 1269–73. New York and London: Garland Publishing.

Einhorn, B., G. Smith, and C. Edwards. 2007. "Intel Inside the Third World: Is Getting Computer to Poor Kids Charity—or Big Business?" *Business Week*, issue 4042, July 9, pp. 38–40. Retrieved April 15, 2008, from the Academic Search Premier database.

Einhorn, Bruce, and Mehul Srivastava. 2008. "WTO: Why India and China Said No to U.S." July 30. http://www.businessweek.com/globalbiz/content/jul2008/gb20080730_027680.htm?chan=t. Last accessed April 24, 2009.

Eliot, Lise. 2001. *Early Intelligence: How the Brain and Mind Develop in the First Years of Life*. London: Penguin Books.

Elshtain, Jean Bethke. 1994. "Catholic Social Thought, the City, and Liberal America." In *Catholicism and Liberalism: Contributions to American Public Philosophy*, ed. R. Bruce Douglass and David Hollenbach. New York: Cambridge University Press.

Enderle, Georges. 2004. "The Ethics of Financial Reporting, the Global Reporting Initiative, and the Balanced Concept of the Firm." In *Corporate Integrity & Accountability*, ed. George G. Brenkert. Thousand Oaks, Calif.: Sage Publications.

Enderle, Georges, and Lee A. Tavis. 1998. "A Balanced Concept of the Firm and the Measurement of Its Long-Term Planning and Performance." *Journal of Business Ethics*, vol. 17, pp. 1129–44.

Enkvist, Per-Anders, Tomas Naucler, and Jerker Rosander. 2007. "A Cost Curve for Greenhouse Gas Reduction." *The McKinsey Quarterly*, no. 1, pp. 34–45.

Esty, Daniel C., and Andrew S. Winston. 2006. *Green to Gold: How Smart Companies Use Environmental Strategy to Innovate, Create Vision, and Build Competition Advantage*. New Haven, Conn.: Yale University Press.

Etzioni, Amitai. 2001. *Next: The Road to the Good Society*. New York: Basic Books.

———. 1999. "The Good Society," *The Journal of Political Philosophy*, vol. 7, no. 1, March, pp. 88–103.

———. 1996. *The New Golden Rule: Community and Morality in a Democratic Society*. New York: Basic Books.

———. 1988. *The Moral Dimension: Toward a New Economics*. New York,: The Free Press.

Eugenio, Ofélia C. 2008. "A Public-Private Partnership for Enterprise Development: The Case of the Angola Enterprise Program." In *Peace through Commerce: Responsible Corporate Citizenship and the Ideals of the United Nations Global Compact*, ed. Oliver F. Williams, C.S.C. Notre Dame, Ind.: University of Notre Dame Press.

Eurosif. 2008. *European SRI Study 2008*. http://www.eurosif.org/publications/sri_studies. Last accessed April 24, 2009.

Evans, James R., and William M. Lindsay. 1999. *The Management and Control of Quality*. Cincinnati, Ohio: South-Western College Publishing.

Feder, Barnaby J. 2007. "Teeny-Weeny Rules for Itty-Bitty Atom Clusters." *The New York Times*, January 14, pp. wk5, 14.

Feinstein, Charles H. 1998. "Pessimism Perpetuated: Real Wages and the Standard of Living in Britain during and after the Industrial Revolution." *The Journal of Economic History*, vol. 58, no. 3, September, pp. 625–58.

"The Final Cut: Business Can Do It, with Governments' Help." 2007. *The Economist*, vol. 383, issue 8531, June 2–8, pp. 28–30 (in special section, "Cleaning Up: A Special Report on Business and Climate Change," between pp. 54–55 of issue).

Finkelstein, Sydney, Donald C. Hambrick, and Albert A. Cannella, Jr. 2009. *Strategic Leadership: Theory and Research on Top Executives, Top Management Teams, and Boards*. New York: Oxford University Press.

Finnis, John. 1980. *Natural Law and Natural Rights*. Oxford: Clarendon Press.

Fisher, Julie. 1998. *Non-Governments, NGOs, and the Political Development of the Third World*. West Hartford, Conn.: Kumarian Press.

Fitzgerald, Michael. 2007. "It Takes Deep Pockets to Fight Global Warming." *The New York Times*, August 12, BU3.

Fombrun, Charles J. 1996. *Reputation: Realizing Value from the Corporate Image*. Boston: Harvard Business School Press.

Fort, Timothy L. 2007. *Business, Integrity, and Peace: Beyond Geopolitical and Disciplinary Boundaries*. Cambridge, Mass.: Cambridge University Press.

———. 2001. *Ethics and Governance: Business as Mediating Institutions*. New York: Oxford University Press.

Fort, Timothy L., and Cindy A. Schipani. 2000. "Corporate Governance in a Global Environment: The Search for the Best of All Worlds." *Vanderbilt Journal of Transnational Law*, vol. 33, pp. 829–76.

Fort, Timothy L., and Michelle Westermann-Behaylo. 2008. "Moral Maturity, Peace through Commerce, and the Partnership Dimension." In *Peace through Commerce: Responsible Corporate Citizenship and the Ideals of the United Nations Global Compact*, ed. Oliver F. Williams, C.S.C. Notre Dame, Ind.: University of Notre Dame Press.

Fortin, Ernest L. 1988. "The Trouble with Catholic Social Thought." *Boston College Magazine*, Summer, pp. 37–38.

Franklin, Daniel. 2008. "Just Good Business: A Special Report on Corporate Social Responsibility." *The Economist*, January 19, pp. 3–24.

Freedom House. 2007. *Freedom in the World Survey, 2007.* http://www.freedom house.org. Last accessed April 24, 2009.

———. 2006. *Freedom in the World, 2006.* New York: Freedom House.

———. 1999. "Democracy's Century: A Survey of Global Political Change in the 20th Century." December 7, http://www.freedomhouse.org/reports/century .html.

Friedman, Milton. 1970. "The Social Responsibility of Business Is to Increase Its Profits." *The New York Times Magazine*, section 6, September 13, pp. 30–32.

———. 1962. *Capitalism and Freedom.* Chicago: University of Chicago Press.

Friedman, Thomas L. 2008. *Hot, Flat, and Crowded: Why We Need a Green Revolution—and How It Can Renew America.* New York: Farrar, Straus and Giroux.

———. 2007. "Going Green with Greenbacks Internet." *Palm Beach Post*, March 17, p. 15A.

———. 2005. *The World Is Flat: A Brief History of the Twenty-First Century.* New York: Farrar, Strauss and Giroux.

———. 2000. *The Lexus and the Olive Tree.* Updated and Expanded Edition. New York: Random House.

Fukuyama, Francis. 2000. "Social Capital." In *Culture Matters: How Values Shape Human Progress*, ed. Lawrence Harrison and Samuel Huntington. New York: Basic Books.

"The Future of Globalisation." 2006. *The Economist*, July 29, p. 11.

"Gartner Says Emerging Markets Hold the Key to Future Telecoms." December 1, 2006, http://www.gartner.com/it/page.jsp?id=499110&format=print. Last accessed April 24, 2009.

Gates, William. 2008. "On Software, Innovation, Entrepreneurship, and Giving Back." Address presented to Stanford University faculty and staff, February 19.

Geczy, Christopher C., Robert F. Stambaugh, and David Levin. 2005. "Investing in Socially Responsible Mutual Funds." Unpublished paper, October.

Genovesi, Antonio. 2005. *Delle Lezioni di Commercio o sia di Economia Civile.* Naples: Instituto Italiano per gli Studi Filofici.

George, Robert P., ed. 1992. *Natural Law Theory: Contemporary Essays.* Oxford: Clarendon Press.

Ghislanzoni, Giancarlo, Risto Penttinen, and David Turnbull. 2008. "The Multilocal Challenge: Managing Cross-Border Functions." *The McKinsey Quarterly,* no. 2, pp. 71–81.

Glade, William P. 1988. "Patterns of Similarity and Difference." In *Multinational Managers and Host Government Interactions,* ed. Lee A. Tavis. Notre Dame, Ind.: University of Notre Dame Press.

Glaser, Danya. 2000. "Child Abuse and Neglect and the Brain—A Review." *Journal of Child Psychology and Psychiatry,* vol. 41, issue 1, pp. 97–116.

Glendon, Mary Ann. 2001. *A World Made New: Eleanor Roosevelt and the Universal Declaration of Human Rights.* New York: Garland Publishing, Random House.

———. 1998. "Reflections on the UDHR." *First Things,* Institute on Religion and Public Life, April, pp. 23–25.

Gordley, James. 1997. "Good Faith in Contract Law: The Problem of Profit Maximization." Paper presented at The Second International Symposium on Catholic Social Thought and Management Education, University of Antwerp, Antwerp, Belgium, July 27.

Greene, Jay, and Mike France. 2005. "Culture Wars Hit Corporate America." *Business Week,* May 23, p. 91.

Greenhut, Marshall, with Bob Corcoran. 2008. "General Electric and Corporate Citizenship: Improving the Health of the Poor in Africa." In *Peace through Commerce: Responsible Corporate Citizenship and the Ideals of the United Nations Global Compact,* ed. Oliver F. Williams, C.S.C. Notre Dame, Ind.: University of Notre Dame Press.

Grossman, Lev. 2006. "Power to the People." *Time,* vol. 168, issue 26, December 25, p. 44.

"Groundbreaking Studies by the United Nations, Goldman Sachs, and McKinsey & Company Show Benefits of Corporate Responsibility." 2007. CSR News from United Nations Global Compact, July 5. http://www.csrwire.com/News/9112.html. Last accessed April 24, 2009.

Guáqueta, Alexandra. 2008. "Occidental Petroleum, Cerrejón, and NGO Partnerships in Colombia: Lessons Learned." In *Peace through Commerce: Responsible Corporate Citizenship and the Ideals of the United Nations Global Compact,* ed. Oliver F. Williams, C.S.C. Notre Dame, Ind.: University of Notre Dame Press.

Guéhenno, Jean-Marie. 1995. *The End of the Nation-State*. Minneapolis: University of Minnesota Press.

Haakonssen, Knude. 1992. "Natural Law." In *Encyclopedia of Ethics*, ed. Lawrence C. Becker, assoc. ed. Charlotte B. Becker, vol. 2, pp. 884–90. New York: London and Garland Publishing.

Haigh, Michael S., and John A. List. 2005. "Do Professional Traders Exhibit Myopic Loss Aversion? An Experimental Analysis." *The Journal of Finance*, vol. 60, no. 1, February, pp. 523–34.

Hamdi, Mohamed Elhachmi. 1996. "Islam and Liberal Democracy: The Limits of the Western Model." *Journal of Democracy*, vol. 7, no. 2, April, pp. 81–85.

Harris, Gardiner and Vanessa Fuhrmans. 2002. "Its Rivals in a Funk, Novartis Finds A Technique to Thrive: Swiss Drug Maker Embraces Bare-Knuckled Marketing." *The Wall Street Journal* (online), August 23.

Harrison, Lawrence E., and Samuel P. Huntington, eds. 2000. *Culture Matters: How Values Shape Human Progress*. New York: Basic Books.

Hart, Stuart L. 1997. "Beyond Freening: Strategies for a Sustainable World." *Harvard Business Review*, vol. 75, issue 1, January–February, pp. 67–75.

Harvey, Fiona. 2008. "World Carbon Trading Value Doubles." *Financial Times*, May 8, p. 27.

Hasnas, John. 1998. "The Normative Theories of Business Ethics: A Guide for the Perplexed." *Business Ethics Quarterly*, vol. 8, issue 1, pp. 19–42.

Hatch, Mary Jo, and Majken Schultz. 2000. "Scaling the Tower of Babel: Relational Differences Between Identity, Image, and Culture in Organizations." In *The Expressive Organization: Linking Identity, Reputation, and the Corporate Brand*, ed. Majken Schultz, Mary Jo Hatch, and Mogens Holten Larsen. New York: Oxford University Press.

Haufler, Virginia. 2000. "Private Sector International Regimes." In *Non-State Actors and Authority in the Global System*, ed. Richard A. Higgott, Geoffrey R. D. Underhill, and Andreas Bieler. New York: Routledge.

Hausmann, David. 2002. "Trustworthiness and Self Interest." *Journal of Banking and Finance*, vol. 26, no. 9, September, pp. 1767–83.

Held, David, Anthony McGrew, David Goldblatt, and Jonathan Perraton. 1999. *Global Transformations: Politics, Economics, and Culture*. Stanford, Calif.: Stanford University Press.

Heydemann, Steven. 2006. "Is the Middle East Different?" *Journal of Democracy*, vol. 7, issue 2, April, pp. 171–75.

Higgott, Richard A., Geoffrey R. D. Underhill, and Andreas Bieler, eds. 2000. *Non-State Actors and Authority in the Global System*. New York: Routledge.

Hill, Charles W., and Thomas M. Jones. 1992. "Stakeholder-Agency Theory." *Journal of Management Studies*, vol. 29, no. 2, March, pp. 131–54.

Hill, Miriam. 2006. "Real Suit Over Virtual Property." *Philadelphia Inquirer*, October 20, http://www.philly.com. Last accessed April 24, 2009.

Hirsh-Pasek, Kathryn A., Roberta M. Golinkoff, and George Hollich. 2000. "Trends and Transitions in Language Development: Looking for the Missing Piece." *Developmental Neuro-psychology*, vol. 16, no. 2, pp. 139–63.

Hobbes, Thomas. 1994. *Leviathan: With Selected Variants from the Latin Edition of 1668*, ed. Edwin Curley. Indianapolis: Hackett Publishing Co.

Hodges, Michael, and Stephen Woolcock. 1993. "Atlantic Capitalism versus Rhine Capitalism in the European Community," *West European Politics*, vol. 16, no. 3, July, pp. 329–44.

Hollenbach, David. 1994a. "A Communitarian Reconstruction of Human Rights: Contributions from Catholic Tradition." In *Catholicism and Liberalism: Contributions to American Public Philosophy*, ed. R. Bruce Douglass and David Hollenbach. New York: Cambridge University Press.

———. 1994b. "Afterword: A Community of Freedom." In *Catholicism and Liberalism: Contributions to American Public Philosophy*, ed. R. Bruce Douglass and David Hollenbach. New York: Cambridge University Press.

———. 1979. *Claims in Conflict: Retrieving and Renewing the Catholic Human Rights Tradition*. New York: Paulist Press.

Holloway, Mark. 2006. "Harnessing the Power of Business to Fight AIDS: Unilever and M·A·C Cosmetics." Paper presented at the conference "Peace through Commerce: Partnerships as the New Paradigm," University of Notre Dame, November 13.

Howard, George S. 2006. *Stan Ovshinski and the Hydrogen Economy: Creating a Better World*. Notre Dame, Ind.: Academic Publications.

———. 1991. "Cultural Tales: A Narrative Approach To Thinking, Cross-Cultural Psychology, and Psychotherapy." *American Psychologist*, vol. 46, no. 3, pp. 187–97.

Howe, Mark L., and Mary L. Courage. 1997. "The Emergence and Early Development of Autobiographical Memory." *Psychological Review*, vol. 104, no. 3, July, pp. 499–523.

Human Development Report 2007/2008: Fighting Climate Change: Human Solidarity in a Divided World. United Nations Development Programme (UNDP). New York: Palgrave Macmillan.

Human Development Report 2001: Making New Technologies Work for Human Development. United Nations Development Programme (UNDP). New York: Oxford University Press.

Human Development Report 1999: Making New Technologies Work for Human Development. United Nations Development Programme (UDNP). New York: Oxford University Press.

Hummels, D., J. Ishii, and Kei-Mu Yi. 2001. "The Nature and Growth of Vertical Specialization in World Trade." *Journal of International Economics*, vol. 54, no. 1, June, pp. 75–96.

Hunt, Scott A. 2002. *The Future of Peace on the Front Lines with the World's Great Peacemakers*. San Francisco: Harper San Francisco.

Huntington, Samuel P. 1996. *The Clash of Civilizations: Remaking of World Order*. New York: Touchstone, Simon & Schuster.

———. 1991. "The Third Wave: Democratization in the Late Twentieth Century." Norman: University of Oklahoma Press.

"In the Twilight of Doha." 2006. *The Economist*, July 29, pp. 63–64.

"INGO Accountability Charter." 2006. International Non-Governmental Organizations Commitment to Accountability, June 6. http://www.ingo accountabilitycharter.org.

Interface, Inc. (press release). 2004. "Interface Celebrates Ten Years of Sustainability in Action," August 31. http://www.interfaceflor.hk/internet/webAU .nsf/webpages/541_AU.html. Last accessed April 24, 2009.

Interfaith Center on Corporate Responsibility (ICCR). 1998. Press Release, "Religious Investor Coalition Declines to Endorse Apparel Industry Partnership Agreement," November 5. On file with authors.

"Intergovernmental Panel on Climate Change, Fourth Assessment Report, Climate Change 2007: Synthesis Report, Summary for Policymakers." Valencia, Spain, http://www.ipcc.ch/pdf/assessment-report/ar4/syr/ar4_syr_spm.pdf. Last accessed April 24, 2009.

"Internet World Stats: Usage and Population Statistics," *The Internet Coaching Library*, http://www.internetworldstats.com/stats.htm. Last accessed April 24, 2009.

Jameson, Kenneth P., and Juan M. Rivera. 1988. "The Mexican Case: Communication under State Capitalism." In *Multinational Managers and Host Government Interactions*, ed. Lee A. Tavis. Notre Dame, Ind.: University of Notre Dame Press.

Jana, Reena, and Aili McConnen. 2006. "Second Life Lessons." *Business Week*, issue 4011, special section, November 27, pp. 17–25.

Jensen, Lionel M., and Timothy B. Weston, eds. 2006. *China's Transformations: The Stories Beyond the Headlines*. Lanham, Md.: Rowman & Littlefield Publishers.

Jensen, Michael C. 2001. *Value Maximization, Stakeholder Theory, and the Corporate Objective Function*. Cambridge, Mass.: Harvard Business School; The Monitor Company; Social Science Electronic Publishing [SSEP], October.

Jensen, M. C., and W. H. Meckling. 1976. "Theory of the Firm: Managerial Behavior, Agency Costs, and Ownership Structure." *Journal of Financial Economics*, vol. 3, no. 4, pp. 305–60.

John XXIII (Pope). *Pacem in Terris*. 1963. http://www.vatican.va/holy_father/john_xxiii/encyclicals/documents/hf_j-xxiii_enc_11041963_pacem_en.html. Last accessed April 24, 2009.

———. *Mater et Magistra*. 1961. http://www.vatican.va/holy_father/john_xxiii/encyclicals/documents/hf_j-xxiii_enc_15051961_mater_en.html. Last accessed April 24, 2009.

John Paul II (Pope). *Fides et Ratio*. 1998. www.vatican.va/holy_father/john_paul_ii/encyclicals/documents/hf_jp-ii_enc_15101998_fides-et-ratio_en.html. Last accessed April 24, 2009.

———. 1993. *Veritatis Splendor. Origins*, 28/297 (1995), Encyclical Letter issued October 5.

———. 1987. *Sollicitudo Rei Socialis. Origins* 17/38 (1988), Encyclical Letter issued December 30.

Johnson, James Turner. 2006. "Searching for Common Ground: Ethical Traditions at the Interface with International Law." *Universalism vs. Relativism: Making Moral Judgments in a Changing, Pluralistic, and Threatening World*, ed. Don Browning. Lanham, Md.: Rowman & Littlefield Publishers.

Johnson, Marcia K. 2006. "Memory and Reality." *American Psychologist*, vol. 61, no. 8, November, pp. 760–71.

Johnson, Mark H., and John Morton. 1991. *Biology and Cognitive Development: The Case of Face Recognition*. Cambridge, Mass.: Blackwell Publishers.

Joy, Bill. 2000. "Why the Future Doesn't Need Us." *Wired Digital, Inc.*, issue 8.04, April. http://www.wired.com/wired/archive/8.04/joy.html. Last accessed April 24, 2009.

Kahana-Kalman, Rohnit, and Arlene S. Walker-Andrews. 1997. "The Role of Person Familiarity in Young Infants' Perceptions of Emotional Expressions." *Child Development*, vol. 7, no. 2, pp. 352–69.

Kant, Immanuel. 1983. *Ethical Philosophy*, trans. James W. Ellington. Indianapolis: Hackett Publishing Co.

Kaplan, Robert S., and David P. Norton. 1996. *The Balanced Scorecard*. Boston: Harvard Business School Press.

———. 1992. "The Balanced Scorecard—Measures that Drive Performance," *Harvard Business Review*, January–February, pp. 71–79.

Karr-Morse, Robin, and Meredith S. Wiley. *Ghosts from the Nursery: Tracing the Roots of Violence*. New York: The Atlantic Monthly Press, 1997.

Kekic, Laza. 2006. "A Pause in Democracy's March." *The Economist: 21st Edition—The World in 2007*, p. 19.

Keohane, Robert O., and Joseph S. Nye, Jr. 2000. "Introduction." In *Governance in a Globalizing World*, ed. Joseph S. Nye, Jr., and John D. Donahue. Washington, D.C.: Brookings Institution Press.

Khanna, Parag. 2008. *The Second World: Empires and Influence in the New Global Order.* New York: Random House.

Kielstra, Paul, Gareth Lofthouse, James Walson, and Sarah Murray. 2008. "Doing Good: Business and the Sustainability Challenge." Economist Intelligence Unit, a white paper published by *The Economist*, February.

Kim, Kwan S. 1988. "The Korean Case: Culturally Dominated Interactions." In *Multinational Managers and Host Government Interactions*, ed. Lee A. Tavis. Notre Dame, Ind.: University of Notre Dame Press.

Kline, John M. 1991. "The Inverse Relationship between Nation-States and Global Corporations." In *Global Corporations and Nation-States: Do Companies or Countries Compete?* Washington, D.C.: National Planning Association.

———. 1988. "Advantages of International Regulation: The Case for a Flexible, Pluralistic Framework." In *International Regulation: New Rules in a Changing World Order*, ed. Carol C. Adelman. San Francisco: Lehrman Institute, ICS Press.

———. 1985. *International Codes and Multinational Business: Setting Guidelines for International Business Operations.* Westport, Conn.: Quorum Books.

Kluth, Andreas. 2006. "When the Hype Dies Down." *The Economist: 21st Edition—The World in 2007*, p. 19.

Komonchak, Joseph A. 1994. "Vatican II and the Encounter Between Catholicism and Liberalism." In *Catholicism and Liberalism: Contributions to American Public Philosophy*, ed. R. Bruce Douglass and David Hollenbach. New York: Cambridge University Press.

Krugman, Paul. 1995. "Growing World Trade." In *Brookings Papers on Economic Activity*, ed. William C. Brainard and George L. Perry. Washington, D.C.: The Brookings Institution.

Kumra, Gautam. 2006. "One Business's Commitment to Society: An Interview with the President of the Novartis Foundation for Sustainable Development." *The McKinsey Quarterly*, no. 3, pp. 71–85.

Küng, Hans. 1999. "A Global Ethic in an Age of Globalization." In *International Business Ethics: Challenges and Approaches*, ed. Georges Enderle. Notre Dame, Ind.: University of Notre Dame Press.

Kurzweil, Ray. 2000. *The Age of Spiritual Machines: When Computers Exceed Human Intelligence.* New York: Penguin Group.

Langreth, Robert. 2001. "Reviving Novartis." *Forbes Magazine*, vol. 167, February 5, pp. 90–96.

Lederach, John Paul. 2008. "The Role of Corporate Actors in Peace-Building Processes: Opportunities and Challenges." In *Peace through Commerce: Responsible Corporate Citizenship and the Ideals of the United Nations Global*

Compact, ed. Oliver F. Williams, C.S.C. Notre Dame, Ind.: University of Notre Dame Press.

Leisinger, Klaus M. 2009a. "On Corporate Responsibility for Human Rights." In *Humanism in Business*, ed. Heiko Spitzeck, Michael Pirson, Wolfgang Amann, Shiban Khan, and Ernst von Kimakowitz. Cambridge: Cambridge University Press.

———. 2009b. "Corporate Responsibilities for Access to Medicines." Novartis Foundation for Sustainable Development, http://www.novartisfoundation .com, p. 23. Last accessed April 24, 2009.

———. 2008. "Stretching the Limits of Corporate Responsibility." In *Peace through Commerce: Responsible Corporate Citizenship and the Ideals of the United Nations Global Compact*, ed. Oliver F. Williams, C.S.C. Notre Dame, Ind.: University of Notre Dame Press.

———. 2007a. "Corporate Philanthropy: The 'Top of the Pyramid.'" *Business and Society Review*, vol. 112, issue 3, September, pp. 315–42.

———. 2007b. "Capitalism with a Human Face: The UN Global Compact." *Journal of Corporate Citizenship*, issue 28, June, pp. 113–32.

———. 2005. "Walking Upright on Forest Trails: Christian Values as a Basis for Corporate Decisions." Lecture given on the occasion of the acceptance of the *honoris causa* doctorate of the theological faculty of the University of Fribourg, Fribourg, Switzerland.

———. 2004. "Business and Human Rights." In *UN Global Compact/United Nations High Commissioner for Human Rights: Embedding Human Rights in Business Practices*. New York and Geneva: United Nations, pp. 50–60.

———. 2003. "Opportunities and Risks of the United Nations Global Compact: The Novartis Case Study." *Journal of Corporate Citizenship*, issue 11, Autumn, pp. 113–31.

Levy, David M. 2006. "More, Faster, Better: Governance in an Age of Overload, Busyness, and Speed." *First Monday* (peer-reviewed journal on the Internet), special issue no. 7: *Command Lines: The Emergence of Governance in Global Cyberspace*, November. http://firstmonday.org/htbin/cgiwrap/bin/ojs/index .php/fm/article/view/1618/1533. Last accessed April 24, 2009.

Lewis, Bernard. 1996. "Islam and Liberal Democracy: A Historical Overview." *Journal of Democracy*, vol. 7, no. 2, April, pp. 52–63.

Li, Jin. 2003. "The Core of Confucian Learning." *American Psychologist*, vol. 58, no. 2, p. 146.

Litow, Stanley. 2008. "IBM and Corporate Citizenship." In *Peace through Commerce: Responsible Corporate Citizenship and the Ideals of the United Nations Global Compact*, ed. Oliver F. Williams, C.S.C. Notre Dame, Ind.: University of Notre Dame Press.

Lohr, Steve. 2007. "Preaching from the Ballmer Pulpit: Can Microsoft Thrive in a New Digital Era?" *The New York Times*, section 3, January 28, pp. 1, 8, 9.

Longworth, R. C. 2001. "A New World Disordered; The Seeds of Terror Thrive in Poor Ground; Tragedy's Economic Roots." *Chicago Tribune*, Perspective, 155th year, no. 273, section 2, September 30, pp. 1, 6.

Lorenz, Konrad. *The Foundations of Ethology: The Principal Ideas and Discoveries in Animal Behavior*. New York: Springer-Verlag, 1981.

Loughran, Tim, Bill McDonald, and Hayong Yun. 2009. "A Wolf in Sheep's Clothing: The Use of Ethics-Related Terms in 10-K Reports." *Journal of Business Ethics*, vol. 89, Supplement 1, May, pp. 39–49.

Lowry, David B. 2008. "International Concord and Intranational Discord: A Study of Freeport-McMoRan." In *Peace through Commerce: Responsible Corporate Citizenship and the Ideals of the United Nations Global Compact*, ed. Oliver F. Williams, C.S.C. Notre Dame, Ind.: University of Notre Dame Press.

———. 2006. "Extractives, Economic Development, Codes of Conduct, and Audits: Creating Peace through Carefully Thought Out Commerce." Paper presented at the conference "Peace through Commerce: Partnerships as the New Paradigm," University of Notre Dame, November 13.

Lucas, Edward. 2008. "The Electronic Bureaucrat: A Special Report on Technology and Government." *The Economist*, February 16, p. 3 (following regular p. 56).

MacIntyre, Alasdair. 1988. *Whose Justice? Which Rationality?* Notre Dame, Ind.: University of Notre Dame Press.

———. 1981. *After Virtue: A Study in Moral Theory*. Notre Dame, Ind.: University of Notre Dame Press.

Madsen, Richard, William M. Sullivan, Ann Swidler, and Steven M. Tipton, eds. 2002. *Meaning and Modernity*. Berkeley: University of California Press.

Malan, Daniel. 2008. "From Being Apart to Being Partners: The Experience of Barloworld." In *Peace through Commerce: Responsible Corporate Citizenship and the Ideals of the United Nations Global Compact*, ed. Oliver F. Williams, C.S.C. Notre Dame, Ind.: University of Notre Dame Press.

Malhotra, Heide B. 2006. "NGOs Losing Privileged Status." *Epoch Times*, New York, January 31.

Malkin, John. 2003. "In Engaged Buddhism, Peace Begins with You." *Shambhala Sun*, July.

Mandel, Gregory N. 2008. "Nanotechnology Governance." *Alabama Law Review*, vol. 59, http://ssrn.com/abstract=1018707. Last accessed April 24, 2009.

Mankin, Eric. "Brain-Computer Link Systems on the Brink of Breakthrough, Study Finds." http://www.eurekalert.org/pub_releases/2007-12/uosc-bls121207.php. Last accessed April 24, 2009.

Manyika, James M., Roger P. Roberts, and Kara L. Sprague. 2008. "Eight Business Technology Trends to Watch." *The McKinsey Quarterly*, no. 1, pp. 61–71.

Margolis, Joshua, and James P. Walsh. 2003. "Misery Loves Companies: Rethinking Social Initiatives by Business." *Administrative Science Quarterly*, vol. 48, June, pp. 268–305.

Maritain, Jacques. 1947. *The Person and the Common Good*, trans. John J. Fitzgerald. New York: Charles Scribner's Sons.

Markoff, John. 2008. "Two Views of Innovation, Colliding in Washington." *The New York Times*, January 13, p. BU3.

Markus, R. A. 1990. "*De ciuitate dei*: Pride and the Common Good." In *Collectanea Augustiniana: Augustine—Second Founder of the Faith*, ed. Joseph C. Schnaubelt and Frederick Van Fleteren. New York: Peter Lang.

Marty, Martin E. 2005. *When Faiths Collide*. Malden, Mass.: Blackwell Publishing.

Maruna, Shadd. 1997. "Going Straight: Desistance from Crime and Life Narratives of Reform." In *The Narrative Study of Lives*, vol. 5, ed. Amia Lieblich and Ruthellen Josselson. Thousand Oaks, Calif.: Sage Publications.

Maslow, Abraham H. 1998. *Toward a Psychology of Being*. 3rd ed. New York: John Wiley & Sons.

———. 1973. *Dominance, Self-Esteem, Self-Actualization: Germinal Papers of A. H. Maslow*, ed. Richard Lowry. Monterey, Calif.: Brooks/Cole.

Mayer, Lloyd Hitoshi. 2007. "Legal Issues for Today's Nonprofit Managers." Unpublished manuscript on file with authors, March 15.

McAdams, Dan P. 2001. "The Psychology of Life Stories." *Review of General Psychology*, vol. 5, no. 2, pp. 100–122.

McAdams, Dan P., and P. T. Bowman. 2001. "Narrating Life's Turning Points: Redemption and Contamination." In *Turns in the Road: Narrative Studies of Lives in Transition*, ed. Dan P. McAdams, Ruthellen Josselson, and Amia Lieblich. Washington, D.C.: American Psychological Association.

McInerny, Ralph. 1987. "The Primacy of the Common Good." In *The Common Good and U.S. Capitalism*, ed. Oliver F. Williams, C.S.C., and John W. Houck. Notre Dame, Ind.: University of Notre Dame Press.

"The McKinsey Quarterly Confronting Climate Change." 2008. *The McKinsey Quarterly*, no. 2.

"The McKinsey Global Survey of Business Executives: Business and Society." 2006. *The McKinsey Quarterly*, no. 2, pp. 33–39.

"The McKinsey Quarterly Intelligent Choices in Global Energy." 2007. *The McKinsey Quarterly*, no. 1.

"The Mensch of Malden Mills: CEO Aaron Feuerstein Puts Employees First." 2003. *CBS 60 Minutes*, July 6. http://www.cbsnews.com/stories/2003/07/03/

60minutes/main561656.shtml?source=search_story. Last accessed April 24, 2009.

Merchi, Robert. 1995. "Value Added." *Financial World*, vol. 164, issue 17, August 1, p. 52.

Milanovic, Branko. 2000. "How Great is World Inequality?" *Wider Angle*, World Institute for Development Economics Research newsletter, vol. 40, no. 1, pp. 10–11.

The Millennium Development Goals Report 2007. New York: United Nations.

Monks, Robert A. G., and Nell Minow. 2000. *Corporate Governance*. Malden, Mass.: Blackwell Publishing.

Mufson, Steven. 2007. "Company Aims to Test Carbon-Trading Waters with Plankton." *Anchorage Daily News*, July 21, p. D-3.

Muller, Jerry Z. 1995. *Adam Smith in His Time and Ours: Designing the Decent Society*. Princeton, N.J.: Princeton University Press.

Mumme, Donna L., Anne Fernald, and Carla Herrera. 1996. "Infants' Responses to Facial and Vocal Emotional Signals in a Social Referencing Paradigm." *Child Development*, vol. 67, no. 6, pp. 3219–37.

Muravchik, Joshua. 1996. "Promoting Peace Through Democracy." In *Managing Global Chaos: Sources of and Responses to International Conflict*, ed. Chester A. Crocker and Fen Osler Hampson with Pamela Aall. Washington, D.C.: United States Institute of Peace Press.

Murphy, Patrick E. 1995. "Corporate Ethics Statements: Current Status and Future Prospects." *Journal of Business Ethics*, vol. 14, no. 9, September, pp. 726–40.

Murphy, Patrick E., ed. 1998. *Eighty Exemplary Ethics Statements*. Notre Dame, Ind.: University of Notre Dame Press.

Murray, Larry. 2008. "The HUE & CRY Against Manmade CO_2 vs.: 'Does It Cause Global Warming Far Less Than Warming Increases Our CO_2?'" Unpublished manuscript, June 2.

"NanoTech: Are Non-Materials Over-Hyped? Part 2." 2004. SpaceDaily.com (New York), October 29.

Nelson, Charles A., and Michelle Bosquet. 2000. "The Neurobiology of Fetal and Infant Development: Implications for Infant Mental Health." *Handbook of Infant Mental Health*, 2nd ed., ed. Charles H. Zeanah, Jr. New York: Guilford Press.

Neuhaus, Richard John. 2000. "A New Order of Religious Freedom." In *Law and Religion: A Critical Anthology*, ed. Stephen M. Feldman. New York: New York University Press.

"New Report: Local Networks Gaining in Strength and Impact." 2007. *The Global Compact, Compact Quarterly*, December. http://www.unglobalcompact.org/

NewsandEvents/news_archives/2007_12_17.html. Last accessed April 24, 2009.

Newton, Lisa, and John Bee. 2008. "Creating Shared Value: Nestlé S.A. in Developing Nations." In *Peace through Commerce: Responsible Corporate Citizenship and the Ideals of the United Nations Global Compact,* ed. Oliver F. Williams, C.S.C. Notre Dame, Ind.: University of Notre Dame Press.

Nobre, Anna C., and Kim Plunkett. 1997. "The Neural System of Language: Structure and Development," *Current Opinion in Neurobiology,* vol. 7, no. 2, April, pp. 262–68.

Nordstrom, Kjell, and Jonas Ridderstrale. 1999. *Funky Business.* Stockholm: Bookhouse Publishing.

Novak, Michael. 1991. *The Spirit of Democratic Capitalism.* Lanham, Md.: Madison Books.

Novartis. 2007. "Chain Reaction: Business Ethics Shouldn't Stop at the Company's Own Gates." http://www.corporatecitizenship.novartis.com. Last accessed April 1, 2009.

Novartis Annual Report 2007: Caring and Curing. Basel, Switzerland: Novartis AG.

Novartis Code of Conduct, Section 6. 2001. See http://www.corporatecitizenship .novartis.com. Last accessed April 1, 2009.

Novartis Foundation for Sustainable Development. http://www.novartis foundation.org. Last accessed April 1, 2009.

Novartis GRI Report 2006. http://www.corporatecitizenship.novartis.com. Last accessed April 1, 2009.

Novartis. *Only One Company, Novartis Operational Review 1996.* Basel, Switzerland: Novartis.

Novartis Policy on Corporate Citizenship. http://www.corporatecitizenship .novartis.com. Last accessed April 1, 2009.

Novartis Third Party Code of Conduct, Version 2.0, April 2007. http://www .pharmaceuticalsupplychain.org. Last accessed April 1, 2009.

Novartis and the UN Global Compact. http://www.corporatecitizenship .novartis.com. Last accessed April 1, 2009.

Novartis UNGC Communications on Progress, 2007 and 2008. http://www .corporatecitizenship.novartis.com. Last accessed April 24, 2009.

Oberman, Justin. 2006. "Beep, Beep! It's Your Local Politician!" Personal Democracy Forum, April. http://personaldemocracy.com/node/874. Last accessed April 24, 2009.

Ohmae, Kenichi. 1995. *The End of the Nation State: The Rise of Regional Economics.* New York: The Free Press.

O'Neill, Donal A. 2008. "Impact Assessment, Transparency, and Accountability: Three Keys to Building Sustainable Partnerships between Business and Its Stakeholders." In *Peace through Commerce: Responsible Corporate*

Citizenship and the Ideals of the United Nations Global Compact, ed. Oliver F. Williams, C.S.C. Notre Dame, Ind.: University of Notre Dame Press.

O'Reilly, Charles A., III, Jennifer Chatman, and David F. Caldwell. 1991. "People and Organizational Culture: A Profile Comparison Approach to Assessing Person-Organization Fit." *Academy of Management Journal*, vol. 34, no. 3, September, pp. 487–516.

"Orion's Belter: The World's First Practical Quantum Computer is Unveiled." 2007. *The Economist*, February 17, p. 81.

Orlitzky, Marc, Frank L. Schmidt, and Sarah L. Rynes. 2003. "Corporate Social and Financial Performance: A Meta-analysis." *Organization Studies*, vol. 24, pp. 403–41.

O'Rourke IV, James S. "Putting Reputation at Risk: The Seven Factors of Reputational Management." Unpublished manuscript.

Pacala, Stephen W., and Robert H. Socolow. 2004. "Stabilization Wedges: Solving the Climate Problem for the Next 50 Years with Current Technologies." *Science*, vol. 305, no. 5686, August 13, pp. 968–72.

Paine, Lynn Sharp. 2003. *Values Shift: Why Companies Must Merge Social and Financial Imperatives to Achieve Superior Performance*. New York: McGraw Hill.

Pandit, Bansi. 1996. *Hindu Dharma*. Columbia, Mo.: South Asia Books.

"Partnering for Success: Business Perspectives on Multistakeholder Partnerships." 2005. World Economic Forum: Global Corporate Citizenship Initiative, in cooperation with the John F. Kennedy School of Government, Harvard University, January.

Paul VI (Pope). *Populorum Progressio*. 1967. http://www.vatican.va/holy_father/paul_vi/encyclicals/documents/hf_p-vi_enc_26031967_populorum_en.html. Last accessed April 24, 2009.

———. *Dignitatis Humanae*. 1965a. http://www.vatican.va/archive/hist_councils/ii_vatican_council/documents/vat-ii_decl_19651207_dignitatis-humanae_en.html. Last accessed April 24, 2009.

———. *Gaudium et Spes*. 1965b. http://www.vatican.va/archive/hist_councils/ii_vatican_council/documents/vat-ii_cons_19651207_gaudium-et-spes_en.html. Last accessed April 24, 2009.

Pavlov, Ivan P. 1927. *Conditioned Reflexes: An Investigation of the Physiological Activity of the Cerebral Cortex*, trans. G. V. Anrep. London: Oxford University Press.

Perry, Bruce D. 1997. "Incubated in Terror: Neurodevelopmental Actors in the Cycle of Violence." In *Children in a Violent Society*, ed. J. D. Osofsky. New York: Guilford Press.

Perry, Michael J. 1998. *The Idea of Human Rights: Four Inquiries*. Oxford: Oxford University Press.

———. 1990. *Morality, Politics, and Law*. Oxford: Oxford University Press.

Poniewozik, James. 2006. "The Beast with a Billion Eyes." *Time*, vol. 168, issue 26, December 25, pp. 63–64.

Pontin, Jason. 2007a. "A Great Leap Forward in Computing? Maybe Not." *The New York Times*, April 8, p. BU4.

———. 2007b. "Awaiting the Day When Everyone Writes Software." *The New York Times*, section 3, January 28, p. 3.

Porter, Michael E., and Claas Van Der Linde. 1995. "Green and Competitive: Ending the Stalemate." *Harvard Business Review*, vol. 73, issue 5, pp. 120–35.

Prahalad, C. K., and Hrishi Bhattacharyya. 2008. "Twenty Hubs and No HQ." *Strategy + Business*, May 29, http://www.strategy-business.com/enewsarticle/enews052908. Last accessed April 24, 2009.

Progoff, Ira. 1956. *The Death and Rebirth of Psychology*. New York: McGraw-Hill Book Co.

Putnam, Robert D. 2000. *Bowling Alone: The Collapse and Revival of American Community*. New York: Simon & Schuster.

———. 1993. *Making Democracy Work: Civic Traditions in Modern Italy*. Princeton, N.J.: Princeton University Press.

Quinn, James Brian. 2005. "The Intelligent Enterprise: A New Paradigm." *Academy of Management Executive*, vol. 19, no. 4, pp. 109–21.

Rand, Ayn. 1957. *Atlas Shrugged*. New York: E. P. Dutton and Co.

Rank, Otto. 1978. *Will Therapy*. New York: W.W. Norton & Co.

Ratliff, Evan. 2006. "Me Translate Pretty One Day." *Wired*, December, pp. 210–13.

Rawls, John. 1993. *Political Liberalism*. New York: Columbia University Press.

———. 1971. *A Theory of Justice*. Oxford: Oxford University Press.

"The Real Digital Divide." 2005. *The Economist*, March 12, p. 11.

Reilly, Charles A. 1998. "Balancing State, Market and Civil Society: NGOs for a New Development Consensus." In *Poverty and Inequality in Latin America: Issues and New Challenges*, ed. Guillermo A. O'Donnell and Victor Tokman. Notre Dame, Ind.: University of Notre Dame Press.

"Reinventing the Internet." 2006. *Economist Technical Quarterly*, March 11, pp. 32–33.

Revkin, Andrew. 2008. "A Shift in the Debate over Global Warming." *The New York Times*, April 6, p. 3.

Richardson, Laurie. 1998. "Three Pillars of Responsibility: A Conversation with Amitai Etzioni." In *Corporate Global Citizenship*, ed. Noel M. Tichy, Andrew R. McGill, and Lynda St. Clair. Lanham, Md.: Lexington Books.

Riding, Alan. 2005. "Unesco Adopts New Plan Against Cultural Invasion." *The New York Times*, October 21, p. B3.

Rieff, Philip. 1961. *The Mind of a Moralist*. Garden City, N.Y.: Doubleday & Co.

"Rio Declaration on Environment and Development." The United Nations Conference on Environment and Development. http://www.unep.org/ Documents.Multilingual/Default.asp?documentid=78&articleid=1163. Last accessed April 24, 2009.

Roberts, Peter W., and Grahame R. Dowling. 2002. "Corporate Reputational and Sustained Superior Financial Performance." *Strategic Management Journal*, vol. 23, September, pp. 1077–93.

Rodrik, Dani. 1997. *Has Globalization Gone Too Far?* Washington, D.C.: Institute for International Economics.

Rogers, Carl. 1961. *On Becoming a Person: A Therapist's View of Psychotherapy.* Boston: Houghton Mifflin.

Rohter, Larry. 2007. "Brazil, Alarmed, Reconsiders Policy on Climate Change." *The New York Times*, July 31, A3.

Romig, Jeff. 2005. "Whirlpool Volunteers Feel Privileged to Give." *South Bend Tribune*, June 24, pp. A1, A6.

Rosenwald, George C. 1992. "Conclusion: Reflections on Narrative Self-Understanding." In *Storied Lives: The Cultural Politics of Self-Understanding*, ed. George C. Rosenwald and Richard L. Ochberg. New Haven, Conn.: Yale University Press.

Roth, Brad R. 2000. "Evaluating Democratic Progress." In *Democratic Governance and International Law*, ed. Gregory H. Fox and Brad R. Roth. New York: Cambridge University Press.

Rowland, Rhonda. 2001. "Cancer Pill Speeds through Testing." CNN.com/ health, March 1. http://archives.cnn.com/2001/HEALTH/conditions/03/01/ leukemia.drug/index.html. Last accessed April 24, 2009.

Rubenstein, Richard E. 2003. *Aristotle's Children: How Christians, Muslims, and Jews Rediscovered Ancient Wisdom and Illuminated the Dark Ages.* Orlando, Fla.: Harcourt.

Ruggie, John. 2008. "Promotion and Protection of All Human Rights, Civil, Political, Economic, Social and Cultural Rights, Including the Right to Development" (Advance Version). Report of the Special Representative on the Issue of Human Rights and Transnational Corporations and Other Businesses. United Nations Human Rights Council, April 7. http://74.125.47.132/ search?q=cache:we2UZKvH-jMJ:www.unglobalcompact.org/docs/issues _doc/human_rights/Human_Rights_Working_Group/29Apr08_7_Report _of_SRSG_to_HRC.pdf+john+ruggie+promotion+and+protection&cd= 1&hl=en&ct=clnk&gl=us&client=safari. Last accessed May 9, 2009.

Ruiz, Alfredo. 1997. *Narrative in Post-Rationalist Cognitive Therapy*, trans. Susana Aronsohn. Santiago, Chile: Instituto de Terapia Cognitiva.

Sacks, Oliver. 1995. *An Anthropologist on Mars: Seven Paradoxical Tales.* New York: Alfred A. Knopf.

Salter, Liora. 1999. "The Standards Regime for Communications and Information Technologies." In *Private Authority and International Affairs*, ed.
Claire A. Cutler, Virginia Haufler, and Tony Porter. Albany: State University
of New York Press.

Santora, Joseph C. 2006. "Crossing the Digital Divide: Do All Global Citizens
Have Their Passports?" *Academy of Management Perspectives*, November,
pp. 118–19.

Sarbin, Theodore R. 1986. "The Narrative as Root Metaphor for Psychology."
In *Narrative Psychology: The Storied Nature of Human Conduct*, ed. Theodore R. Sarbin. New York: Praeger.

Sasmor, R. M. 1996. "Operant Conditioning of a Small-Scale Muscle Response."
Journal of the Experimental Analysis of Behavior, vol. 9, pp. 69–85.

Schachter, Daniel L. 1996. *Searching for Memory: The Brain, the Mind, and the
Past*. New York: Basic Books.

Schein, Edgar H. 1992. *Organizational Culture and Leadership*. 2nd ed. Hoboken, N.J.: Jossey-Bass, Wiley Co.

Scherrer, Brigitte Hélène. 2008. "Producing Generic Medicines in Afghanistan:
Opportunities and Challenges of a Multistakeholder Partnership." In *Peace
through Commerce: Responsible Corporate Citizenship and the Ideals of the
United Nations Global Compact*, ed. Oliver F. Williams, C.S.C. Notre Dame,
Ind.: University of Notre Dame Press.

Schilling, David M. 2000. "Making Codes of Conduct Credible: The Role of
Independent Monitoring." In *Global Codes of Conduct: An Idea Whose Time
Has Come*, ed. Oliver F. Williams, C.S.C. Notre Dame, Ind.: University of
Notre Dame Press.

Schore, Allan N. 2003. *Affect Dysregulation and Disorders of the Self*. New York:
W. W. Norton & Co.

Seigel, Daniel J. 2001. "Towards an Interpersonal Neurobiology of the Developing Mind: Attachment Relationships, 'Mindsights,' and Neural Integration."
Infant Mental Health Journal, vol. 22, nos. 1–2, pp. 67–94.

———. 1999. *The Developing Mind: Toward a Neurobiology of Interpersonal Experience*. New York: Guilford Press.

Selsky, John W., and Barbara Parker. 2005. "Cross-Sector Partnerships to Address Social Issues: Challenges to Theory and Practice." *Journal of Management*, vol. 31, no. 6, December, pp. 849–73.

Sen, Amartya. 1999. *Development as Freedom*. New York: Anchor Books.

———. 1997. "Human Rights and Asian Values." *New Republic*, vol. 217, issue
2/3, July 14–21, pp. 33–40.

Sengupta, Somine. 2007. "Glaciers in Retreat." *The New York Times*, July 17,
p. D1.

Sethi, S. Prakash. 2003. *Setting Global Standards: Guidelines for Creating Codes of Conduct in Multinational Corporations.* Hoboken, N.J.: John Wiley & Sons.

——. 2000. "Gaps in Research in the Formulation, Implementation, and Effectiveness Measurement of International Codes of Conduct." In *Global Codes of Conduct: An Idea Whose Time Has Come,* ed. Oliver F. Williams, C.S.C. Notre Dame, Ind.: University of Notre Dame Press.

Sethi, S. Prakash, and Linda M. Sama. 1998. "Ethical Behavior as a Strategic Choice by Large Corporations: The Interactive Effects of Marketplace Competition, Industry Structures, and Firm Resources," *Business Ethics Quarterly,* vol. 8, no. 1, January, pp. 85–104.

Shachtman, Tom, Joe Mackall, and Richard A. Stevick. 2007. "The Future of the Amish." *Chronicle of Higher Education,* vol. 53, issue 46, July 20, p. B4.

Sherwood, Emily Layzer. 2006. "Corporate Social Responsibility Reports Are On the Rise." *ETHIKOS,* January/February, pp. 13–22.

Shue, Henry. 1980. *Basic Rights.* Princeton, N.J.: Princeton University Press.

Singer, Jefferson A. 1997. *Message in a Bottle: Stories of Men and Addiction.* New York: The Free Press.

Skinner, B. F. 1938. *The Behavior of Organisms: An Experimental Analysis.* New York: Appleton-Century.

Slaughter, Anne-Marie. 2000. "Government Networks: The Heart of the Liberal Democratic Order." In *Democratic Governance and International Law,* ed. Gregory H. Fox and Brad R. Roth. New York: Cambridge University Press.

"Small Wonders: A Survey of Nanotechnology." 2005. *The Economist,* January 1, pp. 1–12.

Smith, Adam. 2000. *Wealth of Nations.* Bibliomania.com.

——. 1976a (1776). *An Inquiry into the Nature and Causes of the Wealth of Nations,* ed. A. L. Macfie and D. D. Raphael. Cambridge: Oxford University Press.

——. 1976b (1759). *The Theory of Moral Sentiments,* ed. A. L. Macfie and D. D. Raphael. Cambridge: Oxford University Press.

"Socially Responsible Investing," *Wikipedia, The Free Encyclopedia,* http://en .wikipedia.org/wiki/Socially_responsible_investing. Last accessed March 12, 2009 (last modified March 11, 2009).

Solomon, Robert C. 1993. *Ethics and Excellence: Cooperation and Integrity in Business.* The Ruffin Series in Business Ethics. New York: Oxford University Press.

"Some Like It Cool." 2007. *The Economist,* December 22, p. 10.

Soroush, Abdolkarim. 2000. *Reason, Freedom, and Democracy in Islam: Essential Writings of Abdolkarim Soroush,* ed. and trans. Mahmoud Sadri and Ahmad Sadri. New York: Oxford University Press.

"A Special Report on Business and Climate Change." 2007. *The Economist,* June 2, pp. 1–30.

"Special Report on Wal-Mart." 2004. *The Economist,* April 17, pp. 9, 67–69.

"Splitting the Digital Difference." 2006. *The Economist Technology Quarterly,* September 23, pp. 3–4.

Stein, Joel. 2006. "My So-Called Second Life." *Time,* vol. 168, issue 26, December 25, p. 76.

Steinfels, Peter. 1994. "The Failed Encounter: The Catholic Church and Liberalism in the Nineteenth Century." In *Catholicism and Liberalism: Contributions to American Public Philosophy,* ed. R. Bruce Douglass and David Hollenbach. New York: Cambridge University Press.

Sternglanz, Sarah H., James L. Gray, and Melvin Murakami. 1977. "Adult Preferences for Infantile Facial Features: An Ethological Approach." *Animal Behaviour,* vol. 25, no. 1, pp. 108–15.

Storme, Mattias E. 1994. "The Validity and the Content of Contracts." In *Towards a European Civil Code,* ed. A. S. Hartkamp, M. W. Hesselink, E. H. Hondius, C. E. du Perron, and J. B. M. Vranded. Dordrecht, The Netherlands: Martinus Nijhoff Publishers.

Sullivan, William M. 1982. *Reconstructing Public Philosophy.* Berkeley: University of California Press.

"Sunlit Uplands: Wind and Solar Power Are Flourishing, Thanks to Subsidies." 2007. *The Economist,* vol. 383, issue 8531, June 2–8, pp. 16–20 (in special section, "Cleaning Up: A Special Report on Business and Climate Change," between pp. 54–55 of issue).

Tavis, Lee A. 2008. "Multinational Enterprises: Interacting with Nongovernmental Organizations." In *Peace through Commerce: Responsible Corporate Citizenship and the Ideals of the United Nations Global Compact,* ed. Oliver F. Williams, C.S.C. Notre Dame, Ind.: University of Notre Dame Press.

———. 2006. "Problems of Wealth Distribution in the Global Apparel Industry: Locating Responsibilities in the Global Supply Chain." In *Rediscovering Abundance: Interdisciplinary Essays on Wealth, Income and their Distribution in the Catholic Social Tradition,* ed. Helen Alford, O.P., Charles Clark, S. A. Cortright, and Michael J. Naughton. Notre Dame, Ind.: University of Notre Dame Press.

———. 2004. "The U.N. Global Compact Principles and Multinational Corporate Standards." In *Human Rights and the Private Sector: International Symposium Report.* Novartis Foundation for Sustainable Development and the Prince of Wales International Business Leaders Forum. Basel, Switzerland: Novartis Foundation for Sustainable Development.

———. 2003. "Novartis and the U.N. Global Compact Initiative." *Vanderbilt Journal of Transnational Law,* vol. 36, no. 2, March, pp. 735–63. (Also published by the United Nations Global Compact Office in "From Principles to Practice," Case Studies Series, Global Compact Learning Forum, June 2004.)

———. 2002a. "Corporate Governance and the Global Social Void." *Vanderbilt Journal of Transnational Law*, vol. 35, no. 2, March, pp. 487–547.

———. 2002b. "Modern Contract Theory and the Purpose of the Firm." In *Rethinking the Purpose of Business: Interdisciplinary Essays from the Catholic Social Tradition*, ed. S. A. Cortright and Michael J. Naughton. Notre Dame, Ind.: University of Notre Dame Press.

———. 2000. "Economic Advantage and Moral Issues in Corporate Governance." In *Die Zukunft des Wissens: XVIII Deutscher Kongress für Philosophie*, ed. Jürgen Mittelstraß. Berlin, Germany: Akademie Verlag.

———. 1997. *Power and Responsibility: Multinational Managers and Developing Country Concerns*. Multinational Managers and Developing Country Concerns (series), vol. 5. Notre Dame, Ind.: University of Notre Dame Press.

Tavis, Lee A., ed. 1982. *Multinational Managers and Poverty in the Third World*. Multinational Managers and Developing Country Concerns (series), vol. 1. Notre Dame, Ind.: University of Notre Dame Press.

Tavis, Lee A., and Timothy M. Tavis. 2004. "The Person, the Market, and the Community." In *The Invisible Hand and the Common Good*, ed. Bernard Hodgson. Studies in Economic Ethics and Philosophy. New York and Heidelberg: Springer-Verlag.

Taylor, Chris. 2006. "Surfing the Web with Nothing but Brain Waves." *Business 2.0 Magazine*, July 24.

Tennesen, Michael. 2007. "Step Lightly, Please." *Audubon Living*, July–August, pp. 89–92.

Tesler, Phillipe. 2008. "Surviving With Sustainable Growth: As Environmental Demands Increase, Companies Must Change Efforts from Opportunistic to Efficient." Corporate Responsibility Officer Monthly Email Newsletter on Business Ethics, March. See http://www.thecro.com/node/645. Last accessed April 24, 2009.

Tesner, Sandrine, and Georg Kell. 2000. *The United Nations and Business*. New York: St. Martin's Press.

"Tired of Globalisation." 2005. *The Economist*, November 3, p. 11, http://www .economist.com/opinion/PrinterFriendly.cfm?story_id=5115177. Last accessed April 24, 2009.

"Top 100 Global Brands Scoreboard." 2005. *BusinessWeek Online*, August 2, http://www.businessweek.com/pdfs/2005/0531_globalbrand.pdf. Last accessed April 24, 2009.

Trevarthen, Colwyn. 2001. "Intrinsic Motives for Companionship in Understanding Their Origin, Development, and Significance for Infant Mental Health." *Infant Mental Health Journal*, vol. 22, no. 102, pp. 95–141.

Trevarthen, Colwyn, and Kenneth J. Aitken. 2001. "Infant Intersubjectivity: Research, Theory, and Clinical Applications." *Journal of Child Psychology and Psychiatry*, vol. 42, no. 1, pp. 3–48.

Trevino, Linda K. 1986. "Ethical Decision Making in Organizations: A Person-Situation Interactionist Model." *Academy of Management Review*, vol. 11, no. 3, pp. 601–17.

United Nations Global Compact. http://www.unglobalcompact.org. Last accessed April 24, 2009.

Valles-Bedregal, Jean Pierre. 2007. "OLPC and Mesh Networking: Bridging Global Rural Disconnection." Paper presented in partial fulfillment of the MBET 70500 course requirements in the MBA Program of the Mendoza College of Business at the University of Notre Dame, December 6.

Value Lines. 2007. "Interface, Inc." July 6, Value Line Publishing.

Vasella, Daniel, M.D. 2001–2002. "CEO Statement." In *Corporate Citizenship at Novartis*, vol. 3.

Väyrynen, Raimo. 2001. "Sovereignty, Globalization, and Transnational Social Movements." *International Relations of the Asia-Pacific*, vol. 1, no. 2. New York: Oxford University Press and the Japan Association of International Relations, pp. 227–46.

Velasquez, Manuel G. 2002. *Business Ethics: Concepts and Cases.* 5th ed. Upper Saddle River, N.J.: Prentice Hall.

Velasquez, Manuel, and F. Neil Brady. 1997. "Natural Law and Business Ethics." *Business Ethics Quarterly*, vol. 7, issue 2, pp. 83–107.

Viscusi, W. Kip, John M. Vernon, and Joseph E. Harrington, Jr. 1995. *Economics of Regulation and Antitrust.* Cambridge, Mass.: MIT Press.

Wagner, Michael K. L., and Amy R. Kaplan. 1990. "State Anti-Takeover Legislation: Necessary Protection or Rationalization of Entrenchment." *Insights: The Corporate & Securities Law Advisor*, vol. 4, no. 2, February, pp. 26–30.

Walker-Andrews, Arlene S. 1997. "Infants' Perception of Expressive Behaviors: Differentiation of Multimodal Information." *Psychological Bulletin*, vol. 121, no. 3, pp. 437–56.

Wallensteen, Peter. 2006. "Strategic Peace-building: Issues and Actors." Inaugural Speech as the Richard G. Starmann Sr. Research Professor of Peace Studies, Kroc Institute, University of Notre Dame, November 5.

"Wal-Mart Urged by Investors to Improve Its Reputation." *Business Respect—CSR Dispatches* no. 83, June 16, 2005, in Corporate Social Responsibility News and Resources, http://www.mallenbaker.net/csr/nl/83.html. Last accessed April 24, 2009.

Weaver, Gary R., and Bradley R. Agle. 2002. "Religiosity and Ethical Behavior in Organizations: A Symbolic Interactionist Perspective." *Academy of Management Review*, vol. 27, no. 1, pp. 77–87.

"Web Server Survey." 2007. *Netcraft*, December. http://news.netcraft.com. Last accessed April 24, 2009.

Weber, James Austin, and Diana Barrett. 2001. "Merck Global Health Initiatives (B): Botswana." Case prepared for class discussion, *Harvard Business School*, 9-301-089, January 26.

Webley, Simon. 1999. "Values Inherent in the Interfaith Declaration of International Business Ethics." In *International Business Ethics: Challenges and Approaches*, ed. Georges Enderle. Notre Dame, Ind.: University of Notre Dame Press.

Weinreb, Lloyd L. "Natural Law and Rights." In *Natural Law Theory: Contemporary Essays*, ed. Robert P. George. Oxford: Clarendon Press, 1992.

Werker, Janet F., and Richard C. Tees. 1984. "Cross-Language Speech Perception: Evidence for Perceptual Reorganization during the First Year of Life." *Infant Behavior and Development*, vol. 7, pp. 49–63.

"When Freedom Stumbles." 2008. *The Economist*, January 19, p. 63.

Whiten, A. 2000. "Social Complexity and Social Intelligence." In *The Nature of Intelligence*, ed. J. Goode. New York: John Wiley & Sons.

Williams, Oliver F., C.S.C. 2008. "Responsible Corporate Citizenship and the Ideals of the United Nations Global Compact." In *Peace through Commerce: Responsible Corporate Citizenship and the Ideals of the United Nations Global Compact*, ed. Oliver F. Williams, C.S.C. Notre Dame, Ind.: University of Notre Dame Press.

———. 2004. "The U.N. Global Compact: The Challenge and the Promise." *St. Augustine Papers*, vol. 6, no. 1, pp. 1–28.

Williams, Oliver F., C.S.C., ed. 2000. *Global Codes of Conduct: An Idea Whose Time Has Come*. Notre Dame, Ind.: University of Notre Dame Press.

Wing, Lorna. 2001. *The Autistic Spectrum: A Parent's Guide to Understanding and Helping Your Child*. Berkeley, Calif.: Ulysses Press.

Woodward, Kenneth L. 2001. "A Peaceful Faith, A Fanatic Few." *Newsweek*, September 24, pp. 67–68.

The World Bank, *Global Economic Prospects 2008: Technical Diffusion in the Developing World*. New York: Oxford University Press.

World Development Report 2006: Equity and Development. Copublication of The World Bank and Oxford University Press. New York: Oxford University Press.

World Development Report 2000/2001: Attacking Poverty. Published for The World Bank. New York: Oxford University Press.

World Economic Forum. 2005. Global Corporate Citizenship Initiative. "Partnering for Success: Business Perspectives on Multistakeholder Partnerships," January, Harvard University.

The World Health Report 2005: Make Every Mother and Child Count. Geneva, Switzerland: World Health Organization.

World Investment Report 2000: Cross-border Mergers and Acquisitions and Development: An Overview. New York: United Nations Conference on Trade and Development.

"World Trade Talks in the Rough." 2005. *The Economist*, November 5, p. 77.

Wright, Robert. 1996. *The Moral Animal: Why We Are the Way We Are: The New Science of Evolutionary Psychology.* London: Abacus.

Wright, Robin. 1996. "Islam and Liberal Democracy: Two Visions of Reformation." *Journal of Democracy*, vol. 7, no. 2, April, pp. 64–75.

"The WTO: A 'Fragile' Body under Attack by Protectionist Policies in the U.S. and EU." 2005. *Knowledge@Wharton* (online business journal), July 27. http://knowledge.wharton.upenn.edu/article.cfm?articleid=1232. Last accessed April 24, 2009.

Wynhoven, Ursula. 2002. "Case Study of How Novartis International AG Has Begun the Process of Delivering on Its Commitment to the Global Compact." July. Unpublished case study.

Yi, Kei-Mu. 2005. "Can Vertical Specialization Explain the Growth of World Trade?" *Journal of Political Economy*, vol. 111, no. 1, February, pp. 52–102.

York, Ryan J. 2002. "Visages of Janus: The Heavy Burden of Other Constituency Anti-Takeover Statutes on Shareholders and the Efficient Market for Corporate Control." *Willamette Law Review*, vol. 38, no. 4, Winter, p. 187.

Zimmer, Carl. 2001. *Evolution: The Triumph of an Idea.* New York: HarperCollins.

LEE A. TAVIS

is C. R. Smith Professor of Finance, emeritus, at the University
of Notre Dame. He is the author of *Power and Responsibility*
(Notre Dame Press, 1997).

TIMOTHY M. TAVIS

holds a Ph.D. in psychology from the University of Texas, Austin,
and is a private practitioner in West Palm Beach, Florida.